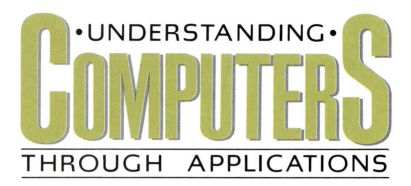

UNDERSTANDING COMPUTERS THROUGH APPLICATIONS

▲
Dr. Barbara Kurshan
Technology Education Consultant

▲
Gail Morse
Classroom Teacher
North Carolina School of Science & Mathematics
Wake County, North Carolina

▲
Alan November
Technology Consultant to the District
Glenbrook Schools
Glenbrook, Illinois

GLENCOE
Macmillan/McGraw-Hill

New York, New York   Columbus, Ohio   Mission Hills, California   Peoria, Illinois

Understanding Computers Through Applications
Copyright ©1993
by the Glencoe Division of Macmillan/McGraw-Hill
School Publishing Company. All rights reserved. Formerly published as
Computer Literacy Through Applications ©1986 by Houghton Mifflin Company.
Except as permitted under the United States Copyright Act, no part of this
publication may be reproduced or distributed in any form or by any means,
or stored in a database or retrieval system, without prior written
permission of the publisher.

Send all inquiries to:

GLENCOE DIVISION
Macmillan/McGraw-Hill
936 Eastwind Drive
Westerville, OH 43081

ISBN 0-02-800813-8

Printed in the United States of America.

3 4 5 6 7 8 RRD 99 98 97 96 95 94 93

CONTENTS

MODULE 1
COMPUTERS IN SOCIETY
2–19

Computers in Society	4
An Overview of Computer History	5
COMPUTERS THEN & NOW	5
Using Computers in Today's Society	6–17
COMPUTERS THEN & NOW	6
Computers in Health and Medicine	7–8
DID YOU KNOW?	7
CAREERS	8
Computers in Business and Industry	9–10
Computers in the Transportation Industry	11
Computers in Government and Law Enforcement	12–13
MULTICULTURAL BYTE	12
READ ALL ABOUT IT: "Astronauts Test Mail by Computer"	13
Computers in Education	14–17
READ ALL ABOUT IT: "Students Don't Fear Her Byte"	14–16
YOU MAKE A DIFFERENCE	17
Debating the Computer Issue	18–19
Module Summary Questions	19

MODULE 2
HOW COMPUTERS WORK
20–37

The Computer Factory	22
Parts of the Computer	23–28
MULTICULTURAL BYTE	24
A Miracle Made of Sand	29
CAREERS/READ ALL ABOUT IT: "My Work as a Computer Technician"	30
Bits and Binary	31
The Software Connection	32–33
DID YOU KNOW?	32
Dialing the World	34
Shopping for a Computer	35–37
YOU MAKE A DIFFERENCE	35
COMPUTERS THEN & NOW	36
Module Summary Questions	37

MODULE 3
GAMES, ENTERTAINMENT, & MUSIC
38–55

History of Electronic Games	40–42
COMPUTERS THEN & NOW	40
DID YOU KNOW?	41
MULTICULTURAL BYTE	42
Today's Computer Games	43
READ ALL ABOUT IT: "*Spaceship Warlock*: Exploring Space and Technology"	44–45
Stretching the Bounds of Reality	46–47
CAREERS	47
READ ALL ABOUT IT: "Good Vibrations: The PC Joins the Band"	48–51
Other Forms of Entertainment	52–55
DID YOU KNOW?	52
YOU MAKE A DIFFERENCE	53
Module Summary Questions	55

MODULE 4
GRAPHICS
56–73

How Graphics Enhance Information	58–59
How Graphics Work in a Computer	60–63
MULTICULTURAL BYTE	61
CAREERS	62
COMPUTERS THEN & NOW	63
Using Software to Create Graphics	64–67
YOU MAKE A DIFFERENCE	66
DID YOU KNOW?	66
READ ALL ABOUT IT: "Computer Graphics Field Keeps Growing"	68–69
Multimedia	70–73
Module Summary Questions	73

CONTENTS

WORD PROCESSING
74–91

What Is Word Processing?	76–78
DID YOU KNOW?	78
AppleWorks Quick-reference Chart for Your Apple II Computer	79
DeskMate Quick-reference Chart for Your IBM Computer	80
ClarisWorks Quick-reference Chart for Your Macintosh Computer	81
Special Features Make You a Better Writer	82–83
COMPUTERS THEN & NOW	83
Word Processors and Schools	84–85
Word Processing with Desktop Publishing	86–87
CAREERS	86
MULTICULTURAL BYTE	87
READ ALL ABOUT IT: "Rules of Thumb for Making Readable, Attractive Pages"	88–91
YOU MAKE A DIFFERENCE	91
Module Summary Questions	91

DATABASES
92–109

What Is a Database?	94–96
COMPUTERS THEN & NOW	96
Creating a Good Database	97
DID YOU KNOW?	97
AppleWorks Quick-reference Chart for Your Apple II Computer	98
DeskMate Quick-reference Chart for Your IBM Computer	99
ClarisWorks Quick-reference Chart for Your Macintosh Computer	100
Pizza Hut® Goes Online	101–102
READ ALL ABOUT IT: "Justice Aims Database at Gun Sales"	103–104
MULTICULTURAL BYTE	104
Alternative Databases	105
Online Careers	106
CAREERS	106
READ ALL ABOUT IT: "High Tech on the Range"	107–109
YOU MAKE A DIFFERENCE	109
Module Summary Questions	109

TELECOMMUNICATIONS
110–127

Computers as Communications Tools	112
MULTICULTURAL BYTE	112
How the Computer Works as a Telecommunications Tool	113–114
COMPUTERS THEN & NOW	113
Creating Communities with Telecommunications	115
Computer Networks	116
YOU MAKE A DIFFERENCE	116
Networking Options	117–120
DID YOU KNOW?	118
CAREERS	120
Schools and Telecommunications	121
READ ALL ABOUT IT: "Classroom TV Brings in World"	122
READ ALL ABOUT IT: "Today's Software, Tomorrow's Children's Workstation"	123
Telecommuting	124
Working Around the World	125
Using an Online Information Service	126–127
Module Summary Questions	127

SPREADSHEETS
128–145

What Is a Spreadsheet?	130–131
How Spreadsheets Work	132–133
Working with Spreadsheets	134
The History of Spreadsheet Programs	135–137
COMPUTERS THEN & NOW	135
DID YOU KNOW?	136
MULTICULTURAL BYTE	137
How Is a Spreadsheet Created?	138
YOU MAKE A DIFFERENCE	138
When Should a Spreadsheet Be Used?	139
CAREERS	139
READ ALL ABOUT IT: "High Tech on the Range" (Continued from Module 6)	140–143
Spreadsheets—Are They All the Same?	144–145
DID YOU KNOW?	145
Module Summary Questions	145

CONTENTS

MODULE 9
PROGRAMMING
146–163

A New Generation of Programmers	148
How You and the Computer Solve Problems	149–150
CAREERS	150
READ ALL ABOUT IT: "How Do You Create Software?"	151–154
MULTICULTURAL BYTE	154
What Is Hypertext?	155
A Look at *HyperCard*	156–160
COMPUTERS THEN & NOW	157
DID YOU KNOW?	157
What Can You Do with Hypermedia Programming?	161–163
YOU MAKE A DIFFERENCE	162
Module Summary Questions	163

MODULE 10
THE HISTORY OF COMPUTERS
164–181

The Age of the Computer	166–167
COMPUTERS THEN & NOW	166
MULTICULTURAL BYTE	167
The Analytical Engine that Could (A One-act Play)	168–169
READ ALL ABOUT IT: "Babbage's Difference Engine Launched—142 Years Later"	170
Hollerith—An Inventor Founds IBM	170
First-generation Computers	171–173
YOU MAKE A DIFFERENCE	172
DID YOU KNOW?	173
Second-generation Computers	174
Third-generation Computers	175
Fourth-generation Computers	175–178
The Story of Apple Computers	176
IBM—The PC Invades the Business World	177
Macintosh—Computing Becomes Less Complicated	178
The NeXT Step	179
Future Generations—What Can We Expect?	179
Generations Past and Present	180–181
CAREERS	181
Module Summary Questions	181

MODULE 11
ETHICS AND PRIVACY
182–199

What Is Ethics?	184
The Fine Print—Who Owns the Software You Just Bought?	185–188
YOU MAKE A DIFFERENCE	186
COMPUTERS THEN & NOW	188
READ ALL ABOUT IT: "Open Up—This Is the Software Police!"	189–191
DID YOU KNOW?	190
Focusing on Information, Accuracy, and Privacy	192–195
CAREERS	193
Help! My Computer Has Chicken Pox!	196–197
MULTICULTURAL BYTE	197
How To Be a Responsible Computing Citizen	198–199
Module Summary Questions	199

MODULE 12
COMPUTERS IN THE FUTURE
200–217

Looking into the Future	202
Computers & You	203–205
COMPUTERS THEN & NOW	203
MULTICULTURAL BYTE	204
Computers & the Community	206–212
READ ALL ABOUT IT: "Dressing for Tech-cess"	206–208
DID YOU KNOW?	208
READ ALL ABOUT IT: "'Smart Cars' Combat Gridlock"	210–211
CAREERS	212
Computers & the Global Village	213–215
MULTICULTURAL BYTE	213
A Letter to My Future Son or Daughter	216
YOU MAKE A DIFFERENCE	217
Module Summary Questions	217
Student Glossary	218–225
Index	226–230
Acknowledgments	231
Credits	232

MODULE 1
COMPUTERS IN SOCIETY

People everywhere use computers at work, at home, at school, and even at play. Computers are useful because they serve many purposes—from helping doctors diagnose health problems, to designing the cars of the future, to tracking business expenses, and more.

In Module 1, you will learn how a wide variety of people and businesses use computers and how you, too, can use these valuable tools!

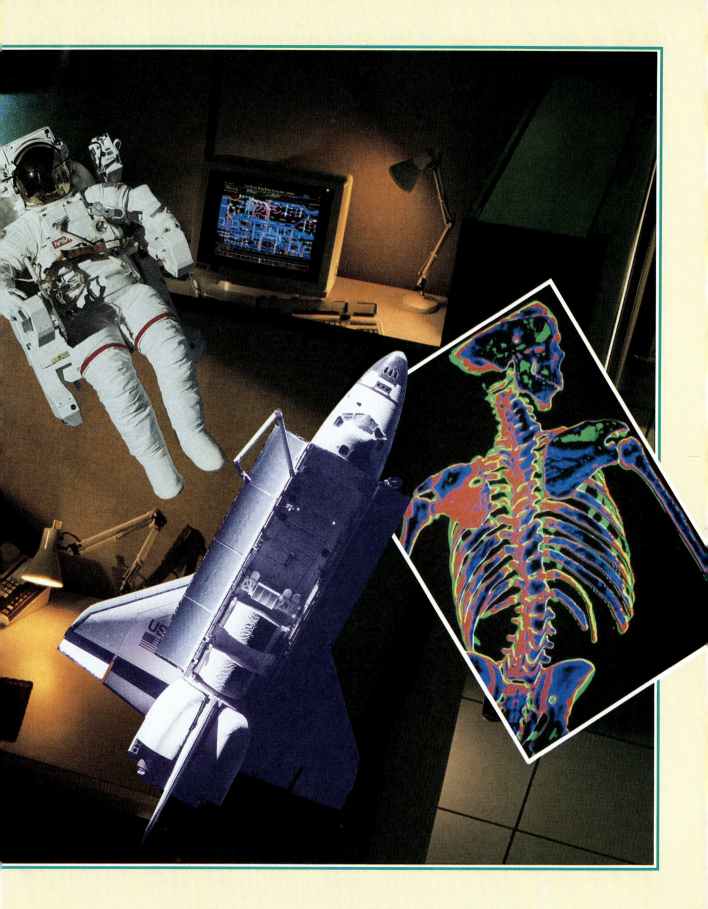

COMPUTERS IN SOCIETY

Teachers, farmers, auto mechanics, weather people, pilots, newspaper reporters, artists, the writers and editors of this book—and even kids like me—have something in common. We all use *computers* in our homes, at work, and in our communities.

Hi. My name is Kellie. I'm in Mrs. Johnson's computer class in Valparaiso, Indiana. Until I took this class, I didn't know what a computer was. Now, I'm learning to use *spreadsheets, databases, word processors,* and other *programs,* to help me with my schoolwork.

Today, people use computers every day at home. Can you think of what in your home has a computer in it? There are computers in microwaves, videocassette recorders (VCRs), compact-disc (CD) players, telephone answering machines, *calculators,* and yes, even cars!

People also use computers at their jobs. I want to be an environmental engineer. These people conduct experiments to determine the short- and long-term effects of pollution on our planet. I will use computers to help me gather the *data* and run simulations, or models, of what pollution could do to us in the future.

But first, what is a computer? Who are the men and women who deserve the credit for inventing and improving this tool? Read along as we learn what computers are and how they are used in our society.

Learning to use computers for today's schoolwork and tomorrow's career

MODULE 1

An Overview of Computer History

Almost since the beginning of time, people have been interested in inventing machines that can help them work faster and more efficiently. First, it was the wheel; then came the lever, the cotton gin, and the steam engine, just to name a few. Over the years, these simple, labor-saving devices have become more complex and have helped solve many problems that face us. Today, machines such as the computer—an electronic device that performs calculations and processes information—help us solve problems in our schools, homes, workplaces, communities, and around the globe.

How did the modern computer come to be invented? You will learn more about the history of the computer in Module 10, *The History of Computers*. But, in brief, the invention of the modern computer was sparked by World War II (1939–1945). The United States military needed to make many complex calculations quickly about ballistics—the study of how artillery shells move toward a target. Military leaders already had hundreds of people calculating tables and performing all kinds of complex tasks, but these tasks needed to be calculated more quickly and with greater accuracy. What was really needed was a machine that could process and interpret many pieces of information, or data.

In 1944, at Harvard University in Boston, a team of engineers designed one of the first general-purpose computers. The Mark I was 51 feet (16 m) long and eight feet (2 m) tall. It filled a large room and weighed several tons.

At the end of World War II, the first all-electronic computer was built. It was called ENIAC, which stands for Electronic Numerical Integrator And Calculator. ENIAC was much faster than the Mark I because it processed and stored information electronically, rather than mechanically. The ENIAC was even more enormous than the Mark I. It took up over 3,000 cubic feet (84 cubic m) of space—more space than is found in most really big houses!

You will learn more details about the ways different generations of computers—from *mainframes* to *minicomputers* to *microcomputers*—were developed, and how they were used to help people and society, in Module 10.

COMPUTERS THEN & NOW

Thousands of years ago, people in the Middle East, China, and Greece used a tool called an *abacus* (A buh kuhs). The abacus used units of tens, hundreds, and thousands to help early peoples add and subtract large numbers. Once a person learned how, it was an easy tool to use. Today, we still use the base 10, or decimal, number system for the math we study.

Many people think that the modern computer is a descendant of the abacus—one of the world's first calculators.

COMPUTERS IN SOCIETY

Using Computers in Today's Society

Laptop computers, today's solution for the on-the-go businessperson

COMPUTERS THEN & NOW

The early computers were not only very large but also slow and hard to use. They also used lots of energy.

Today, most *personal computers,* or *"PCs,"* as they are known, weigh less than 20 pounds (9 kg). Some *laptop* models weigh only four or five pounds (2 kg). Today's PCs are faster, do more, and consume less energy than did the models of only last year!

It seems like almost every day new computers show up on the market. You'll be surprised at how quickly technology is changing our world. To find out what's the newest computer on the market, scan a newspaper, visit a library, or check out a computer store.

The following articles and interviews describe a number of people in a wide variety of fields. In fact, some are your age. What, if anything, do all these people have in common? They all rely on computers to help them do their jobs. (After all, school is a job, too!)

Read the selections that follow. Then, work with your classmates to make two lists. First, think of as many people as you can in your community who use computers in their jobs or at home. Write the names of these people in a vertical column on a sheet of paper. Then, next to each name, identify what career or business that individual is involved in. How many uses for computers did you find in your community?

Do you know yet what career you want after you graduate from school? What are your interests? How do you think the profession you choose will use computers five or 10 years from now? In what ways can you prepare yourself now for using computers in the field you select?

Computers are used in a variety of businesses and industries. You can probably name several careers in which computers play a major role. You can probably also name many people in your town or city who use computers in their jobs.

MODULE 1

Using Computers in Today's Society

COMPUTERS IN HEALTH AND MEDICINE

Staying healthy doesn't depend on computers— or does it? Samuel and Krista talked with two doctors to find out how computers are used in medicine. Here's part of their report:

MEDICAL DOCTORS

Dr. Rivera is a pediatrician, a children's doctor. "I see children of different ages, from babies to teens," he told us one day after school in his office. "One child may have a cold, another a high fever, and another a broken leg."

Sometimes Dr. Rivera can't tell what's wrong with a seriously ill patient unless he uses a computerized axial tomography (CAT) scanner. A *CAT scan* is a sophisticated medical test that uses a computer to look at all or part of the human body by making a "3-D," or three-dimensional, picture. In the case of a head-injury patient, for example, Dr. Rivera can use a computer, a *monitor*, and a type of television camera to "see" the location and extent of the injury from the outside, rather than performing exploratory surgery on the patient.

"The CAT scan lets me see where my eyes can't see," Dr. Rivera said. "If I didn't have the picture, I might not be able to tell what's wrong. By studying the picture, I can usually determine the best way to treat my patient."

The CAT scanner is just one piece of computer equipment that Dr. Rivera uses. The doctor also uses computers to record patient information and keep up-to-date medical records, as well as to research and study the newest medical techniques and findings.

"There's no doubt about it," says Dr. Rivera at the conclusion of the interview. "Using computers and all they have to offer definitely helps to make me a significantly better doctor."

DID YOU KNOW?

Did you know that, thanks to a special type of computer, some individuals who are deaf or very hard of hearing may be able to hear?

The cochlear (KAHK leer) implant is a new electronic hearing device. When it is placed in a person's ear, the implant changes sound into electrical impulses. These impulses travel almost instantly to the brain. In many cases, the brain is then able to translate the electrical impulses into sound.

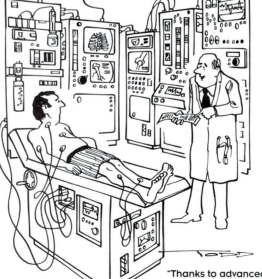

"Thanks to advanced technology we can start treating you immediately . . . for one of five things!"

SURGEONS

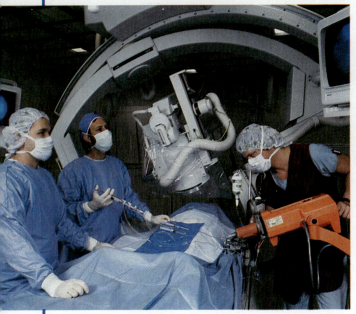

Doctors using computers to perform surgery

Dr. Siano is a surgeon, a doctor who performs operations, at the community hospital. She specializes in arthroscopic (ahr thrah SKAH pihk), or joint, surgery. "Surgery is only used when it's absolutely necessary," Dr. Siano said, as we visited her making her rounds to check on recovering patients. "When surgery is needed, computers play an important role in the operating room, or O-R, as we call it. Computers help me monitor my patient's progress by keeping track of blood pressure, heart and breathing rates, and more. With computers to help us, surgery is safer, too," she said. "It takes teamwork in the O-R—and computers are part of our team."

Dr. Siano also told us that computers help her perform delicate operations, such as knee-joint surgery. The doctor diagnoses the problem by inserting a tiny, tubelike instrument into the joint through a small incision. A kind of camera lens at the end of the instrument is then inserted, so that the doctor can actually see what the problem is. If needed, a second incision can be made to perform the surgery, without making a large incision.

C·A·R·E·E·R·S

SALESPERSON • ELECTRICIAN • ASTRONAUT • MECHANIC • ENGINEER • PHYSICIST • DENTIST • FARMER • NURSE • DOCTOR • TEACHER • SURGEON • OPTOMETRIST • PILOT • PROFESSOR • SECRETARY • ARTIST

My name is Adele Mimnaugh, and I'm an occupational therapist at St. Joseph's Hospital in Paterson, NJ. I help people become as independent as possible so that they can function in society.

One of the really neat things that I use with my patients who are unable to walk is a special, voice-operated wheelchair. By speaking into a device on the wheelchair, I can show you how to make it do things. If you tell it to turn left, it turns left. If you want to stop, just say "stop" and it does.

There are a lot of other voice-operated devices. What do you know about voice-operated (or voice-activated) devices? Find out more about how these devices are helping people all over the world.

Because the cut is so small and the discomfort slight, most patients experience less pain than in traditional surgical procedures. Another benefit of computer-assisted surgery is that the computer actually saves the patient the additional cost of lengthy hospital stays.

What other ways can computers help us stay healthy? Why not find out? Visit a local clinic or hospital, or ask a doctor, nurse, or technician to visit your class. If you're interested in a medical career, these professionals can tell you what kinds of schooling you'll need and what subjects you should take.

Using Computers in Today's Society

COMPUTERS IN BUSINESS AND INDUSTRY

Today, computers are playing a big role in how we drive. Almost all cars today use computers to regulate the flow of fuel, monitor maintenance, and prevent brakes from locking.

David, a seventeen-year-old, has a part-time job at a gas station. Do gas stations use computers? Well, the people that work there certainly do!

AUTO MECHANICS

"I work at City Garage on Saturdays. I pump gas, check the oil, wash windshields, and help fix cars. I guess you can tell that I want to be a mechanic. My boss, Harry, is the greatest, and I'm getting a lot of on-the-job experience from him. Someday, I hope I'll be as good a mechanic as Harry is.

When Harry was 45, he went back to school. He wanted to learn how to use a computer to repair cars. Today's cars aren't simple driving machines that just gas up and go. They are very complicated machines that need regular maintenance to keep them in good running condition. Without computers to help him find a problem, Harry could spend a whole day on just one car. Now, Harry can fix more cars much more quickly and accurately than he could without the help of computers.

Right now, I'm learning all I can about cars. I take auto shop and a computer class at school. After I graduate from high school, I'm planning to go to auto mechanic's school and become a mechanic—just like Harry."

AUTOMOTIVE ENGINEERS

My Aunt Denise works for a car manufacturer, and she uses computers to help design new cars. She's what is called an "automotive engineer."

As part of her job, Aunt Denise uses a computer to test the fuel efficiency of a car. The more fuel-efficient, the better gas mileage the car gets, the less fuel the car consumes, and the less gas we have to buy.

My aunt also uses computer *software* called *computer-aided design/computer-aided manufacture* (CAD/CAM) to draw designs of how the new cars will look. She draws different shapes for the body of the car. Then, still using a computer, she tests each body shape to see which one is most fuel-efficient. Aunt Denise is even working with a team of engineers to design cars for the future. They are using

Computers aiding in automotive manufacturing

computers to design a solar-powered car that will be powered by energy from the sun—not a fossil fuel like gasoline.

How will computers change what we drive and the way we drive in the future? If you're interested in cars, why not ask an auto mechanic or an automotive engineer to visit your class?

Using computers on the farm to track expenses, keep records of supplies, and monitor weather reports

FARMERS

Of course, computers don't grow like corn or wheat. Yet, computers are helping more and more farmers feed the world. Find out how one farmer uses computers.

"Hi, my name is Sarah, and I'm from a tiny town in Virginia. You may be surprised to know that I'm a farmer. A number of women farm these days. Farming is hard work, but I love it!

I didn't grow up on a farm. My family lived in the city of Roanoke. My parents had a lot of plants at home. They also had a small plot in a community garden. I guess that's where I first became interested in farming.

I worked in our garden every summer. In high school, I had my own garden. I even made money selling the flowers and vegetables I grew. That money helped me go to college to study agriculture.

I never thought I would need to use a computer to farm, but on a good-sized farm like my husband's and mine, computers are important. I use mine to help me plan which crops to grow—such as corn—and in which fields to grow them.

Computers also help me run my farm as a business. I use it to keep track of my expenses. It helps me decide when I need to order more supplies, such as seed, fertilizer, and feed for my animals.

Weather is always important to a farmer. I use my computer to keep track of up-to-date weather reports. The weather reports I get through a *network* help me decide if I should water my fields or wait for rain.

It's difficult enough to be a farmer these days; why make it more difficult on myself? I use every tool that I can, including my computer. I 'read up' on new technology—using my computer, of course—to help me increase crop production. I keep track of my expenses and my income. A farming life is still not easy, but it is easier thanks to the computer."

COMPUTERS IN THE TRANSPORTATION INDUSTRY

People in the transportation industry—who deal in the shipping and receiving of cargo or people—use computers to make more efficient use of time, distance, and labor. Computers are used by people who work on the railroads, in the trucking industry, at shipping companies, and at the airlines to move goods and people around the world.

Exactly how are computers used to ensure that people and goods arrive safely, on time, and on budget to their proper destination? To answer this question, the authors of this book spoke to a number of people at Southwest Airlines, a regional airline serving Texas and other states in the Southwest, to find out what they said.

The airline industry uses computers for many reasons. Ground

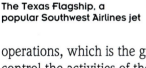

The Texas Flagship, a popular Southwest Airlines jet

operations, which is the group of workers who control the activities of the airline on the ground, uses computers to keep track of ticketing. Passengers who make reservations to fly to one of the various Southwest Airlines destinations do so by speaking with a ticket agent. Once the agent receives the necessary information, the reservation is entered into the computer. At the airport, passengers with a valid credit card can use a touch-screen computer to indicate their final destination, select the fare they are to pay, and receive their tickets—all without meeting anyone face-to-face. And, once the passenger arrives at the airport, the most recent arrival and departure information is posted on computer monitors throughout the airline terminal.

Once the reservation is confirmed, the airline uses a computerized information system called AMRIS to track the number of seats that are sold on each flight. The computer also identifies which cities are so popular that they might need additional flights. The less popular routes, however, might see a decrease in the number of flights each day!

Flight crews are scheduled by using the computer, as well. Not only does Southwest's computer identify who flies where, it schedules how long a flight attendant might be out of town, and the maximum number of flight hours a pilot can log between rest periods. Training time and vacation time are also scheduled via the computer.

Safety is a big concern to any airline. Southwest Airlines maintains an up-to-date database of aircraft maintenance and engineering information. When was the aircraft last serviced? Check the computer.

Looking for a replacement part on an aircraft with a mechanical problem? Check the computer for the location of the nearest spare part.

Records and interoffice communications are handled through—you guessed it—the computer! Lost baggage, employee payroll, and interoffice messages are communicated through various databases, spreadsheets, and *electronic mail (E-mail)* systems.

Ask your friends and family if they know anyone who works in the transportation field. Your teacher might want to invite a guest speaker to class to talk to you and your classmates about careers in aviation.

COMPUTERS IN GOVERNMENT AND LAW ENFORCEMENT

LAW ENFORCEMENT OFFICERS

Can computers help fight crime? Read how one police officer uses computers to help him do his job.

"I've been a police officer for over 15 years. I never thought computers would help me in my job. Was I ever wrong!

We depend on computers for fast and accurate information. We have computer *files* about all sorts of things—stolen cars, criminal records, and arrest warrants, just to name a few.

Our computer files on criminals include descriptions about hair and eye color, height and weight, and recognizable marks, such as scars. Our computer files on stolen cars record license numbers, the color and make (or model) of the car, and registration information.

Our computer lets me get the information I need, when I need it. For example, if I'm looking for speeders on our highways, I can simply point a computerized radar "gun" at the vehicle and record its speed. If I have to arrest a suspect, I can use the computer to see if that individual is wanted anywhere else. I have a terminal right in the patrol car that's hooked into the main computer by radio. It's called a *mobile data terminal*.

I've also worked with federal law enforcement agencies on a few cases. The Federal Bureau of Investigation (FBI) has a computerized file of fingerprints that is unbelievable. Agents can match up an unknown fingerprint with one in their files in a matter of seconds. Our local precinct sometimes calls the FBI headquarters in Washington, DC, to ask for help and information.

Today, I depend on computers to help me do my job well. Computers make great crime-fighting partners."

MILITARY CAREERS

Our military leaders and troops use computers to help protect the citizens of the United States. Radar planes and computerized radar systems help track satellites (ours and those of foreign countries) and provide us with up-to-the-minute information on issues of national security. Military aircraft, equipped with a variety of computers, routinely search the skies for signs of increased activity to alert us to a possible problem.

Computers are used, too, in times of military alert. Pilots can use laser-guided missiles to shoot down enemy planes and missiles. Computers are used to plan troop maneuvers and strategies. In times of peace, the military uses computers to analyze data, simulate battle situations, and to develop advanced machinery.

MULTI CULTURAL BYTE

As Chairman of the Joint Chiefs of Staff, General Colin Powell played a key role in 1991's Operation Desert Storm, removing Iraq's army from Kuwait. How did he accomplish this goal? "There are no secrets . . . ," Powell says. "Success is the result of perfection, hard work, learning from failure." By using computers to simulate, or role-play, battle scenarios and to test new equipment and strategies, Powell can keep America's armed forces at peak effectiveness, while maintaining the overall defense budget.

READ ALL ABOUT IT

**From *The Boston Globe*
August 6, 1991**

Astronauts Test Mail by Computer

HOUSTON—A battle for communications supremacy is raging in space, where electronic mail could replace the fax machine on the shuttle Atlantis and on space craft of the future.

Yesterday the space shuttle astronauts continued a first test of an electronic mail system that would enable them to converse by computer with NASA ground controllers.

If it works, it could replace the Text and Graphic System, or space fax machine, that is the primary method NASA uses to communicate with the astronauts, officials say.

"It is quite possible, even likely, for the space station Freedom that electronic messaging could become the first means of communication," the National Aeronautics and Space Administration's project investigator, Mark Dean, said in an interview.

Word of the experiment has leaked to computer users around the world, about 80 of whom have sent their own such mail to a special, separate electronic basket set up for the public to send messages to the astronauts.

The crew will receive the messages when they return home, Dean said.

"I'll bet you 10 bucks it's Mrs. Platt's form again."

THE INTERNAL REVENUE SERVICE

The Internal Revenue Service (IRS) is the branch of the Department of the Treasury responsible for collecting federal income tax. To perform this function, the IRS uses computers in many ways.

Over 120 million tax returns are filed each April. The IRS processes these returns by matching the figures submitted on each individual return to the corresponding figures supplied by employers, banks, mortgage companies, and other financial institutions that are required to report interest and income.

The IRS also uses computers to keep track of common errors made by taxpayers and to create new versions of the income tax forms so that taxpayers can avoid making the same errors year after year.

A taxpayer can even file a tax return electronically by taking the return to a specified location, where the return is transmitted via computer to the IRS office. Now, people who are due a tax refund can receive their checks more quickly just by taking advantage of the electronic filing option.

Using Computers in Today's Society

COMPUTERS IN EDUCATION

COMPUTERS IN THE CLASSROOM

Look around your classroom. Notice all the different hair colors, eye colors, heights, and weights. Each one of you is unique, different in your own way. Just as you all have an individual look, you all have individual ways of learning. Computers help students learn "hands-on" about the world around them in their own learning styles.

Computers can help you build success at your own pace. You'll use math skills and learn new ones, you'll improve your reading and spelling skills, and you'll learn about different areas of interest—science, social studies, health, music, art, and so on. You'll learn how you can write stories, business letters, and advertisements using a word-processing program. You'll be able to create logos and greeting cards and animate pictures using a *graphics* program.

When using a computer, the possibilities are almost endless! But whether you are learning how to enter data, word process a letter to a pen pal, or create a graph, you are in control of your learning. Discover the wonderful world of computers and how they can bring the world to you!

A world of computers

TEACHERS USE COMPUTERS

★ READ ALL ABOUT IT ★

From *People Weekly Extra,*
Amazing Americans!
October, 1991
By Gail Wescott

Students Don't Fear Her Byte

Gail Morse created
a high-tech classroom
to prove that
today's kids won't
drop out if they can
tune in (the TVs)
and turn on
(the computers)

In these times of shrinking school budgets and sagging morale, chagrin is about all that most harried teachers have time for, while disengaged students dash home to the tube—in front of which the average American kid camps an astonishing 23 hours a week. But far from tsk-tsking such couch potato conduct, North Carolina science teacher Gail Morse went eyeball-to-eyeball with the enemy and turned her students' passion for electronic entertainment into a technique for learning. "Adults were paper-trained—books, scissors, glue," explains Morse. "Kids today are used to lights—by lights, I mean TVs, VCRs, Nintendos, computers."

Continued on next page

MODULE 1

★ READ ALL ABOUT IT ★

Gail Morse, a teacher in Huntersville, North Carolina, and an author of this book

Continued on next page

READ ALL ABOUT IT

To both interest and educate her classes at J.M. Alexander Junior High in Huntersville, just north of Charlotte, Morse has begged and borrowed from local and national businesses a smorgasbord of plug-ins that she values at $25,000: PCs, televisions, laser-disc and videocassette units, video cameras and camcorders and even a satellite dish on the roof. These are the tools she feels will best reach today's technologically literate youngsters.

Two years ago Morse's theories were put to the test when she and colleague Pam Shillinglaw took on a group of students the school considered "at risk." Recalls Morse of the 56 seventh graders with low grades and spotty attendance records: "They were kids other teachers are glad to see in *your* classroom." But once they entered the wired environment, they seemed transformed. Students readily took to such InfoAge skills as desktop publishing (they composed letters that they zapped to other schools around the country) and videotape production (they created term cassettes, rather than papers). In the process, they also polished their math, science and language abilities. A year later, 48 of the students tested at least one level higher in science, and 20 went on to an advanced class.

Their progress was especially gratifying for Morse, who remembers being a "mediocre student" herself while growing up in Roselle, NJ. After graduating from high school, she landed a job fielding complaints for AT&T in South Plainfield, NJ. "I started noticing that the people who got promotions all had degrees," Morse says. "That got my attention." It also spurred her to work her way through Ohio's University of Dayton, where she majored in science. Currently, she lives in Mooresville with the youngest of her seven children, Susan, 17, and Gina, 14.

Morse credits the in-class boredom of her own children with her changing attitude toward teaching others. "Traditionally, we have been dispensers of information, standing in the front of the room like dictators. Those days are over. I see myself as a collaborator, a researcher, a catalyst." Yet electronics alone are not the answer, she says. "There are teachers filling up their rooms with what I call the stuff. But the stuff is not what makes a difference. It's how you use it to help kids learn. If we're going to teach them how to achieve in the 21st century, then we're going to have to change the whole culture of the classroom."—T.C.; GAIL WESCOTT in Huntersville ■

MAKE A DIFFERENCE

Does your school have enough computers? Computer equipment costs a lot of money. Many school systems have limited budgets. They can only spend a given amount of money on computers because they need money for other expenses, too.

If your school budget is tight, you don't have to go without computer equipment. You can help your school raise money to buy equipment, or you can help set up "computer-loan" programs with local businesses.

Here are some ways to help your school earn money to buy more computer equipment.

GROCERY STORE GIVEAWAY

Some grocery stores sponsor computers for schools. Customers give their register receipts to the school. When enough receipts have been saved, the school exchanges the receipts for computer equipment.

FUND-RAISERS

Some schools use dances, recycling efforts, bake sales, and other projects to earn money for computer equipment. Often, other organizations help sponsor, or support, fund-raising efforts for education. Check with your teacher or principal. Ask if your school's Parent-Teacher Association (PTA/PTO) will lend support for a worthwhile cause.

COMPUTER LOANS

Perhaps a local business will let you borrow its old computer equipment. Make a deal with the owner or manager. For example, offer to include a free ad in your school newspaper if the business lends you a piece of computer equipment.

Getting computers for your school is a joint effort, not just an adult's responsibility. Help in whatever ways you can and ask your fellow classmates to pitch in, too.

DEBATING
THE COMPUTER ISSUE

*Are computers the answer to our world's problems?
Derrick and Allison disagree on the answer to this question.
Read along as they debate the issue in their science class.*

I'm Derrick. I think computers are the answer to many of our world's problems. Computers already touch all parts of our lives. We use computers at home, at school, and at work. When we travel, computers are at work, helping us get where we're going—safely and on time.

Computers help us protect our environment and discover cures for many diseases. New inventions and products are often designed and tested using computers.

The future uses of computers are limitless! They can help us solve a number of our problems and create a better world. Are computers the answer? You bet!

Derrick, I disagree. Computers are only a tool. Only we human beings can solve the big problems we face today, as well as those we will face tomorrow, and in future generations.

Computers can help us study the environment, but they can't stop acid rain. Computers can tell us how quickly we are using up our landfills and how much paper and waste we discard, but they can't recycle for us. Computers can be used to help deliver food to starving nations, but they can't solve world hunger.

Computers can help us, but they can't create a better world. That's up to each of us, as members of one *global village*.

Students debating the impact computers have on the global village

WHAT'S YOUR OPINION?

Are computers the answer to solving world problems? Or, are computers just a tool?

Find out what others think about computers solving world problems such as hunger and pollution. Here are some ideas to help you get started.

1. **Take a survey.** Plan a list of questions you want to ask classmates, teachers, friends, and neighbors. Record the answers you get.

2. **Conduct a debate.** Divide your class into two teams. Have each team research the "pros and cons" of using computers to solve world problems. Conduct a debate like Allison and Derrick did. Ask a panel of judges to determine which side presented the strongest arguments.

3. **Interview experts in your community.** Talk with people who work with computers—scientists, engineers, auto mechanics, doctors, and other businesspeople. How do they think computers will be used in the future to solve global problems?

4. **Write a report.** Go to your school library and ask your librarian to help you locate current information about computers. If your school is linked to an "information" network, ask someone to assist you in finding the most up-to-date information. Write a report on your findings, and share it with your class.

5. **Write for information.** Contact local, state, national, or world hunger organizations. Find out if they use computers and, if so, how. Share the information you find with your class.

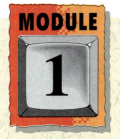

MODULE SUMMARY QUESTIONS

In order to check your comprehension of how computers affect people in our society, you may wish to discuss the following ideas.

1. Computers are used by many kinds of people for a variety of purposes. Name five careers mentioned in Module 1. Then describe how someone in each field might use computers to perform his or her job.

2. Computer-based medical inventions, such as the cochlear implant and the voice-operated wheelchair, are often used to help people attain goals they might otherwise be unable to achieve. How do you think braille touch-screen computers and voice-activated computers help blind students learn in the classroom?

3. Learning how to use computers will help you achieve greater success in school, at work, and in life in general. As you see it, what are three advantages of knowing how to use computers? Explain.

MODULE 2

How Computers Work

Computers are complicated, fascinating machines that are made up of many different parts. A hard drive (pictured here), the Central Processing Unit, and chips are only some of the necessary components that a computer needs to function.

In Module 2, you'll learn about *all* the parts that work together to make up the incredible machine we call a computer. And, you'll learn what to keep in mind when shopping for a computer.

THE COMPUTER FACTORY

What does a computer really do? Think of the computer as an information factory and compare it to a factory that makes cookies. A computer makes a product, just as the cookie factory makes cookies. The computer's product is information.

To make cookies, raw ingredients are needed such as flour, shortening, sugar, vanilla, and eggs. The cookie factory takes food of one form, the sugar and the other ingredients, and changes it, through a process, into food of a different form—the cookies.

Just as the cookie factory makes food from food, the computer makes information from information. The computer's raw ingredients are facts called data. The computer takes data, or information, in one form and works with it to change it into a different form.

A baker, who supervises the factory's operations, follows a recipe to make cookies. The recipe is really just a list of instructions to be followed. The computer has a supervisor, too. Its "baker" is called a *Central Processing Unit,* or *CPU* (the main component, or "brain" of the computer). The CPU follows its list of instructions, called a program, to perform its tasks. The computer program works like a baking recipe. Instead of food, however, the CPU uses data as "ingredients."

In the cookie factory, the baker has helpers who form a system for cookie making. A computer is often called a system, too, for much the same reason. The computer's CPU does not do all of the work. Following a program's instructions, the CPU gathers data and information from *input* devices, such as the *keyboard* or the *mouse.* A mouse, in computer talk, is a small hand-held device moved around on a surface to cause the *cursor* to move on the screen and to make selections within a program. The cursor is a spot of light or symbol that you see on the screen that shows the exact place at which you are entering data. The instructions of the program, the "recipe," tell the CPU what to do with the data, or "ingredients," it receives. The data, in the form of electrical pulses that the computer understands, is stored in the computer's memory until it is needed.

At very high speeds, the CPU "supervisor" routes data to other devices so that special jobs can be performed with the data. When the instructions of the program are completed, the CPU routes the data, in its final form, to an *output* device, such as the screen or *printer,* where you can see the results.

Just as the cookie factory can change the raw ingredients for cookies into something you can enjoy, the computer changes its raw ingredients—data— into another form of information.

Inputting ingredients to make a product

PARTS OF THE COMPUTER

"Dad, may I use the computer to do my homework?" asks John Fenton, a computer literacy student in Santa Clara, California. "I need to take it apart to see what makes it work."

"Whoa! Wait a minute, John," says his dad, a college computer instructor. "What are you doing?"

John replies, "I have to write a report to explain how a computer works, so I thought I'd take this one apart and see what's inside." John lays the tools down on the table and says, "Maybe I should ask you to do this with me. Then, you could explain what the parts are."

"And get them back in the right place," adds his dad. "First of all, we don't need to use any tools to open up this machine," says dad, "and we need to be careful because some of the parts are delicate. Let's start with the system unit, this big box you call the computer. You know, the computer is really all of these things: the system unit, the keyboard, screen, mouse, and printer, all together. That's why it's called a 'system.' It's a group of devices that work together; sort of a computing team."

As his dad lifts the lid off of the system unit, John sees hundreds of black and colored objects. "Are these chips?" asks John.

"Yes, some of them are," answers his dad. "Most of these black, rectangular things in here are *integrated circuits (ICs);* those are the ones we call *chips*. They're tiny, but complete, electronic circuits, which may contain up to hundreds of thousands of *transistors* and other electronic components. They're used in place of other, much larger, electronic components which were used in earlier computers. Thanks to these tiny chips, today's computers are much smaller, faster, and more reliable than the older computers I first used."

Looking inside a computer

THE CENTRAL PROCESSING UNIT

One of the most important chips inside the personal computer is the *microprocessor.* This is the Central Processing Unit (CPU). The computer's basic *functions* are to receive input information, process that information, then produce a new form of it for output. The CPU's job is to make these functions work correctly.

The CPU is made up of two major parts. One part is called the *control unit.* The control unit is the computer's "traffic cop," making sure that the program's instructions are followed correctly and at the right time. The control unit

Parts of the Computer

also controls the movement of data from input to the computer's memory, and from memory to output.

A second part of the CPU is the *Arithmetic Logic Unit (ALU)*. This is where all of the computer's arithmetic is performed. If you want the computer to add, subtract, multiply, or divide, the control unit routes the data to the ALU where the actual math work is done. When the ALU has the answer, the control unit will move the answer to some location in the computer's memory.

Logic functions are also performed by the ALU. A logic function is one where the computer compares data using some conditions. The data can be a number, an equation, or even a word. The computer tests the relationship between items of data to determine whether they are equal to each other, or not equal, or whether they relate in any of the other logical ways in which data can be compared. Just as someone might use a comparison to make a decision (for instance, comparing the price of one brand of shirt to another), logic functions are used by the computer to decide what operation is to be done next.

MEMORY—RAM AND ROM

"Where is the computer's memory?" John asks his dad. The computer's memory is also made up of chips.

"You know how the computer goes through a system check process when you first turn it on?" asks his dad. "Well, that process is controlled by computer instructions which are built into the *Read-Only Memory (ROM)*. Read-only means that the computer can only read what is contained in these chips and cannot change what is there. When you are using the computer and you type in data, the computer stores the data in *primary storage* called *Random Access Memory (RAM)*. That is the type of memory we usually talk about when someone wants to know how much memory our computer has. The memory capacity of a computer is measured in *bytes*. A byte is equal to one *character* (a letter, a number, a symbol, or a space). Your friend, Brian, says his computer has 640K of memory. The letter "K" stands for *kilobyte*, which means about 1,000 bytes, or characters, of *storage* in memory. (The exact number of bytes in a kilobyte is 1,024.) So Brian's computer can store about 640,000 characters in its main memory. My computer has 2 *megabytes*, or million bytes, of memory, which means it can store about 2 million characters.

We call the memory 'random access' because the computer can access any one of these thousands—or millions—of *address* locations in memory. (Actually, ROM also can be randomly accessed.) It's like going to a friend's house. If you have the address, you can go right to it. You don't have to knock on every door in the neighborhood to find the right house.

RAM is also changeable memory. When data is stored in RAM, you can have the computer read the data as often as you need to. But you can also change the data stored there by letting the

---

MULTICULTURAL BYTE

At age 25, An Wang immigrated to the United States from China. He landed a job working on one of the world's first computers. Wang worked on improving the computer's memory. Memory lets a computer store data. Wang designed a core memory that helped computers store more data, work faster, and make fewer errors.

Wang's personal goal was to make computers that everyone would be able to use. In 1951, Dr. Wang started his own computer company. He became one of the leaders in the computer industry. In the 1970s, Wang computers were synonymous with office word processing.

Parts of the Computer

"I know it's been three days since installation, as soon as we find the OFF-ON switch you can start operations."

Parts of the Computer

computer access the data's storage location in RAM and putting new data there. Then, when you read the data again, you will be reading the new data instead of the old value that was replaced.

A big difference between ROM and RAM is that the information stored in ROM stays there when you turn the computer off and is there, ready for you, when you turn the computer back on. RAM, on the other hand, is *volatile,* or temporary, memory. When you turn on the computer, RAM is empty and anything that is put into RAM while the computer is on will be erased and lost whenever the computer is turned off again."

STORAGE

"Dad, I thought the computer's memory was on these disks we put into the machine," John remarks. "If the computer's memory is in those chips, then what's on these disks?"

His dad explains, "Well, although some people do use the word 'memory' for their disks, the correct word would be storage. It's also called *secondary storage,* to show the difference between disk storage and the computer's primary memory. Disks are also called *peripheral* devices because they're not part of the CPU, as are the control units and memory. All other items of equipment attached to the CPU electronically, such as the input and output devices, are peripherals as well.

Disks provide a place where you can store your data and your programs, or sets of instructions, when you're not using them or when the computer is turned off. Remember, the computer's main memory erases anything stored in RAM when the power is turned off, so disks provide permanent storage.

Data and programs are stored on a disk in a coded form understood by the computer. The codes are made up of magnetic signals stored on the surface of the disk. Both *hard disks* and *floppy disks* store data in this way. Hard disks store more data than floppy disks and are able to store and retrieve data faster. On the other hand, floppy disks offer the convenience of being removable, so that they can be carried to another computer, which is not always possible with the hard disk.

A magnetic tape cartridge is an alternate form of storage, one often used to make a permanent *backup copy,* or a duplicate of the original, of the data stored on hard disks to guard against loss. This unit uses a magnetic tape, somewhat like those used for cassette tapes to record music. Data stored on a magnetic tape cartridge is stored in the same magnetic coded form as on the disk.

More recent forms of storage are optical discs, which use tiny laser beams to read and, depending on the type of drive, write information onto discs. *CD-ROM* (Compact Disc Read-Only Memory), WORM (Write Once, Read Many) drives, and erasable optical drives all use optical discs. A CD-ROM uses laser beams to read information. You cannot write on a CD-ROM.

MODULE 2

Parts of the Computer

A CD-ROM can store up to 650 megabytes. WORM discs and drives allow a file to be saved only one time, but to be opened and read many times. Erasable optical discs and drives are different from CD-ROMs in that they allow the user to write over a file many times and to read it many times."

INPUT DEVICES

"So, how does all of this stuff get in and out of the computer?" asks John. "I mean, how does the computer know what to do with the button I press on the keyboard, or when to show something on the screen?"

"First, let's get clear what the 'stuff' is," John's dad replies. "The computer gets data as input. Data are the numbers, letters, words, or other facts that you feed into the computer so that it can do its work. Data do not have to be typed in on the keyboard. There are many types of data, and many ways to get it into the computer. In every case, though, the purpose of an input device is to receive the data and change it to a form that the computer can use and store."

The most familiar input device may be the keyboard. The letter and number keys make it possible to enter the words for a report or numbers for a math assignment. Keyboards contain other keys, too, which have special uses. Many keyboards have *command keys* or *function keys* that might be labeled F1, F2, and so on. Function keys help to simplify the keystrokes used to perform computer operations. The actual action performed by a function key is assigned by a program, so a function key does not necessarily always have the same purpose.

A mouse is certainly a popular input device, and one that makes computing easier. As you have read, the mouse is a pointing device that points to a location on the computer's screen. A program then senses the place you have pointed to on the screen and interprets the action you have indicated at that location. There are other devices that do just about the same thing as a mouse. A touch-sensitive screen has a special panel that senses where your finger is pointing, and a light pen uses a signal to indicate a position on the screen. With either of these, the program then works the same as it would with a mouse.

A different way to get data into the computer is to use a *scanner*. There are many forms of scanners. You may have seen one type, a laser scanner, at the supermarket check-out counters. This device scans the bar code printed on the grocery items and converts the bars into codes for numbers and letters that the computer understands. Other scanners read pencil marks on tests, coded characters on checks, and many other things. Some scanners can even read the text out of a book or newspaper, and convert it into input for the computer. Just think of the millions and millions of keystrokes that would save.

An exciting form of computer input has to do with image processing. Scanners that read pictures, drawings, photographs, or television images have been developed to convert these images into computer data that can be processed.

HOW COMPUTERS WORK

Some computers can use voice recognition equipment —peripherals that can recognize something you say and convert it to computer input. Simple commands, such as "Go" or "Up," and even more complicated commands and input, such as complete spoken sentences, are being used more and more by newly developed voice recognition devices.

OUTPUT DEVICES

While sound (including voice output) and images (such as full-color television pictures) are becoming popular, monitors and printers are the most commonly used computer output devices. Monitors, sometimes known as *CRTs (Cathode Ray Tubes),* show information on a screen. Because the image on a screen is only temporary, this form of output is called soft copy. The monitor can have a color screen, displaying many colors at the same time, or a monochrome screen, which displays data in only one color. Most computer users today prefer graphics monitors because they are able to show pictures as well as words and numbers.

To have a more permanent form of output, such as a report to hand in for homework, you need a device that produces *hard copy.* This generally means that you will use a printer, the second most common computer output device.

Printers come in many types. A low-cost type of computer printer is the *dot-matrix printer.* This printer uses a moving bundle of very small wires to form letters by making small dots that are in the shape of a letter or number. They can also produce graphic designs in the same way— by making a pattern of dots in the desired shape. Some printers can form characters by shooting out tiny droplets of ink. These are known as *ink-jet printers.* If the printer has a colored ribbon or uses colored ink, the output can be in color as well as in black.

Laser printers, which produce a superior image at much higher speeds than dot-matrix printers, are really a cross between a copying machine and a special, computer-controlled dot-matrix printer. Inside the laser printer, a special computer directs laser light to make very small dots, at 300 or more dots per inch, on a light-sensitive drum. The drum then works as a copier would by printing the image on a piece of paper. Specialized forms of laser printers can also produce high-quality, full-color output.

Producing high-quality images with laser printers

BACK TO WORK

"Well, I guess we'd better get this computer back together now so you can do your report. I hope this helped you," John's dad says to John.

"Wow, that's a lot of stuff to learn," John replies. "I don't know if I can remember it all. Uh, Dad? Do you think you could stay and help me type the report?"

A Miracle Made of Sand

The next time you take a walk on the beach, look down at the sand under your feet. You could be walking over millions of future computer chips. Sand contains silicon, which is the second most common element found on earth (oxygen is the most common). Silicon is also found in the mineral quartz. Quartz is mined in small pieces to supply most of the silicon used to make the integrated circuits (ICs) in microcomputer chips.

To create these electronic marvels, engineers first design the chip's circuits and components on diagrams that might be wall-sized. When the design is complete, the diagrams are reduced hundreds of times until they are only about one-fourth of a square inch (one square centimeter) in size. Next, the reduced diagrams are copied onto glass squares, called photomasks.

While the photomasks are being made, other workers are using a special vacuum oven to change pieces of silicon-laden quartz into a rod-shaped crystal that is 99.99 percent pure silicon. Next, the rod is sliced into thin wafers. The wafers are then heated until they are red-hot so that they will produce a thin coating of silicon dioxide. Electricity cannot flow through silicon dioxide. It is this property that is at the heart of integrated circuit technology.

The cooled wafers are then coated with a light-sensitive chemical called photoresist. A photomask is placed over the wafer. Ultraviolet light, shining through the photomask, changes the photoresist to form the circuit pattern. Next, special materials are placed on the exposed silicon patterns. These materials eventually form the electronic components that make up the integrated circuit. The wafers are then reheated in ovens and the whole process is repeated again. The same steps must be done to produce each layer of circuits and components designed for the integrated circuit. Thin metal pathways are laid over the wafers to form electrical connections between components.

Computer technicians examining chips in a "clean room"

After testing, the wafer is cut with a diamond saw or laser to separate the individual chips. The bad chips are discarded. Then, using thin, gold wires, assembly workers bond metal pads at the edge of each good chip to connectors on a metal frame. The chip and its frame are then enclosed in a case. The frame has a row of metal pins that are used to plug the chip into sockets built into computers and other equipment.

★ Read All About It ★

From *Boys' Life*
August, 1991
By Robert W. Peterson

My Work as a Computer Technician

Adolfo González

As a boy, Adolfo González loved to take things apart to see what made them tick. "I was always curious," he says. "My parents used to punish me a lot because when I got a new toy, I would take it apart and it might never work again."

Today, Mr. González takes apart some really big "toys" and puts them back together so they do work. He is a computer service technician for big computer company IBM.

His job is to install, maintain, and repair computer systems. It is an important job because almost every business, industry, school, and government agency relies on computers.

González spends much of his working day in computer rooms of IBM's client companies in northern New Jersey. He checks out computer systems, cleans and lubricates tape and disk drives and printers, and makes adjustments.

He is never far from his own computer terminal that links him with IBM's service division in West Orange, NJ. When he hears beeps from the terminal, he knows there is computer trouble at a company in his area.

Punching buttons on the terminal, González learns where and what the trouble is. And off he goes to fix it.

"You've got to drop everything and run when a computer breaks down," he says, "because sometimes all work stops when a computer is down."

When he gets to the trouble site, González checks a printout on which the computer has logged its own internal workings. Often the log will show where and what the problem is. Using small hand tools, a Multimeter, and an oscilloscope, he fixes or replaces the balky component.

González, who is 25 years old, has been a computer service technician for three years. "I love the work," he says.

He knew when he finished high school that he wanted to work in electronics. He attended the DeVry Technical Institute in Woodbridge, NJ, for two years and graduated with a 4.0 grade point average as an electronic technician.

That was not the end of González' schooling. In his first year with IBM, he spent six months at the company's service school in Atlanta. "And training never stops," he says. "IBM keeps coming out with new machines, and so we go away and get trained to work on them."

González recommends that young people thinking about becoming computer service technicians take lots of math and physics courses in high school. "Math is a must," he says, "especially if you're going to electronics school." (Not every technician does; some are hired with no background in electronics.)

A technician must be mechanically inclined. Most computer system repairs are on drives and printers, which are mechanical devices.

"Another thing he needs is the ability to think logically," González says. "If you can't you're going to have a problem finding out what's wrong with a computer."

A technician needs good communication skills, says Pete Emmel, González' boss. "The technician has to be able to talk to a customer and deal with him one-on-one," he says. "That's equally important as his technical skills." ◼

Bits and Binary

When you press the keys on the computer's keyboard, everything you type is converted into numbers inside the computer. The numbers you type, however, are not the same ones that the computer uses.

When you count, or type numbers, you are using a system based on the number 10, called the decimal system. The digits of the decimal system are 0, 1, 2, 3, 4, 5, 6, 7, 8, and 9. The computer uses a system based on the number 2—a *binary system.* Can you guess which two digits are used in the binary system? If you answered 0 and 1, then you are correct. These binary digits are better known by their nickname: *bit* (a contraction of BInary and digiT).

Bits reflect the way a computer works. The only thing a computer really understands is two electrical states: on or off. The bit 0 stands for off, while 1 means on. While this may seem confusing, it actually simplifies things for the computer.

Using binary digits is not all that new. Gottfried Leibniz used binary digits in his computing machine, designed in 1694. At the foundation of computer instructions is a logic system developed in the 1850s by the English mathematician, George Boole (bool).

Two codes would not be enough to represent all of the letters, numbers, special characters and instructions used by the computer, so a group of 7 bits was created. A standard code table, called *ASCII (American Standard Code for Information Interchange),* is used by computer manufacturers so that data from one computer can be understood by other computers.

You and your friends can write messages to each other by using the binary ASCII code. For example, the message "Hi Mary," which has seven characters (the space counts as one character), would look like this:

1001000 1101001 0100000 1001101
1100001 1110010 1111001

How would you write "I am fine"?

Codes a computer understands

Binary Chart

ASCII Code (7 Bits)	Capital Letters	ASCII Code (7 Bits)	Capital Letters	ASCII Code (7 Bits)	Lower-case Letters	ASCII Code (7 Bits)	Lower-case Letters
1000001	A	1001110	N	1100001	a	1101110	n
1000010	B	1001111	O	1100010	b	1101111	o
1000011	C	1010000	P	1100011	c	1110000	p
1000100	D	1010001	Q	1100100	d	1110001	q
1000101	E	1010010	R	1100101	e	1110010	r
1000110	F	1010011	S	1100110	f	1110011	s
1000111	G	1010100	T	1100111	g	1110100	t
1001000	H	1010101	U	1101000	h	1110101	u
1001001	I	1010110	V	1101001	i	1110110	v
1001010	J	1010111	W	1101010	j	1110111	w
1001011	K	1011000	X	1101011	k	1111000	x
1001100	L	1011001	Y	1101100	l	1111001	y
1001101	M	1011010	Z	1101101	m	1111010	z

ASCII Code for Space (7 Bits) 0100000

The Software Connection

THE SOFTWARE

How does the computer know how to do what we want it to do? The answer is that the computer doesn't really know what to do until we give it specific instructions, known as a program. A wide variety of programs is available for computers of every type—from games to geometry, from spreadsheets to word processing.

Another name for computer programs is software. The keyboard, system unit, and monitor are called computer *hardware* because you can see them, touch them, and pick them up. You can't really see a program, although you could read the computer program code used to create it. A program is usually stored in the binary code understood by the computer—its machine language.

In fact, the first computers were programmed entirely in machine language binary code. This code appeared on paper as pages and pages of 0s and 1s. Everything the computer had to do was coded.

Eventually, computer engineers recognized that some of the computer's functions were always the same, such as recognizing the characters typed on the keyboard. These standard functions, together with other routines that made the operation of the computer more efficient, were combined into a program known as an *operating system*. The operating system has to be loaded into the computer's memory before the computer can be used.

The process of loading the operating system into memory is called *booting* the system. Programs that are used to run the computer or to manage systems-related tasks, such as *formatting* or initializing disks, are called *systems software*.

Using an operating system, such as DOS or the Macintosh System, you are able to tell the computer what you would like to do. By typing a command or using a mouse to indicate an activity, you tell the computer that you want to start using a program to accomplish a specific task. Programs that are used to do specific tasks are called *applications software*.

It takes the combination of two types of software, systems and applications, to accomplish anything with the computer. Whether the computer will be used to write a paper or draw a picture, you will start the computer with an operating system. Next, indicate your chosen activity using a *command* (which is a request to the operating system), and then use the applications software.

The applications software will use functions that are a part of the operating system. To get data from a disk, the applications software will issue a request for the data to the operating system, which then gets the data and sends it to the applications program. When a *printout* is requested, the applications system sends output to the printer through the operating system.

Did you know that the term *booting* the system comes from an old expression about a self-made person pulling himself or herself up by the bootstraps? To apply the concept to computers, think of the computer as lifting itself by its own bootstraps in order to begin functioning.

MODULE 2

CONNECTION

The Software Connection

Software enemies—sunlight, magnets, ballpoint pens, and cleaning fluids

TEN TIPS ON CARING FOR SOFTWARE

1. Label disks and tapes carefully. When labeling disks, don't write directly on them. Write on the sleeve or on a self-adhesive label that you can affix to the disk jacket. Always use a felt-tip pen.
2. Never leave cassettes or disks in the drive when they aren't being used.
3. Avoid exposing tapes or disks to magnetic fields. Keep them away from telephones, televisions, and other electrical appliances.
4. Be careful not to record over material you want to keep.
5. Don't touch the surface of a disk. Never remove a disk from its hard plastic jacket.
6. Keep backup copies of important disks.
7. If possible, store disks in storage boxes. If disks are kept in binders, store the binders upright.
8. Keep disks and plastic boxes of disks out of direct sunlight.
9. Remove disks from the drive before turning the power off.
10. Don't try to clean disks with any kind of liquid.

DIALING THE WORLD

What do you get when you combine a personal computer and a telephone? You get the world!

This isn't a joke—it's the truth. A computer can use a device called a *modem* to send and receive signals over a telephone. Modems permit one computer to "talk" to another, regardless of where the computer is actually located.

Using a modem, you can contact a friend who has a computer and share data or just send letters electronically. One American high-school English class set up a computer and modem to correspond with a high-school class in Norway. The two classes shared their reports on books and life in their own countries. The students also wrote papers on their impressions of the culture of the other country and sent the papers to their partner class for corrections before they handed in their work.

See if you can hook up a modem and telephone to a computer at your school or public library, and then see if there is a way to communicate with students elsewhere (it doesn't have to be around the world). Electronic services such as *Prodigy* or *CompuServe* can, for a fee, link you to students and other users in other cities. Sharing ideas and information electronically is the way of the future. Can you think of some ways that modems can help you *now*? Read Module 7 on telecommunications to find out more about how a modem works and how to use one.

Contact people around the world using a modem and a computer

MODULE 2

SHOPPING FOR A COMPUTER

After reading about computers (and perhaps using one for a while) it's natural to want to have one of your own. "So, let's go down to the computer store and pick one out," you say.

Hold on! A personal computer is a major investment, and not just for the money it represents. What good would it do to buy a computer and then find that it doesn't do the job you had hoped it would? Here's a checklist to help you evaluate computer hardware and software.

I. Ask yourself, "When I get the computer home, what do I want to be able to do?" Knowing how you plan to use your computer helps you to select the right one. Make a list of how you, and anyone else in the house, plan to use the computer. Have a list that shows what you need to do now, as well as what you might like to be able to do in the future. Your computer should be able to "grow" as your needs do.

II. Look for software *first,* before you purchase the computer itself. The applications software you select will determine what the computer will be able to do. No matter how powerful the computer hardware is, it can only accomplish what the software enables it to do. Match the software to your list of things you want to do now *and* later. Then, choose programs that seem to offer the best chance for growth. You'll be surprised at how quickly your skills will improve and how much more you'll demand of your system.

III. Do your "homework." Get information and advice from the pros. Use computer magazines, newspaper articles, and the experience of others who have done some of the things you would like to do with a computer. Compare notes and select one or two software packages that seem to be best suited to your needs. Find out which computer system is required to run the software you select. Talk to professionals as well as other computer users.

IV. Try it out! Using a friend's computer, a computer at school, or a demonstration system in a computer store, spend some time using the software and hardware you

You MAKE A DIFFERENCE

In 1976, while still in high school, Jonathan Rotenberg formed a computer users' group called the Boston Computer Society (BCS). It had a great name but only two people showed up at the first meeting. By the fifth meeting, however, there were enough people that Rotenberg was able to attract guest speakers. From these small beginnings, BCS grew into the world's largest personal computer group.

▬ A group such as BCS provides a great opportunity for people of similar interests to get to know one another and share ideas.

▬ By sharing information, Rotenberg and the members of BCS were able to advance their knowledge and use of computers beyond what they could have done alone.

▬ Perhaps you can start a user group for yourself and your classmates at your school.

 Apple II

store or bookstore? Are there classes where you can get training?

It's exciting to purchase your own computer, and it can open up a whole new universe of possibilities. In your excitement, however, don't get caught up in the flash and dazzle of advertising and promotion. Don't choose a computer based only on popular opinion about what is "best" or "easiest to use." Your time spent on research will be rewarded by the purchase of

 Macintosh

a system that will help you for years to come.

VII. After you have purchased your new computer, try to join or organize a users' group, or computer club. This is a great way to learn more and share ideas with others.

selected. If you are not certain which type of computer you prefer, try to find the same, or similar, software on more than one computer and compare the way each works.

V. Set a realistic budget for your computer purchase. Spending money just to buy the most powerful computer on the block may make absolutely no sense. Spending too little, however, might cause you to buy a computer that barely works for your needs today and allows no room for growth.

VI. Look beyond the first day of your computer usage. Is the computer expandable so that you can add new features when you want to? What warranty or provision for service is there should something go wrong? Where can you go for help? What books or manuals are provided with the system or in the computer

COMPUTERS THEN & NOW

The IBM Personal Computer was introduced August 12, 1981. The original system had 64K of RAM, an optional single-sided floppy disk drive, a keyboard, and either a monochrome or color monitor. The system unit and keyboard alone sold for $1,565. Adding a color monitor, disk drive, and an operating system pushed the price to $2,665. Bring a local newspaper or a computer magazine to class and look up a comparable IBM PC offered for sale. How does the 1981 price differ from today's purchase price?

Window shopping for a computer

MODULE SUMMARY QUESTIONS

In order to check your comprehension of how computers work, you may wish to discuss the following ideas.

1. Computers have many parts that make them work, including input and output devices. Make a chart, naming as many of these parts as you can.

2. One of the great benefits of a computer is its ability to store lots of information. Explain how RAM works. Then, compare and contrast RAM and ROM.

3. Many homes, offices, and schools have computers. If you were planning to purchase a computer for your home or school, what information would you need to help you decide which computer to buy? Where would you find the information? How would you determine what kind of hardware and software you need?

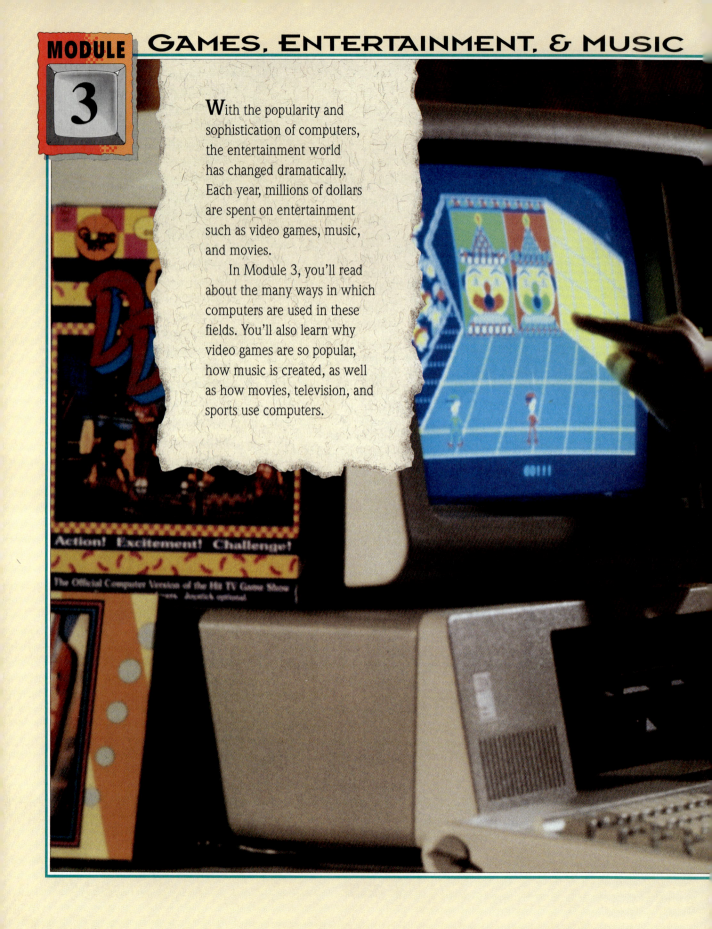

MODULE 3
Games, Entertainment, & Music

With the popularity and sophistication of computers, the entertainment world has changed dramatically. Each year, millions of dollars are spent on entertainment such as video games, music, and movies.

In Module 3, you'll read about the many ways in which computers are used in these fields. You'll also learn why video games are so popular, how music is created, as well as how movies, television, and sports use computers.

History of Electronic Games

COMPUTERS THEN & NOW

Players of the first home video game, Magnavox's *Odyssey,* had to tape a transparent overlay on their TV screens to represent the playing court. The game's simple microchip, or integrated circuit, didn't even have enough memory to draw the background on the screen!

By contrast, today's games have enormous memory capacities which allow them to store and use a great deal of information. So your favorite game may not only show one screen, but literally hundreds.

If you've ever played a game on a computer, you've contributed to the popularity of electronic games. Of course, computers weren't invented to play games, but ever since scientists created the first electronic contest, computers and games have been a great match.

In the 1950s, computer scientists wrote the first computer versions of games like chess and tic-tac-toe for their own enjoyment. But it would be about 10 years before these inventions were made available to the general public.

The first computer game to become widely available was *Space War,* which first surfaced in 1961 in the electrical engineering department of the Massachusetts Institute of Technology (MIT). Although the game was an immediate hit, it ran on a computer the size of a huge laboratory, so it wasn't something most people could afford—or fit inside their house!

That changed in the 1970s as computers became smaller and programmers learned more about their craft. Still, the first video games would seem incredibly boring compared to even the simplest game on the market today.

The object of Atari's *Pong* was like Ping-Pong™. Players attempted to hit the "ball" with an electronic "paddle" that they could move up or down. The public was fascinated with the idea, and people began feeding millions of dollars into coin-operated video games. Almost overnight, a powerful industry had been born. Ask your parents if they remember the first video games. Which ones were their favorites?

Pong—the first coin-operated video game

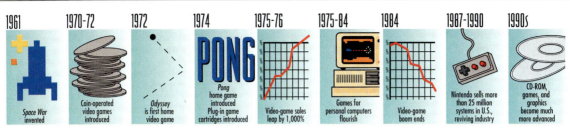

Over thirty years of the history of electronic games

In 1972, the video game moved from public locations to people's living rooms. Magnavox's *Odyssey,* which cost a little less than $100, was the first video game designed for home use. *Odyssey* was so simplistic that its only graphic was a ball that moved around on the screen. The game's technology was quickly outdated, however, and more advanced games began flooding the home video-game market.

Electronic games took a new direction in 1974 as Atari released *Pong* to the home market. The next year, Atari found even more success with its *2600* model, which gave home users a choice of several different plug-in cartridges.

Each cartridge for the Atari contained a microchip with the instructions for a particular game. In other words, these cartridges were a form of software. Now, people no longer had to buy separate hardware, or computer components, for each game they wanted to play. With just one computer, they could play tennis, hockey, baseball, and a number of other games.

With the development of plug-in cartridges, game sales went through the roof. Between 1975 and 1976, video-game manufacturers saw their sales leap by as much as 1,000 percent. Everywhere, people became knob-twiddling, button-punching fanatics of their favorite video games.

During this same period, the first personal computers (PCs) began hitting the market. The development of games for the personal computer gave the public an exciting glimpse into the future. The new versions of games like solitaire and tic-tac-toe used detailed computer graphics for the first time. In just a short time, games had come a long way from *Pong*'s ball and paddle.

Did you know a mechanical computer game can be built using nothing but Tinkertoys®?

The Mid-America Center in Hot Springs, AR, has a Tinkertoy® computer that was built during the 1970s by six MIT students.

The computer was designed to play tic-tac-toe. The computer isn't totally automatic, though; it requires a human being to turn a crank.

People were also fascinated by the new things they could do with computer games. For instance, users could now change the whole structure of a game—not just play it. Fantasy games like *Wizardry, Adventure,* and *The Hitchhiker's Guide to the Galaxy* allowed the player to choose his or her own path through an ever-changing world of text and pictures. By typing simple instructions, a computer game player might be a knight slaying a dragon in a lost civilization, a detective searching for clues to a mystery, or a futuristic time traveler—without ever leaving home!

History of Electronic Games

These computer games remained popular for a while, but by 1984, sales of traditional video games like *Pac Man, Space Invaders,* and *Asteroids* had slumped and players became bored. There just weren't enough new game ideas to keep them interested. The video-game boom had ended.

In 1987, however, a Japanese company called Nintendo single-handedly brought about the rebirth of the home video-game industry. Nintendo Entertainment Systems (NES) took the world by storm arousing game players with its state-of-the-art graphics and sound capabilities. By the end of 1990, Nintendo had sold more than 25 million NES systems in the United States and millions more worldwide. The success of such Nintendo games as *Donkey Kong* and *Super Mario Brothers* created a whole new industry of game-related merchandise. People now not only played their favorite game at the video arcade, they also bought the video-game cartridge, read the book, watched the television program, wore the T-shirt, and even ate the breakfast cereal.

As of 1990, video games were in nearly one third of all homes in the United States. This success caused the market to virtually explode with new products. As NEC created *TurboGrafx-16* and Sega introduced *Genesis,* another invention burst onto the scene—CD-ROM. With CD-ROM's enormous memory capacity, game makers were able to produce amazing graphics and sound.

Today, video and computer games are a worldwide phenomenon. In Europe, a popular home video game can sell more than 100,000 copies in its first month of release. Children in Tokyo stood in lines up to four blocks long just to purchase the latest version of Nintendo's *Super Mario Brothers*.

A Soviet scientist, Alexey Pazhitnov, invented *Tetris,* a popular NES game. *Tetris* is also available on MACs, IBMs, and GameBoys.

Just as computer games have affected people the world over, they are, in turn, being shaped by the world's imagination. With so many minds involved in the world of computer gaming, it is hard to imagine what the products of the future will be like.

SUPER MARIO BROTHERS merchandise: doll, shirt, calendar, game cartridges, radio with microphone, and magazine

MULTICULTURAL BYTE

Can you imagine playing video games for homework? Some students in Japan attend specialized trade schools that train them for careers in the video-game industry.

Students in these schools learn how computer games are designed. Each student is allowed to specialize in a specific discipline, such as planning, programming, graphics, or music.

The schools are part of a national strategy to retain Japan's 90 percent market share in video-game sales.

MODULE 3

TODAY'S COMPUTER GAMES

Track a criminal through a back alleyway in Paris. Outwit enemy fighter planes thousands of feet in the air. Rule your own kingdom. Thanks to the advanced technology of today's computer games, you can experience all of these things without ever leaving your home!

Some game programs combine wild adventure with a new opportunity for learning. For example, Broderbund's *Where in the World Is Carmen Sandiego?* gives you geographic clues to help you track down and apprehend "Carmen." The trick is, you have to know—or learn about—world geography to make sense of the clues.

Other games feature flight simulators much like the ones used in military and commercial pilot training. In fact, many users of Spectrum Holobyte's *Falcon* and Microsoft's *Flight Simulator* have been so fascinated by the games that they've gone on to earn pilot licenses.

You might not ever really rule a country, but with Sierra On-Line's *King's Quest V: Absence Makes the Heart Go Yonder* boys and girls can at least practice being a king. As "King Graham," you must liberate the kingdom and rescue your family. The game tests your ability to deal with changing situations and a large cast of characters. The CD-ROM version of the game even lets the game's characters talk to you!

Today, literally thousands of computer games are on the market with special effects that are approaching arcade quality. This modern technology allows today's game players to defy the limits of reality in new and exciting ways. Just choose a computer game program and take off for worlds that were, worlds that are, or worlds that will never be— it's all up to you.

Experiencing new adventures through video games

★ Read All About It ★

An interview
by Dennis L. Whiteman

Spaceship Warlock:
Exploring Space and Technology

In 1991, *Spaceship Warlock,* an interactive science fiction movie, was released on CD-ROM by Reactor Inc., an entertainment developer and publishing company based in Chicago. In *Spaceship Warlock,* you, the player, start out penniless, hungry, and wandering the streets of a dirty, drab planet. If you can scrape up enough money, you might leave on an interplanetary shuttle and meet some interesting characters or take off on a luxury cruise. But beware—danger lurks everywhere. Reactor Inc. president Mike Saenz [Signs] talks, below, about his experiences in creating computer games.

DLW: How are CD-ROM games different than traditional games?

Saenz: They're bigger, first of all. More graphics, more animation, more sound. All a game is comprised of is graphics, animation, sound and programming and how you configure all of those things.

DLW: How did you come up with the idea for *Spaceship Warlock?*

Exploring space through CD-ROM games

Saenz: When somebody asks me, 'How did you come up with something?' I say: 'Nothing's really original.' We're definitely influenced by movies, television, books and games—that kind of stuff. I've been a professional entertainer for years. I've been in computers for seven years. Before that, I spent six years in the comic book industry. That amounts to thirteen years of experience designing comic books, graphic novels, software games and software programs. Our problem isn't how to come up with ideas. Our problem is how to make them happen.

DLW: How do you make them happen?

Saenz: A lot of elbow grease. Just getting the nose down to the grindstone and doing it. It's 10 percent inspiration, 90 percent perspiration.

DLW: Why did you choose to develop in CD-ROM?

Saenz: Basically, it's the future of games. I've been researching CD-ROM since I first heard about it in 1985. You talk to anybody in the game industry and they'll tell you that

Continued on next page

★ Read All About It ★

CD-ROM is the medium of the future —at least for the near future.

DLW: The Japanese have trade schools where developers learn how to design games.

Saenz: People in the world of game development are not taking a couple of computer night courses and then bingo—they're ready to design games. It's not getting any easier just because there are a whole lot of multimedia tools on the Macintosh that allow people to do things they've never done before. That doesn't make it any easier. Everybody still has to go through the process of learning how to create professional entertainment products.

DLW: More than just learning how to use a computer?

Saenz: You've got to learn the craft of entertaining, telling a story, animation, and in terms of computer games, you also have to be very familiar with the technology. Your knowledge of the technology has to extend beyond what's commonly known, as well as the graphics strengths, the animation strengths and music strengths.

DLW: Is designing computer games a good career field?

Saenz: I wouldn't wish it on my worst enemy —it's extremely difficult. The game industry has its ups and downs and I wouldn't want to lead anyone on.

DLW: How many people worked on *Spaceship Warlock*?

Saenz: Mainly two people, but we had other people do other types of things.

DLW: What about the graphics?

Saenz: All of the graphics were originally done for the product, but that's pretty much true of any computer game. There was one minor exception. There was some video of a character moving around where we digitized it [changed visual information into computer data] off of a human. And then we changed it drastically. We only used it to create a series of silhouettes to create a crowd scene at the end of the game.

DLW: You used *Swivel 3-D, Studio 8, Adobe Photoshop,* and *Macromind Director*. Are those tools that are commonly used in creating computer games?

Saenz: Game companies use whatever tools work. They just don't publicize it. The tools we used pretty much matched up to the tools that are being used for multimedia on the Macintosh today. Other game companies use similar tools. The computer is like a new pencil. Ultimately, it's not what the pencil does, it's what you're doing with the pencil.

DLW: Where did you get the sounds?

Saenz: Where we couldn't do our own sounds, we used public domain sounds—and that wasn't an extensive amount.

DLW: Where did the characters' voices come from?

Saenz: We did the voice-overs—pretty much like a movie.

DLW: How long did it take to create *Spaceship Warlock*?

Saenz: Eight months. But it took the experience of my thirteen years in the industry, Dave's eight years in the computer industry and Joe Sparks' seven years in the computer industry. It takes that level of experience. Even so, we're not happy. Our next product is going to be better, but that's the way it works. ■

STRETCHING THE BOUNDS OF REALITY

A tiger, a woman, or both?

For years, video-game players have been able to control the actions of the tiny electronic characters who seemed to "live" inside video-game monitors. In 1991, Sega took that fantasy one step further. With Sega's *Time Traveler* arcade game, players can now control tiny human images.

The state-of-the-art game creates this illusion by combining a computer brain with *laserdiscs,* or disks with recorded pictures and sound that are read by a laser beam, and space-age *optics,* or light images. In response to players' actions, the game's computer selects footage of human actors and projects it onto a spherical blackened mirror. The result is a holographic, or three-dimensional (3-D), image. A whole new reality is created within the confines of the machine.

Just a few years ago, we never could have dreamed of advances such as these. In fact, even experts admit that predicting the future of electronic games is pure speculation. "Travel back in time a decade or so and ask someone playing *Pong* or *Space War* what the future held, and the speculation would doubtless be too conservative by half," wrote Bob Lindstrom in the January 1991 issue of *Compute!* magazine.

Scientists a decade ago couldn't have imagined the impact CD-ROM would have on technology. The adoption of CD-ROM as a standard by both video-game makers and computer users has resulted in huge changes in the industry. CD-ROM allows game makers to squeeze millions of bytes of information into a game. As a result, they are able to create amazingly detailed moving pictures, crystal-clear sounds, and hundreds of different plots and storylines within a single game.

Perhaps the most exciting advance in gaming made its debut in 1989 when Mattel, Inc., released a $90 computer glove that allowed players to control some Nintendo games with hand movements. This new technology was named *virtual reality.* Virtual reality, a name coined by Jaron Lanier, founder of VPL Research, Inc., is, simply put, an artificial world created by a computer that allows a person to interact through the use of special clothing and gear, such as the Mattel glove or a pair of special goggles.

In 1990, one of the first commercial applications of virtual reality was the introduction of Fredonian Aeronautics and Space Administration's arcade game *BattleTech*. The game involves two teams of four players who sit in closet-sized cockpits that are outfitted with 25-inch, high-resolution television montors. As players operate the robotic controls, more than 19,000 3-D animated images rotate, flip, and move in response to their actions. Game players pay by the half-hour.

In the future, virtual reality will have real-world applications, as well. Scientists say that architects will be able to design buildings and have people actually walk through them before they are built. Doctors will be able to perform surgery—without spilling a drop of blood—simply by using a pair of virtual-reality goggles and gloves.

Primitive virtual-reality machines—the product of 25 years of research by NASA and the United States Air Force—already played a major role in training pilots who fought in the Persian Gulf War in 1991. Outfitted with special goggles and headphones, pilots could practice their bombing runs without ever having to leave the ground.

No one knows how far this technology can lead. No doubt, we will continue to use science and our imaginations to stretch the bounds of reality in thousands of new and exciting ways.

CAREERS

SALESPERSON · ELECTRICIAN · ASTRONAUT · MECHANIC · ENGINEER · PHYSICIST · DENTIST · FARMER · TEACHER · DOCTOR · NURSE · PILOT · PROFESSOR · SECRETARY · ARTIST

Thinking of a career in the competitive field of computer game design? If you are, it's important to learn as much as possible about the elements that make up good games—sound, graphics, and plot.

The right training can start at your school. Enroll in classes such as art, film, and video production, and fiction writing—but don't stop there. Read everything you can about computer graphics and interactive media, such as CD-ROM. With this background, you'll be well on your way to an exciting career in video games.

Experiencing virtual reality through the use of special gear

GAMES, ENTERTAINMENT, & MUSIC

★ Read All About It ★

Excerpted from *PC Computing*
February, 1989
By Tim Tully

Good Vibrations:
The PC Joins the Band

A scenario for the next Grammy Awards: The lights are low and the tension is high. The host pauses, then tears open the envelope. Applause. The year's biggest star walks to the podium with a producer on each arm. One producer is tall, dark, and handsome. The other is small, beige, and has a handle; it's a Compaq Portable 386.

PCs—the newest music stars

It's not as far-fetched as it sounds. In the past five years, supporting roles of PCs have grown at an astonishing rate. Currently, the PC assists in playing, composing, and producing everything from pop music to movie sound tracks.

The PC has fine-tuned the music industry in three ways. Computerized synthesizers and digital samplers, devices that can record and alter the qualities of any sound, allow artists to produce customized tones, pitches, and timbres to suit a particular situation. Computer-driven sequencers help arrange, compose, and produce music with greater ease. Programs can synchronize audiotape with visual images, translate music into notes on paper, and even indulge in the artistically controversial practice of algorithmic composition, which uses the computer's logic capabilities to create new works of music.

For better or worse, when you hear a tune these days, it's a good bet that some part of it has seen the inside of a PC. This means that the music we hear today is different from what we heard ten or even five years ago. Some of the differences are easy to hear; others exist more in the process than in the product.

DESIGNER SOUND

Digital samplers are instruments built around microprocessors that can digitally record (or sample) any sound, then let a musician play it back from the sampler's piano-type keyboard in a full range of pitches.

Rather than attempting to snatch another musician's sound outright, people with samplers and the right software tend to specialize in custom-designing new and unusual sounds for specific applications.

Los Angeles-based Jeff Rona is a professional sound designer who works with a roomful of synthesizers, samplers, and a Macintosh, creating sounds for new compositions, especially film scores. He recently completed a project for composer Phillip Glass's score for the film *Powaqqatsi*. A sound crew followed the camera crew and sampled noises on location: voices, machines, natural sounds, and so on. Using the sampler, Rona turned ambient sounds from the original setting into music for the film's score.

Continued on next page

READ ALL ABOUT IT

"I sampled the sound of a train that appears in one scene, then altered the length and color of the sound in subtle ways," says Rona. "We played the modified 'ka-chunk' of the train along with a drum in the sound track; you can actually hear the train sound playing a drum pattern."

Whether it is sampling great musicians or the great outdoors, the personal computer is a star on the rise. "I could never process this material in so sophisticated a way without the computer," says Rona. "It's really a powerful extension of the musical instruments."

But while the PC helps expand the universe of musical sounds, these sounds still need to be arranged into music.

GETTING THE NOTES RIGHT

A sequencer is a kind of multitrack tape recorder in a computer, used for engineering sounds into music. You can buy a hardware sequencer—a box housing a computer dedicated to just that job. But software versions tend to be more powerful by virtue of the PC's greater memory, more detailed interface, hard disk storage potential, and comparative ease of upgrading. Sequencers use a standardized language known as the Musical Instrument Digital Interface (MIDI), which allows them to talk to electronic musical instruments such as synthesizers, samplers, and drum machines. A PC loaded with one of the two dozen or so available sequencing programs records the data generated by someone playing a MIDI-equipped instrument. The sequencer can send the data back to the instrument on demand, making it play an almost exact duplicate of the original performance, like a player piano. And sequencer software turns a PC into a workstation on which you can shape, manipulate, and otherwise edit music, much as a word processor massages text.

THE NEW COMPOSER

Sequencers have been a boon to struggling musicians. Small bands will, for example, sequence the drum and bass parts of a whole night's worth of music beforehand, then put two people onstage playing the lead parts while the sequencer plays the background.

Continued on next page

An electronic layout of a soundstage

★ Read All About It ★

But sequencers have an even bigger impact on music composers. Unlike its analog forebear, the tape deck, the sequencer records music in easy-to-manipulate digital form. Once a line is recorded, the musician/composer can copy, transpose, or delete the data, shift its pitch or its position in time, change its tempo or volume, have it play a different sound on the synthesizer, or play a different instrument entirely.

The uses of sequencers are as varied as the musicians who use them. To help him write songs, Stevie Wonder carries a Compaq 386 wherever he goes. According to Rob Arbittire, who writes "nonvisual software" for the musician, Wonder uses a Versabraille—a small pad that delivers computer output in braille form—and customized software that communicates with beeps and clicks. Wonder uses the sequencer Texture 2, which is particularly suitable. "Its user interface and keystrokes are laid out so that you're not required to look at the screen," says Arbittire.

According to Arbittire, Wonder typically writes by first sequencing, say, 16 bars of a bass pattern. With that bass line playing in the background, he'll electronically transform the keyboard into another instrument, such as an electric piano, and jam. Then the master songsmith can play everything back, pick and choose while he listens, and keep adding parts. Because the Texture program records in discrete sections, or patterns, of any length, Wonder is free to arrange and rearrange sections of the song until he finds what he likes.

SEQUENCING HEAT

Some of the most innovative PC music-making, however, is happening outside the record studios. In 1984, keyboardist/composer Jan [Yahn] Hammer, formerly of the Mahavishnu [Mah hah VISH new] Orchestra, a rock instrumental group, got a gig scoring [or putting music to] a new TV show called *Miami Vice*. His advanced sounds and sequencer-based techniques put the state of the art into America's living rooms and radically changed the way TV shows and movies are scored.

Stevie Wonder on keyboard

Hammer computer-locks a videotape of the episode he is scoring to his sequencer and audiotape deck. While watching the video, he plays his instruments—a drum part, a piano melody, or maybe just a rhythm figure—into his sequencer. Then he can play back the sequence and modify tempo, orchestration, and so on. The result is a score composed

Continued on next page

READ ALL ABOUT IT

directly to the onscreen action, accompanying it the way a good pianist follows a singer. Within months of the debut of *Miami Vice,* many other new shows were copying Hammer's style and techniques.

Hammer uses an IBM PC-XT, a Macintosh Plus, and a Commodore 64 for everything from sequencing to automating his mixing console. "I can organize my thoughts, like on a word processor. Before, if I wanted to record a piece of music and hear it, I had to tape it and splice different pieces of tape together—a very time-consuming process.

"...And when I hit 'Gently Down the Stream,' you come in with 'Row, Row, Row your Boat.'"

Here it's instantaneous; I can audition different themes and musical ideas and hear how they fit together. I can try anything."

Computers don't make his music better or worse, Hammer says, just appropriate for the era we live in: "In the 1700s, when the piano was being perfected, the music sounded a certain way, which was different from the music 100 years before that. Technology can't help but shape what the artist does—and the creative tools today are computers."

THE HOME STUDIO

Musicians also use PCs to print what they play. William Goldstein, who wrote the music for the TV show *Fame* as well as for such Hollywood films as Shelley Long's *Hello Again* and Chuck Norris's *An Eye for an Eye,* uses a 386 clone with Windows and a program from Ronald called MESA that does sequencing and produces a score in standard music notation. MESA gives Goldstein the dual compositional luxury of hearing his work played on his synthesizers at any point during its creation and seeing it written out, which gives him an overview.

For works that will be recorded by live musicians, PC programs such as Temporai Acuity's Music Printer Plus allow a composer to write a piece on a computer using traditional notation, and then extract and print individual parts for each musician. That saves considerable time and expense when the composer is ready to record.

The personal computer has found a home in the music world. It records, organizes, prompts, and calculates, just as it does in the office or the laboratory.

But the main ingredients are still inspiration. If no human conceives a musical idea and infuses it with shape, meaning, judgment, and labor, then there is no music. The algorithmic composer or random note generator sounds like what it is: a random compilation of noise. If the world at large comes to accept randomly played notes, without the structure and direction of human will, then we will have created the ultimate in least-common-denominator culture, and the instrument will be the artist. But the choice of how we use our tools is always our own. To borrow an expression from the political world: we deserve the music we get.

Other Forms of Entertainment

Whether you realize it or not, computers have already had a tremendous impact on nearly every form of entertainment you enjoy—movies, television, print materials such as books, sports, and even amusement-park rides. Sometimes, this influence is easy to recognize; other times it's hidden behind the scenes.

MOVIES AND TELEVISION

The film industry is an area where we can easily see the difference computers have made. For instance, computers have been mentioned or shown in a wide number of American films since 1985. One of the first movies to deal extensively with the subject of computers was *War Games*. The film told the story of a computer whiz-kid who tapped into the military's early warning system, nearly starting World War III.

Filmmakers have not only rushed to include computers in movie plots, they have also been quick to realize computers' potential for shaping the way movies are made.

Most people are familiar with such animated Disney classics as *Fantasia, Snow White and the Seven Dwarfs,* and *Bambi*. The *animation* in these films was created entirely by hand during the 1930s and 40s. Today, Disney animators use computers to help with the initial stages of a film.

During these early stages, animators spend much of their time experimenting with different drawings. Since the computer can redraw pictures with amazing speed, animators are able to quickly outline the movements of characters in a particular scene. This allows the artist to get a rough idea of how the finished product will look before weeks are committed to hand-drawing a scene that doesn't work.

In the not-too-distant future, computers may be able to recreate Disney-like animation. However, today's computers cannot yet match the rich colors and crisp images that the artists are able to draw by hand.

DID YOU KNOW?

Did you know that the first *interactive animation,* or a film showing both humans and cartoons working together, was probably shown to audiences more than 80 years ago?

In 1909, cartoonist Winsor McCay toured the United States with an unusual show. McCay would stand next to a movie screen and talk about *Gertie the Dinosaur,* who would appear beside him.

At one point, Gertie would appear to snatch off McCay's hat and eat it, much to the audience's surprise.

Today, of course, people are more accustomed to interactive animated films, such as *Who Framed Roger Rabbit,* but in 1909, *Gertie the Dinosaur* actually frightened some people.

Behind the camera, computers are becoming an increasingly popular tool. LucasFilm Ltd.'s Industrial Light and Magic division uses Macintosh II computers to control camera movement for special

A scene from George Lucas's film RETURN OF THE JEDI

effects shots. What we see on the screen are space ships flying at us, but when these scenes are shot, a model of a space ship is actually held still while the camera moves toward it. This creates the illusion that the ship is flying. Since the computer can duplicate the camera's movements exactly every time, each frame can contain three to 100 different moving models, all shot at different times—which makes for a fantastic battle scene.

Computers are also used in virtually all aspects of the television industry. Just turn on your TV for a minute or two and you're likely to see dozens of ways that the computer has influenced the medium. As you may have guessed, commercials make the widest use of this technology, but if you've ever watched a news program, you've seen a computer at work during the opening titles and graphics.

Besides producing special effects, computers are used in many other ways in television video production. The editing of videotape—for news, sports shows, or even your favorite soap opera—is much quicker and more precise when it's done with the help of computers.

ELECTRONIC PRINT MATERIALS

For years, computers have been used for turning ideas into print. However, the print was almost always transferred to paper. In the years to come, you may read your favorite books on a computer. This method of producing text will be much less harmful to the environment. There is no paper to be produced—which saves trees—and no paper to be disposed of—which saves landfill space.

Electronic books, magazines, and newspapers will give readers many exciting options. In 1991, Apple Computer introduced *QuickTime*, a program that combines video, sounds, and graphics on the computer screen in remarkable ways. Dan Sorenson, a developer at WordPerfect

You MAKE A DIFFERENCE

Using a personal computer, teenager Wendy Roy publishes the newsletter *Wendy's Gazette* in Lincoln, RI. The newsletter is a nonprofit enterprise, providing a service to Wendy's community. Twenty families subscribe to *Wendy's Gazette*.

Wendy's newsletter features information that is important to her family, friends, and neighbors. Stories have covered Wendy's performance on a Boston TV talent show and the news that her sister Tracy made the dean's list at Bryant College. The newsletter also features letters to the editor and classified ads.

Corporation, has created an interactive newspaper that uses the new software. In Sorenson's newspaper, the reader can change an ad for a movie into a full-fledged video preview just by clicking the computer's cursor, or input indicator, on the ad. The possibilities of such a device boggle the imagination.

SPORTS

Computers are also affecting coaching decisions made in the sports world. At the University of Michigan, a computer shoots video from several different camera angles during each Wolverine football game. It then edits the video into custom tapes so that specific coaches can see how their players performed. In Colorado Springs, the United States Olympic Team videotapes athletes in motion and analyzes their movements on a computer to help improve performance. And nearly every major-league baseball team has a computer that provides useful information to help the manager decide when to pull a pitcher or batter out of the game in certain situations.

AMUSEMENT PARKS

Computers have found their way into leisure-time activities in many ways. Have you ever ridden on a roller coaster? If so, and your knees were knocking and your stomach was doing flip-flops, you can probably thank modern technology. If the ride was built recently, chances are that a computer designed it for maximum chills and thrills.

Besides roller coasters, engineers are using computer models to create water slides and other rides. This way, the machines can be tested before they are actually built. Water-slide designers can even take into account the friction caused by different types of bathing suits. This kind of information helps them determine how fast riders can go and how closely they can be spaced for maximum speed and safety. The result of the computer's help is fewer accidents.

Roller coaster electronically designed for maximum speed and safety

Other Forms of Entertainment

A library of digital images—eliminating the need for live actors

ENTERTAINMENT IN THE FUTURE

Some people are already imagining future applications for the technology bursting onto the scene today. One idea is to create interactive versions of movies. Imagine how exciting it will be to project your own image right into a movie on your computer screen. Just click a few buttons and you can try your hand at being your favorite movie hero or heroine! Or, if you decide that a character shouldn't die at the end of a sad movie, simply punch a button, and everyone lives happily ever after.

With this ability to manipulate the actors within a film, future movies may not feature actors at all, but rather digital images that look like actors. Of course, real-life actors may not like this idea, but just think of the possibilities!

Although technology hasn't quite caught up with our imaginations yet, changes are happening every day. To be sure, the future will offer exciting new ideas in entertainment.

MODULE SUMMARY QUESTIONS

In order to check your comprehension of how computers have affected games, entertainment, and music, you may wish to discuss the following ideas.

1. What do you most like to do in your spare time? According to what you have read, how have computers affected this form of entertainment over the past 10 years? How do you think this activity will continue to change in the years to come?

2. Can you think of a type of entertainment that has not been affected by computers? Could computers be adapted to make that activity better? If so, explain.

3. If you were to choose a career in the entertainment industry, what job would you most like to do? Based on what you have read in this module, how might computers help you do that job better?

MODULE 4

GRAPHICS

Imagine what the world would be like without pictures. Fortunately, graphics programs allow us to create graphs, charts, and pictures to make our messages clearer and more appealing.

In Module 4, you will learn how to create computer graphics with paint and draw programs. You will also learn about how graphics are used in animation and multimedia. In addition, you will read how many areas of business are using graphics today.

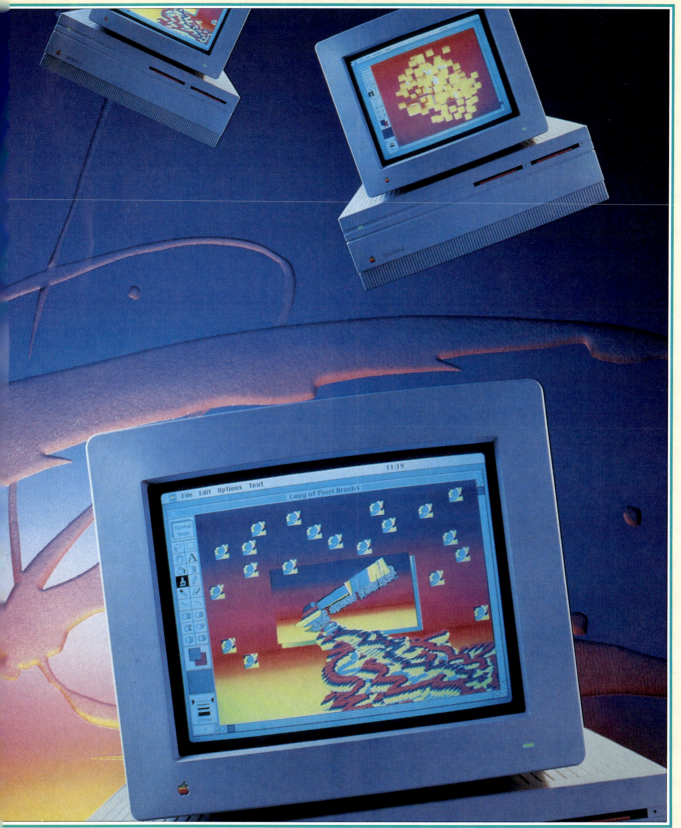

HOW GRAPHICS ENHANCE INFORMATION

By the time you become an adult, you'll have heard many times the expression, "a picture is worth a thousand words." We live in a society that is becoming more oriented toward graphic images every day. So what exactly is a graphic—especially one that's worth so many words?

A graphic can be a picture—like a photograph or a work of art—or a symbol, an image to which your brain assigns a meaning.

Have you ever traveled by car down an interstate highway? Did you notice any signs without words—just pictures—that indicated to you where you could find food, make a telephone call, or buy gasoline?

If you are asking yourself, "Why didn't the sign makers just put the words *food, telephone,* or *gas* on the sign instead?", consider the following. First, if you couldn't read English, wouldn't it be very difficult to understand the meaning of the words? Second, driving down the highway requires utmost concentration on the part of the driver. Any distractions at all can be hazardous. Third, graphics, or visual images, communicate meaning to your brain more quickly than printed words do. Try the following example yourself.

ROAD CURVES AHEAD

Which example at left lets you know at a glance that the road curves ahead? You probably said that the yellow one does.

Computer graphics are also used to expand the meaning of information. For example, imagine for a moment that you work for a record company that sells cassettes, CDs, and record albums. Last year, the cassettes accounted for $7.5 million (75 percent) of your total sales, the CDs accounted for more than $2.4 million (24.9 percent) of sales, and the albums brought in only $100,000 (less than one percent) of your sales.

Roadside symbols, an effective use of graphics

MODULE 4

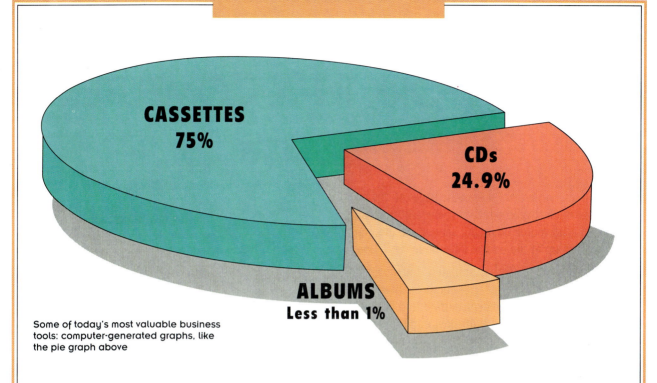

Some of today's most valuable business tools: computer-generated graphs, like the pie graph above

If you used a pie chart to graph your sales by percentage, you might reach the conclusion that you should concentrate your resources on selling cassettes and CDs instead of the albums, which didn't generate much money, and you would probably be right. In this case, the graphic told you more about your business than did the printed words or the total sales figure.

Book, magazine, and newspaper publishers use graphics to convey additional meaning to the words they print in their publications. Moviemakers and video producers also use computer graphics to create the special effects that amaze us in the movies, on television, and on video. Almost $90 million was spent on the computer-generated graphics that viewers saw in the movie *Terminator II.*

So what's wrong with using paper and pencil to create graphics? Why do we need computers to create our visual images for us? Well, it takes a lot of time for any one individual to sketch, paint, or draw a graphic. Computers eliminate a lot of tedious, time-consuming work, freeing up the graphic artists and illustrators for other tasks and making their work easier. By using a computer, there's no need to erase or use a new sheet of paper to make changes to the original, or even to start over—just *delete* and make changes right on the computer.

Computers can help graphic artists, architects, advertisers, designers, engineers, and movie makers produce graphics more quickly, efficiently, and cost-effectively. Computer-generated graphics can also create images of things that are not ordinarily visible, such as the inside of the human brain, or close-up shots of the surface of far-away planets.

In Module 4, *Graphics,* you will learn how graphics enhance the way we "see" information, how graphics work, how graphics are created, and what equipment is needed to produce computer graphics. In addition, you will learn the names of some contemporary graphics packages.

HOW GRAPHICS WORK IN A COMPUTER

Almost everything you see on the pages of this book began as an electronic signal traveling around the inside of a computer, bouncing between microchips and ending up at the end of a Cathode Ray Tube.

From there, it was manipulated, transformed, and output into an image that could be interpreted by your brain to mean something. But how did it get there? Let's find out how computer graphics work.

PIXELS

Computer screens consist of thousands of tiny boxes of light, called *pixels,* that work together as a unit. The computer turns the pixels on and off, like a light switch, to create a pattern. When combined, the pixels (short for **pic**ture **el**ements) show us the shape and color of a graphic on the screen. Look closely at the letters on your computer screen. Can you see the individual pixels that make up each letter?

Low-resolution image

High-resolution image

On a black-and-white screen, black pixels are energized to different light intensities, creating shades from dark black to light gray. On a color screen, the pixels consist of dots of varying intensities of red, blue, and green.

The quality of graphics you see on the screen can be either *high resolution* or *low resolution,* depending on the number of dots that can be displayed in one square inch (6.5 sq cm). High-resolution graphics have sharp, clear images. Low-resolution graphics often appear with jagged, blurred edges. A high-resolution monitor might contain as many as 307,200 pixels. A low-resolution system might have only 64,000 pixels.

STORING COMPUTER GRAPHICS

Two basic methods are used to store and manipulate computer graphics: *bit-mapped* (or raster) *graphics* and *vector graphics.*

A close-up of a pixelated image

Bit-mapped graphics consist of patterns of dots. The image seen on your television set is a bit-mapped graphic. So is the image you see on most computer screens. There are a number of disadvantages to bit-mapped graphics. First, because the image is "seen" as a number of tiny dots, and not a whole object, it is difficult for someone to move just one part of an image without touching the other dots that make up the graphic. Second, a change in the size of the graphic—either larger or smaller—creates distorted, jagged lines. Therefore, it is difficult to resize a bit-mapped graphic easily.

A vector graphic, instead, is made up of lines —not individual dots—and is treated as a whole object. For example, a square is made up of four vectors—one for each side. Vector objects can be moved onto other objects without combining the pixels into one object. Enlarging or reducing the vectors produces smooth, steady lines, rather than the jagged images produced with bit-mapped graphics. An entire object can be stored in the computer and changed at another time.

INPUT/OUTPUT DEVICES

Being a graphic designer is a difficult job. But, before the computer, it was an even tougher assignment. First, people had to use paper and pencil to create (and re-create) their designs. Then, they had to physically "send" their designs—in person or by mail—to the customer. Using a computer to create graphic design helps the designer input (make) and output (send) changes to the design faster and more easily.

A number of input devices can be used to create computer graphics. They range from the more awkward, such as using text commands on a keyboard, to a joystick, which offers minimal control, to light pens, *touch pads, graphics tablets,* and scanners.

The most basic graphic input device for computers is the mouse. The mouse was invented at Xerox's Palo Alto Research Center (PARC). The mouse has become a basic part of the way we create and interact with graphics on the computer screen.

MULTI *CULTURAL* BYTE

Pasqual Vincenzo Minervini combines his love for cycling with his career as a graphic artist. He works at Gita Sporting Goods, a wholesale bicycle dealer in Charlotte, NC, designing bicycle frames, riding clothes and gear, bicycle decals, and the company's retail catalog. Minervini uses the paint program *Studio 32* and the draw program *Adobe Illustrator* on a Macintosh FX. He also works with a scanner, a graphics tablet, and a stylus (a pen used to draw on the tablet). Minervini uses these graphics programs and input devices to design color schemes, determine the location of paint on bicycles, and to design shirts, shorts, tights, jackets, and gloves. Sometimes, he scans in a pattern or image and then manipulates it on the screen. The software has some CAD capabilities such as 3-D, which Minervini takes advantage of when designing frames and clothing. For output, he uses both a color ink-jet and a laser printer.

How Graphics Work in a Computer

Some variations of the basic mouse design are the *trackball,* light pen, and graphics tablet (or digitizer). A trackball is basically a mouse turned on "its back." A ball on the "stomach" rolls around, guiding the cursor.

A light pen allows the user to draw directly on a screen by turning the pixels on or off. Touch pads or graphics tablets are flat pads that connect to a graphics program and allow the user to draw with a special pen. The drawing appears immediately on the screen. Many designers and graphic artists use

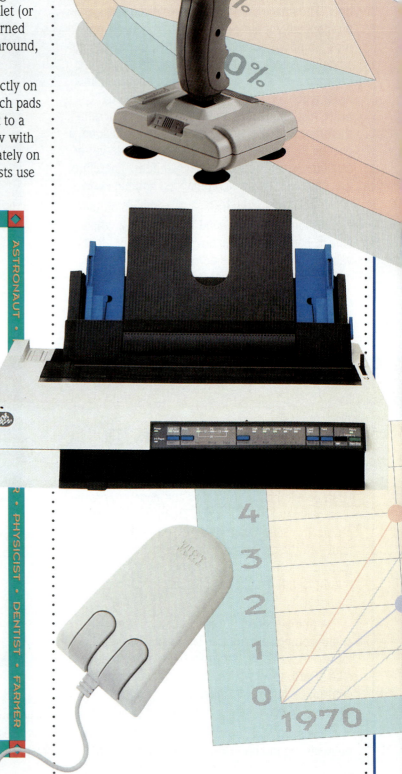

C·A·R·E·E·R·S

SALESPERSON • ELECTRICIAN • ASTRONAUT • PHYSICIST • DENTIST • FARMER • NURSE • DOCTOR • TEACHER • SURGEON • OPTOMETRIST • PILOT • PROFESSOR • SECRETARY • ARTIST

Do you know what a cartographer (kahr TAH gra fur) does? This is a person who makes maps. Look at a map, perhaps one found in your social studies textbook. Many maps are scribed, or drawn, entirely by hand by using sharp tools to cut away the color coating on sheets of plastic. Today, more and more cartographers are using computer tools called *plotters* to help them draw maps accurately. A beam of light from a laser can be used, too, through a light pen. Other times, a scanner can "read" a printed image, then use the data to create a duplicate, or second, map.

MODULE 4

How Graphics Work in a Computer

Modern input and output devices, clockwise from top left: joystick, laser printer, monitor, keyboard, mouse, dot-matrix printer

COMPUTERS THEN & NOW

Did you know that doctors at the University of Texas have developed a new technique for X-raying patients' teeth?

Instead of a traditional X-ray, where images of the patient's teeth are "shot" on film, new technology allows dentists to use digital computer imaging to view the teeth on screen. Not only faster than traditional film X-rays, this new technique exposes the patient to less radiation than the film process.

either—or both—of these tools to create a variety of graphic designs, from those on clothing to prototypes for new aircraft designs.

A scanner lets you transfer images and text from paper into a *digital* format that can be edited and manipulated. Scanners work on the principle that white paper reflects light, black absorbs light and grays (or colors) reflect light depending on the color.

After you've created your images, you'll want to show them to people. Computers provide several output options for showing your creations. Images can be printed on anything from low-resolution dot-matrix printers to high-resolution laser printers and higher-resolution imagesetters.

No matter what you've produced or want to produce on a computer, there is an input or output solution that makes it possible. Which input and output devices have you used?

GRAPHICS

USING SOFTWARE

CREATING EARLY GRAPHICS

In the years before Apple's Macintosh computer brought WYSIWYG (What You See Is What You Get) graphics to the desktop, people created computer graphics by typing in coordinates in computer languages like *BASIC* or *Logo*.

For example, to create a simple box using an Apple II and BASIC, you would have had to type the following commands:

HLIN 10,30 AT 10

HLIN 10,30 AT 30

VLIN 10,30 AT 10

VLIN 10,30 AT 30

This would draw four lines to make a box. The command HLIN (horizontal line) would draw two horizontal lines 20 pixels wide—one beginning at the tenth pixel from the top and one beginning at the thirtieth pixel from the top. VLIN (vertical line) would draw two vertical lines 20 pixels high—one beginning at the tenth pixel from the left side and one beginning at the thirtieth pixel from the left side.

CHARTS AND GRAPHS

Fortunately, computers have come a long way from the days of typing in coordinates to create graphics. With modern software, you can simply tell the computer what type of chart or graph you want and then type in your information. It creates the illustration for you. The computer may even recommend the best way to chart or graph your information!

For instance, if you want to show and compare percentages or parts of a whole, the computer might recommend that you create a pie graph.

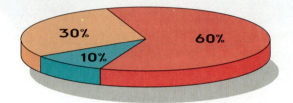

If you want to show and compare facts, a bar graph might be more appropriate.

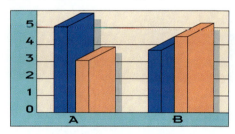

For showing a change over time, the computer would most likely recommend creating a line graph.

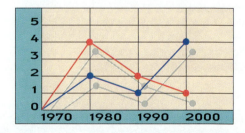

These are just a few of the ways you can use computer graphics. Why not try a graphics program to see what kind of charts and graphs you can create!

TO CREATE GRAPHICS

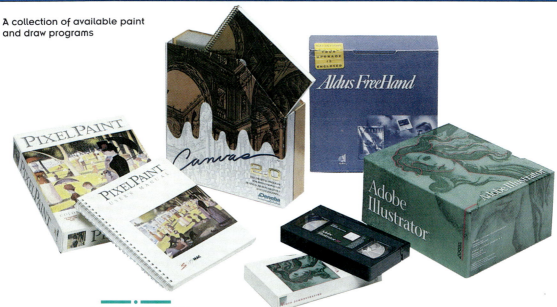

A collection of available paint and draw programs

PAINT PROGRAMS

Using existing information to create graphs is simple if you use special software. The first software for Apple's Macintosh was *MacPaint,* a bit-mapped *paint program* that set the standard for all paint programs that were to follow it.

With *MacPaint* if you want a box, you simply grab the rectangle tool, point where you want it to begin and drag, while holding down the mouse button, until the position looks about right. If you want it to contain a pattern, you select one from the pattern palette, grab the paint bucket, and pour in the pattern. Presto! Your box is painted!

To edit individual dots, you select the pencil tool. Click on a black pixel and turn it white (on) and click on a white pixel to turn it black (off). By selecting parts of a painting with the lasso tool or the selection rectangle, you can move things around or change their pattern.

Newer paint programs have added many enhancements, but all are descended from *MacPaint.* Even more complex programs, which let you edit color scanned photographs, are direct descendants of *MacPaint.*

DRAW PROGRAMS

All *draw programs* have one thing in common: the ability to manipulate graphics as whole objects rather than as dots. Because these programs deal with an object as a whole, they are known as *object-oriented programs.* Paint programs treat circles as series of dots, but draw programs treat circles as groups of lines, with beginning and ending points for each. Clicking on an object in a draw program makes it active. The object can be moved, stretched, or manipulated by selecting the handles, or black squares, at its outer corners.

Using Software to Create Graphics

As was mentioned earlier, clicking on the rectangle tool in *MacPaint* allows you to create a box by selecting where you want it to begin and dragging it to an ending point. The rectangle tool in *MacDraw* works exactly the same way, except that once you've created the box you can click on a handle and change its dimensions. Dragging it up makes the box shorter. Dragging it down makes the box longer.

Whereas *MacPaint* has a paint bucket, adding patterns and colors to *MacDraw* is as easy as picking a color. You can even change the color of the lines that surround the box by holding down the option key while you select the pattern.

COMPUTER-AIDED DESIGN

Some programs allow things meant for the real world to be designed and tested on personal computers long before they exist. Using specialized computer-aided design (CAD) programs, manufacturers of everything from toys to airplanes can design products on a computer and try them out before they are actually built. Exporting CAD information to computer-aided manufacturing (CAM) systems can shave years off the design and manufacturing of products.

You MAKE A DIFFERENCE

When David Kohlmeier was 13 years old, he decided to start his own business. By working hard in a local computer store, David learned to use computer graphics. By using an Apple IIGS computer, *Print Shop* and *Deluxe Paint II* programs, he created greeting cards and signs. His business was so successful that 3 years later David was able to sell about 200 cards in less than a month and earn about $100 doing so!

Draw programs also allow you to move objects around on a page. To move an object, you select it and, while holding down the mouse button, move it to where you want it—to the right, to the left, up, down, even on top of other objects. Some draw programs also allow you to rotate objects in small increments by selecting a special tool or command.

DID YOU KNOW?

Did you know that a number of new-car manufacturers use computer graphics to design their new cars instead of building models?

Using a CAD/CAM system, in the first step, the engineer creates the skeleton of the car, using a series of grid lines. Next, the spaces between the lines are filled in to give an idea of what the body surface of the car might look like. By revising and manipulating the patterns, the engineers can change the shape or design of the car.

Last, the designer adds details, such as color, wheels, and hubcaps to create a realistic picture of the "model."

Using Software to Create Graphics

An artist using a computer, graphics tablet, and stylus to create animation

ANIMATED PIXELS

Another area in which new computer technology is used is in the entertainment industry, in producing animated motion pictures, television shows, and commercials. In the past, animation was a painstaking process. Animators had to draw each frame by hand. Subtle differences between one drawing and the next made the cartoon characters appear as if they were moving, talking, and alive.

Today, computers are changing the way computer animation is created. Computers help speed up the process by allowing the animator to create only the first and last frames of a sequence; the computer fills in the frames in between.

New forms of animation are developing, as well. Movies with both human and animated characters are popular today, and have a high-polished, natural look. Films like Disney's *Fantasia* and *Who Framed Roger Rabbit* prove that animation is no passing fad. With new improvements in animation software, it appears that our favorite animated characters are here to stay.

Learning graphics programs, CAD programs, and CAM systems takes time and patience. However, your investment in time is well worth the return—the ability to generate more complex, more appealing graphics to support your text. Who knows, some of you may even be the ones to create the next generation of graphics software!

★ Read All About It ★

From the pages of *The Office*
March, 1990
By Gloria M. Curry

Computer Graphics Field Keeps Growing

The computer graphics field has grown so rapidly that industry and corporate users are hard put to keep pace with it.

According to Bob Johnson, graphics software product manager at Corporate Software in Westwood, Mass., graphics packages have come a long way in the past three years, both in capability and ease of use. "The old adage, 'a picture is worth a thousand words' is true for graphics," Mr. Johnson says. His company, which has an information center within the management information system and data processing department, assists people in the corporate community by providing technical support for software buyers, and publishes a 500-page software guide. In choosing a computer graphics system, Mr. Johnson says an end user should first identify the purpose in mind. "Are they looking to analyze data? Is it for creating more effective audience presentations, or for applications? Users should really understand what type of data they want to display."

There are painting, drawing and charting packages. A painting package is pixel—maps by dot. It differs from a drawing package, which is vector—maps by line. Both are best for on-screen presentations. For application, if it is to be used for financial or stock market programs, the program should have a high-low-close chart. For trends, bar charts are good for observing time periods, such as comparing sales over quarters. Pie and line charts are also good for displaying trends. "The user should consider the type of data intended for the program, and choose the program with chart types that will best display it."

The use of graphics packages increases productivity and is a time-saver. On-screen presentations of a series of images can now be done, eliminating the need to make 35mm slides. The program simultaneously produces slides, audience hand-outs and speaker notes. Graphics drawing programs and charting packages can also be incorporated into desktop publishing programs. For newsletters, sales charts can be produced, and "Pagemaker" is useful for fliers, according to Mr. Johnson. Another factor is the ability to import data from spreadsheets. It eliminates the need to rekey data, so there is no needless duplication.

Integration is the new trend in graphics programs, and is particularly useful in the organizational chart. Graphics programs now make it easy to produce them, bringing an invaluable degree of intelligence as well. A package that formerly did charting now can also do drawing and painting, and clip-art libraries have hundreds of images that can be used, even if one is not an artist, when making a chart for presentation. You see the image on the screen and it matches, pixel by pixel or dot by dot. This is called "screen-capture utilities" and is valuable in enabling the user to take programs from one file format and convert it to a file format that another program can read. In effect, different programs can "speak" to each other.

Continued on next page

★ READ ALL ABOUT IT ★

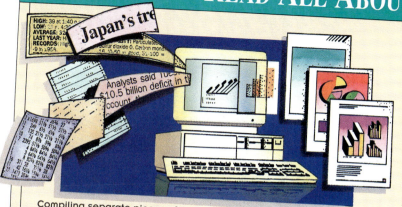

Compiling separate pieces of data into user-friendly graphics

Other future trends include:

Colors. Programs will help the user select colors. Certain colors are matched for background, text, and most effective usage.

Font styles. Future programs will ask the user questions about the type of audience he is trying to reach, then tailor the graphic to that audience and provide a font style with the most impact.

Chart types. Programs will ask questions about the nature of the data to be presented and recommend the appropriate type chart.

Knowledge-based software. Formerly known as artificial intelligence or expert systems, this speeds production of the presentation's creation, and helps ensure its level of professionalism.

According to John Veenhuizen, who designs computer software programs at Buyers Laboratory in Hackensack, N.J., desktop publishing is the new way to link word processing software and graphics programs. One major drawback he sees, however, is lack of standardization. When designing a program, he has to adapt it for the various differences in PCs. "They're just covering too much," he said. "I wish they could give me one video graphics board and standardize it. They should simplify the choice for the end user. That's what this industry needs more than anything." Investing in a color printer is also important for the most effective presentations, Mr. Veenhuizen believes. Least expensive is the dot matrix color printer, but it is not as attractive, as colors are "washed-out or distorted." Laser printers are better, but best is an ink jet printer, he feels. For low-end use, these can be bought for anywhere from $750 to $10,000. The colors are true, bright and vivid, and the detail is good.

PRIMARY ADVANTAGES

Speed and ease of use are the primary advantages of the new graphics programs. Victor Otsuch, a senior technical editor at Datapro Corp., Delran, N.J., agrees. Using computers to give presentations provides the ability to customize and actually change the presentation to show "live data" like a spreadsheet, bar charts or pie charts at a meeting, he points out. "This is available even in portable laptop computers, and any salesperson, for example, can take it along like an attaché case," he said.

"You can get a laptop package that would be comparable to a desktop computer for as little as $1000, and for another $1000 to $1500 can obtain the display device for use with any overhead projector," Mr. Otsuch noted.

"You need speed and performance to show graphics," said Mr. Otsuch. With the new graphics trends, this has been made a reality. ■

MULTIMEDIA

For about a century, people have flocked to see the latest movie and for decades have stayed at home to watch their favorite television shows. What's the appeal? It's the moving image that keeps people watching.

The earliest movies offered no sound. Later, as sound made the movies (known as "talkies") even more real, theaters on Saturday afternoons would be filled with children catching the latest adventures of their movie heroes.

In the 1950s, television brought moving pictures into our homes. Some people predicted that television would signal the death of the motion picture industry. It didn't happen, however, because people love images that are larger than life.

The future's new *multimedia* technologies, such as High-Definition television (HDTV) and the merging of computer and video images, promise to make television more interactive and to make moving visual images even more important in the years ahead.

Multimedia is the merging of traditional computer creations, such as word processing and graphics, with TV sound and video. And why is this important to you, you might ask. The following example shows you why.

Early movie star Gene Autry (pictured), idolized by thousands of moviegoers anxious to experience the combination of sound and pictures

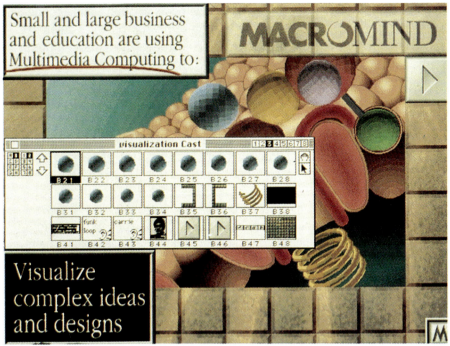

Sophisticated graphics programs, which help computer users manipulate sound, video, and graphics elements

Imagine that your social studies teacher has asked you to find out what a certain president said in a speech. Most likely, to complete the assignment you'll thumb through pages of text and pictures. Even after lots of searching, you may or may not find what you're looking for.

Compton's Multimedia Encyclopedia, a CD-ROM product, uses icons (or symbols) such as a camera, an open book, a pair of eyes, or a set of headphones to tell you that more information is available on a given topic. To find out more, you simply click on the camera icon and the screen fills with a high-resolution picture, such as that of Abraham Lincoln. Clicking on the headphones plays a sound relevant to the subject you're looking at, for instance, a speech by John F. Kennedy.

How are such diverse graphic and sound elements combined to create multimedia productions? The tools include such traditional computer graphics tools as paint and draw programs along with animation programs that make still images move and *authoring systems* that tie everything together.

The first multimedia tool for the Macintosh was a program called *VideoWorks* that was created by MacroMind Inc., during the mid-1980s. *VideoWorks* allowed you to take graphics created with *MacPaint* and add movement by treating each graphic as a separate frame of information. You could even add digitized sounds and create a movie. This simple program brought traditional animation techniques, used since the turn of the century by filmmakers, to computers.

VideoWorks lets you move a picture—a beach ball, for example—around the screen, creating the illusion that the ball is a living object. *VideoWorks* tools included the ability to *tween* objects; that is, to move the ball by selecting it with your mouse and have the program draw the frames between the beginning and ending points.

After new features were added, *VideoWorks* was renamed *MacroMind Director* in the late 1980s. Since then, it has become the favorite tool of many multimedia artists. Along with its new name, the program was given the ability to create interactive (or two-way communication) movies. By adding *buttons*—or commands—to *Director* movies, multimedia artists could create the option of allowing the viewer to choose which scene in a movie to watch next. Later, *Director* added a simple *programming language* called LINGO that allowed both sound and external visual elements—such as live video—to be played back without having been part of the original movie. This was accomplished by controlling external hardware devices, such as CD-ROM players, videodisc players, and videotape recorders.

Multimedia

With these improvements, *Director* has joined *LinkWay, Tutor-Tech, Authorware, HyperCard,* and *SuperCard* to become an authoring system. An authoring system is to a multimedia program (as was *VideoWorks* in the beginning) as a director is to the making of a film. In other words, authoring systems allow you to edit, or change, images, sound, and motion to create a personalized product that makes sense to the user. With *HyperCard,* for example, you can create buttons that play back sequences of video, take you to a text-based sequence of information, or play back a recorded speech.

By combining the elements of sound and motion with the information "printed" on the computer screen, personalized learning and entertainment tools can be created.

One example of this technology at work is ABC News Interactive's *Martin Luther King, Jr. HyperCard* stack and videodisc. This multimedia package enables the user to use a variety of media to explore King's life, times, work, philosophy and impact on civil rights in the United States. The *HyperCard* stack contains text information about King as well as buttons that allow you to search the videodisc, which contains still photos, maps, and film clips about Dr. King. You can even watch

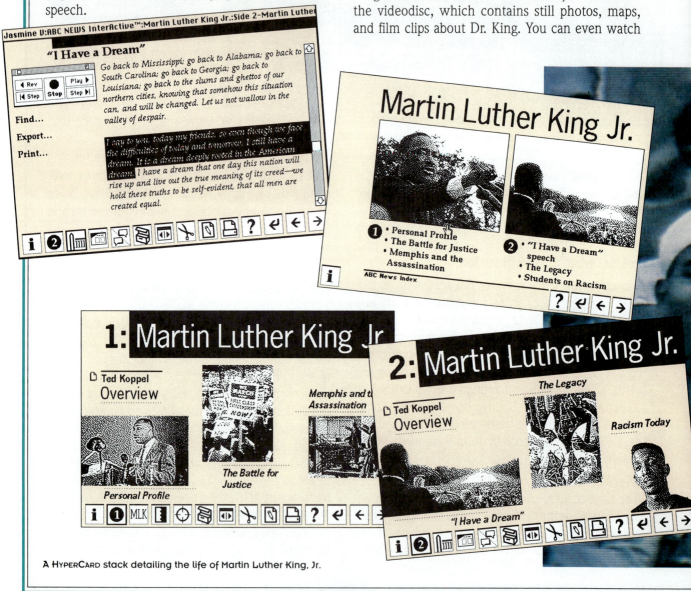

A HYPERCARD stack detailing the life of Martin Luther King, Jr.

Multimedia

all, or part, of the "I Have a Dream" speech on a TV while following the text in the *HyperCard* stack on your Macintosh.

New developments in multimedia promise to get us thinking more about incorporating visual images in our work. In 1991, Apple Computer introduced *QuickTime. QuickTime* is a system software extension that creates standards for using time-based media, such as video and sound. *QuickTime* makes it possible to combine moving visual images with documents like those created by word processors and page layout programs. It also offers a way to condense these images so that they can be stored on hard drives and CD-ROM.

MODULE 4

MODULE SUMMARY QUESTIONS

In order to check your comprehension of computer graphics, you may wish to discuss the following ideas.

1. What are pixels, and how are they used to create computer graphics?

2. What is a computer-aided design (CAD) program, and what purpose does it serve?

3. Imagine that you are a documentary filmmaker. You have been hired to produce a real-life look at the advances in computer graphics in the 1990s. Which multimedia technologies would you use to make your movie? Explain your answer.

GRAPHICS

Module 5: Word Processing

Word processing has made reports, letters, and other writing easier and faster and the results are more accurate than ever before. Using a computer to write allows you to change text without ever picking up a pencil or an eraser!

In Module 5, you will learn how special features in word-processing programs can help you write, edit, and proofread. You'll also read about how desktop publishing combines graphics with text to enhance the look of a page.

What Is Word Processing?

What Is Word Processing?

Angela, a ninth-grader, is learning how to use a word processor to do her schoolwork better and faster. At right is a report Angela wrote for her computer class, explaining the advantages of word processing.

After reading Angela's report, you may be wondering how you can begin word processing. A good way to start is by learning about word-processing programs.

There are many different word-processing programs available. How you operate a program depends on which program you are using. Before you use a word-processing program, you should read the documentation carefully in order to determine exactly what that particular program does and exactly what you have to do to run it.

After you've gained some experience in using word processors, you'll find that most word-processing programs perform the same basic functions. A few simple commands are all you really need to know to begin creating, changing,

How Word Processing Helps Me

By Angela Costner

Using a word processor at school helps me do my schoolwork faster. It also helps me write more neatly and correctly. I'll tell you how, but first, you should know a few things about word processors.

A word processor is a computer program that helps you create text, or words that are displayed on a monitor or printed. A word processor creates text by using light. All you do is type the letters on the keyboard and the letters show up in light on the monitor. These "light words" are easier to change and move around than written or typewritten words. In fact, with a word processor, I can copy a whole paragraph in a split second!

When I want to write at school, I just load a word-processing program into one of the school's PCs, or personal computers. Then, I call up the program from the computer menu and start! The equipment is easy to use. I learned how in just a few hours—and it was worth the effort!

With a word processor, I don't worry about mistakes because it's so simple to "erase" them or change them on the monitor. Best of all, the word processor corrects me when I spell a word wrong. So, I'm always sure that my homework is letter-perfect before I turn it in. The word processor is an amazing writing tool!

MODULE 5

What Is Word Processing?

and moving text around on your computer. It's easy!

As you begin using your word processor, you will want to know how to perform the following functions:

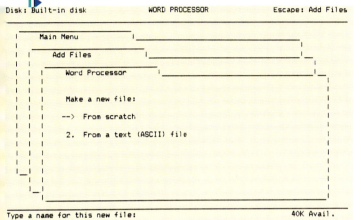

Menu display for opening a document on the Apple II

1. Create a document (also called a "file")
2. Cut and paste text (move it around)
3. Insert and delete text
4. Search for and replace text
5. Format text
6. Save text

Word-processing software usually has other special functions, too. But, for now, let's just learn the basics.

CREATING A DOCUMENT OR FILE

As you begin, the first thing you will want to do is create a document or file. In a word-processing program, a document is anything that you write. A document could be a school report, a letter to a friend, or a list of things that you have to do.

When you start your word processor, the screen will probably show either a blank document or a main *menu,* which lists several options for using your computer. If you see a blank document, you are ready to enter text. If you see a main menu, select the option that says "Create a document" or "Open a file." A blank document will then appear on your screen and you'll be ready to write!

CUTTING AND PASTING TEXT

"Cutting and pasting" is another name for moving text from one place to another in your document. Before word processing, writers actually had to cut out a block of text with scissors, then paste or tape the text in its new position.

With a word processor, all you do is select the text that you want to move, show the computer where you want it and, with a click of a button, it's moved. You can move one sentence, a paragraph, or a whole page to a new location—it's all done in an instant!

To *highlight,* or select, text, simply place your cursor at the beginning of the first word that you want to move and mark it by pressing one or two keys for selecting or highlighting text. Your computer will provide instructions as to which key(s) to use.

After you have marked the beginning of the text, move your cursor to the end of the last word that you want to move and press the select key(s) again. Now you have defined, or selected, the text that you want to move.

The next step is to move the cursor to the spot where you want to place your text selection. Once the cursor is in the correct spot, simply press the button or buttons for "paste," and the selected copy will move to the new position. The computer will close up the hole where you removed the text, and it will open up a hole for the text in the new position. The result is a neat, uniform correction—a lot better than could be done with scissors and paste!

INSERTING AND DELETING TEXT

Inserting means that you add new text to old text. Depending on the software, you may be able to insert new text into an old block of text, or just type new text over old text, totally replacing it. Most programs allow you to do both.

When you set the command to "insert," all you do is move the cursor to the space where you want to place the new text. Then, you type it in. The computer moves the old text over to make room for the new text. Nothing is erased.

When you set the command to "typeover," or "replace," you can simply erase old text by typing over it. All you do is move the cursor to the first letter of the text that you want to replace, and begin typing. The new takes the place of the old.

If you want to delete, or remove, text, simply select the unwanted text and press the command key(s) for deleting copy. Just follow the directions for your particular computer to learn which key or keys to use for deleting.

SEARCHING FOR AND REPLACING TEXT

If you find that you have misspelled or used an incorrect word, you don't have to look through your whole document to find that word—the word processor will do it for you. By using the "search" and "replace" functions, you can have the computer find every instance where you used the word, and then correct it. The computer can do a thorough check for the word (or words) in mere seconds, saving you a considerable amount of time!

FORMATTING TEXT

Formatting tells the computer how you want your text to look on paper. For example, do you want your text to have special margins on the sides, top, and bottom? Do you want certain words to appear in boldfaced (darker) type and other words to be underlined? Do you want your text to be single-spaced or double-spaced? Do you want your titles centered?

Different word processors have different keys that control formatting. Just follow the directions for your particular computer, and you can customize your finished text!

SAVING YOUR DOCUMENT

Saving means that you store your text on the computer's hard disk (internal, long-term memory) or on a floppy disk. Saving stores your document safely in the computer's memory so you can go back later and make changes to the text, print the document, or just see what you have written. To save a document or file, you will have to name it. Name it anything you wish, but it's a good idea to use a name that will remind you of the text that the file contains.

DID YOU KNOW?

Did you know that word processing is even available to people who do not have the full use of their hands?

IBM's *Voice Recognition System* allows physically challenged individuals to use a word processor by speaking into an adapter, or microphone. As the person speaks, the computer changes the spoken words into text on the screen. By examining the context of what the person is saying, the computer is even able to distinguish between words that sound the same, such as "write" and "right."

If the user wishes, he or she can attach a printer to the system and watch the spoken words translate into print—making it possible to dictate letters, memos, and more in mere seconds!

AppleWorks Quick-reference Chart for Your Apple II Computer

To use the *AppleWorks* word-processing program with your Apple II computer, you will need to know a number of commands. You may wish to make a copy of the following quick-reference chart and post it near your computer as a handy guide.

Here's how to use your quick-reference chart: the left-hand column lists several basic functions of *AppleWorks*, the center column provides a short explanation of these terms, and the right-hand column lists the key or keys to press in order to complete each function.

APPLEWORKS WORD-PROCESSING FUNCTIONS

Function	Explanation	Keystroke
Insert	Places new text in an existing block of text	⌘ + I
Edit/Cursor Switch	Switches cursor from insert to replace mode (typeover)	⌘ + E
Delete	Erases selected text block Erases character left of cursor Erases character at cursor	⌘ + D Delete ⌘ + Delete
Copy	Makes a duplicate copy of selected text and stores it temporarily	⌘ + C
Move	Moves selected text to a designated new position	⌘ + M
Find	Locates occurrences of a specific word, phrase, or page throughout a document	⌘ + F
Replace	Lets you replace a specific word or phrase throughout a document	⌘ + R
Bold	Makes selected text appear in boldfaced type	Ctrl + B (Press Ctrl + B again to remove boldface)
Underline	Makes selected text appear underlined	Ctrl + L (Press Ctrl + L again to remove underline)
Center	Centers a line of text in a document	Ctrl + C starts centering text Ctrl + N ends centering
Save	Stores changes to current drive Stores changes to original drive	⌘ + S ⌘ + Ctrl + S
Print	Prints the currently displayed document on paper (via a printer)	⌘ + P
Help	Gives you instructions about what to do next	Click cursor on ?

DeskMate Quick-reference Chart for Your IBM Computer

▼▼▼▼▼▼▼▼▼▼▼▼▼▼▼▼

To use the *DeskMate* word-processing program with your IBM computer, you will need to know a number of commands. You may wish to make a copy of the following quick-reference chart and post it near your computer as a handy guide.

Here's how to use your quick-reference chart: the left-hand column lists several basic functions of *DeskMate,* the center column provides a short explanation of these terms, and the right-hand column lists the key or keys to press in order to complete each function.

DESKMATE WORD-PROCESSING FUNCTIONS

Function	Explanation	Keystroke
Insert	Places new text in an existing block of text	Ins
Delete	Erases selected text	Del
Copy	Makes a duplicate copy of selected text and stores it temporarily on the clipboard	Ctrl + Ins
Cut	Removes selected text and stores it temporarily on the clipboard	Shift + Del
Paste	Inserts cut or copied text from the clipboard into a designated spot in a document	Shift + Ins
Find	Locates occurrences of a specific word or phrase throughout a document	Ctrl + F
Substitute	Lets you replace a specific word or phrase throughout a document	Ctrl + S
Bold	Makes selected text appear in boldfaced type	F4 (Bold)
Underline	Makes selected text appear underlined	F4 (Underline)
Plain	Changes selected text back to plain type	F4 (Plain)
Center	Centers a selected line of text in a document	Ctrl + C
Save	Stores changes you have made to an existing document	F2 (Save)
Save as	Allows you to name and store a new document or rename an existing one	F2 (Save as)
Print	Prints the currently displayed document on paper (via a printer)	F2 (Print)
Help	Gives you instructions about what to do next	F1 (ESC to exit Help)

MODULE 5

ClarisWorks Quick-reference Chart for Your Macintosh Computer

To use the *ClarisWorks* word-processing program with your Macintosh computer, you will need to know a number of commands. You may wish to make a copy of the following quick-reference chart and post it near your computer as a handy guide.

Here's how to use your quick-reference chart: the left-hand column lists several basic functions of *ClarisWorks*, the center column provides a short explanation of these terms, and the right-hand column lists the key or keys to press in order to complete each function.

CLARISWORKS WORD-PROCESSING FUNCTIONS

Function	Explanation	Keystroke
Insert	Places new text in an existing block of text	Move cursor to desired position and type text
Delete	Erases selected block of copy Erases character left of cursor	Delete Delete (or) Backspace
Copy	Makes a duplicate copy of selected text and stores it temporarily on the clipboard	⌘ + C
Cut	Removes selected text and stores it temporarily on the clipboard	⌘ + X
Paste	Inserts cut or copied text from the clipboard into a designated spot in a document	⌘ + V
Find	Locates occurrences of a specific word, phrase, or page throughout a document	Shift + ⌘ + E
Find/Change	Lets you replace a specific word or phrase throughout a document	⌘ + F
Bold	Makes selected text appear in boldfaced type	⌘ + B
Underline	Makes selected text appear underlined	⌘ + U
Undo	Reverses last command	⌘ + Z
Center	Centers a line of text in a document	⌘ + \
Save	Stores changes you have made to an existing document	⌘ + S
Save as	Allows you to name and store a new document or rename an existing one	Shift + ⌘ + S
Print	Prints the currently displayed document on paper (via a printer)	⌘ + P
Help	Gives you instructions about what to do next	⌘ + ?

SPECIAL FEATURES MAKE YOU A BETTER WRITER

Many of today's word-processing programs have special features to help you with writing, editing, and proofreading your text. Now, computers not only help you create text quickly, they help you make sure that it is correctly written, as well. Let's take a closer look at some of these useful word-processing features.

Menu display for using a spelling checker on the Apple II

SPELLING CHECKER

Your word processor may contain a feature called a *spelling checker* or dictionary. With this function, a computer will scan all the words in your document and compare them to an internal dictionary. When it finds a word not contained in its dictionary, the computer will highlight it and stop and wait for your instructions.

After the spelling checker marks your misspelled word, you have a choice: change the spelling or leave it alone. Most computers will offer other spellings for you to choose from. However, if the word is a proper name or an unusual technical term, you may want the computer to ignore it. Some spelling checkers will let you add words like this to the dictionary so they won't be pointed out the next time you check. But, be sure to double-check the spelling first. You don't want to add a misspelled word to your dictionary!

After you use a spelling checker to correct your work, you still need to proofread the entire document. Proofreading means that you read your text carefully, looking for mistakes. Why should you proofread? Because a spelling checker only finds words that are misspelled. It doesn't find words that are used improperly.

Here's an example. If you wrote the sentence, "My cat it old," the spelling checker wouldn't find the error because the word "it" can be found in its dictionary. As long as the word is spelled right, the spelling checker does not care how it is used. You need to proofread your text so you can find mistakes such as these and correct them (change "it" to "is").

Special Features Make You a Better Writer

GRAMMAR CHECKER

A grammar checker works much like a spelling checker. A *grammar checker* helps you make sure that the grammar and punctuation within your document are correct. Grammar checkers may also be called "style checkers."

The grammar checker reads your document, looking for grammatical errors. It highlights your mistakes, just as a spelling checker highlights misspelled words. In some cases, the grammar checker will then suggest ways for you to correct these errors. You can choose to use one of the computer's alternatives, make your own change, or leave the "error" alone. When writing poetry, advertising copy, or some other forms of text, you may not want to follow traditional grammar rules.

THESAURUS

A thesaurus is a dictionary of synonyms. Synonyms are different words that have the same meaning. For example, synonyms for "help" include "aid" and "assist." If your word-processing software has a built-in thesaurus, it can help you make your writing more colorful and interesting.

Suppose you are writing about a famous athlete who has won hundreds of races. Without using synonyms for words like "run" and "fast" your story could quickly become tiresome for the reader! A thesaurus can help you avoid repeating the same words too often within the document. All you have to do is call up the word "run" on your screen, and the thesaurus will suggest alternatives, such as "dash," "dart," "sprint," and "jog."

After using the thesaurus for a while, you will find that you will be able to think of these alternative words on your own. As your vocabulary grows, these words will start coming to mind automatically. In this way, the thesaurus—like the spelling checker and grammar checker—not only helps you create fine documents, but also helps you become a better writer!

COMPUTERS THEN & NOW

Before word processors, typewriters were about the only means by which people, other than professional typesetters, could quickly produce neat, uniform text.

Many of the early typewriters didn't even have keys. Words were formed by turning a dial to each letter and pressing that letter onto the paper.

Today, word processors show us how far we have come since the days of the first typewriter. But there is some irony in this progress. People are now able to create text by speaking into an adapter or touching the computer screen. So, word processors of the future may be "keyless," much like the old typewriters!

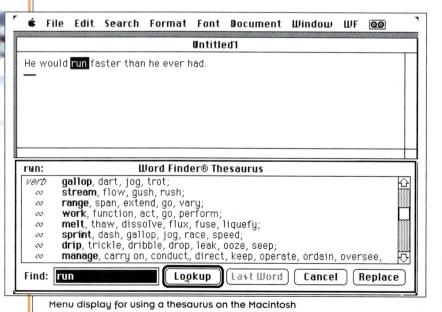

Menu display for using a thesaurus on the Macintosh

WORD PROCESSING

WORD PROCESSORS

Today, English Class . . . Tomorrow, *The Times*!
By Rae Smith

A year ago, if my teacher had assigned a report in English class, I would have said, "Ugh!" But, now that I've learned to use a word processor, I love to write! These days, I think of writing assignments as practice for my future career—writing for *The New York Times*!

With a computer, I've learned to write faster and much better. The word-processing program that I use at school helps me check my work for errors, so my reports are always written correctly. That will be really important at a newspaper. The word processor also lets me rearrange copy easily, so my work is logical and easy-to-read. That's a useful skill for any writer!

Adding emphasis to words is fast and simple with a word processor. Just by pressing a key, I can make words **boldfaced**, *italicized*, <u>underlined</u>, or plain. I can even create headlines, if I want!

Who knows? Maybe I'll just create my own newspaper and give *The Times* some competition!

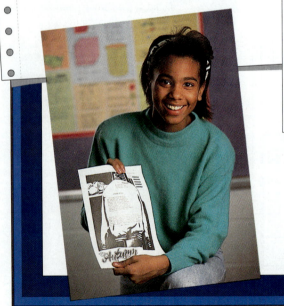

Processing More than "Words"
By Enrique Rodríguez

Did you ever think of using a word processor to improve your *math* skills? I discovered that word processors can make math—or any other subject—much easier to understand. In fact, I think they should be called "thought processors" instead!

At first, writing in math class seemed strange. But, the more I wrote about math, the more I began to understand what my teacher was saying in class. Using my own words to describe a math problem helps me to understand it better—and it's a lot easier for me to solve a problem when I understand it!

I also type my class notes into the word processor every day. Then, before a test, I boldface the important terms and have the computer arrange them alphabetically. That way, they're neat, orderly, and easy to remember. When I print out a copy of my notes, I have an instant study guide!

My math grade has gone from a C to an A- since I started using a word processor. If you ask me, I think word processing is a great invention!

AND SCHOOLS

"Experimenting" with Word Processors

By Roxanne Diller

The lab in my ninth-grade science class is stocked with all the essentials for conducting experiments: chemicals, test tubes, burners, goggles—and a word processor!

Each week, one student in our class is responsible for recording notes about our experiments and other important information on the word processor. At the end of the week, he or she edits the notes, making them easy to read and understand.

For instance, last week we studied acids and bases in class. In the lab, we mixed baking soda and vinegar in an experiment, and the journal-keeper recorded what happened. With the notes neatly recorded, we can simply look up the results of our experiment any time we have a question. Also, each student gets a printout of the notes to use when studying for tests or doing homework.

Now that we include a word processor in all of our experiments, our class understands science better and makes better grades!

The Whole World at Our Fingertips

By Mark Peña

When our social studies teacher told us that we'd be writing a letter to every country on earth, my classmates and I thought it would be impossible. But, that was before we knew how to use the word processor.

The word processor allowed us to edit different addresses onto the same basic letter so we could send out a large mailing in a short time. We've already received several responses. Our next step is to create a chart on the word processor that lists all our new friends around the world!

Once we've compiled all the information about our project, we plan to invite parents, teachers, and other classes to see what we've done. I'm creating the invitations, and a few of my friends are making fliers to post around the school. With the word processor, our invitations and fliers will be easy to read, and they'll look great!

People will be surprised to see how quickly we completed our project—but it was really easy using the word processor. In fact, you might say a computer put the whole world at our fingertips!

Word Processing with Desktop Publishing

Desktop Publishing, or DTP, is a system which combines typeset text and graphics on a single page through the use of a personal computer. Because it is easy to use and has a number of practical applications, DTP has become increasingly popular over the past few years. This, in turn, is having a profound effect on word-processing technology.

PostScript is a page description computer language from Adobe Corporation that was initially used with Apple's *LaserWriter* printers. *PostScript* allowed text and graphics to be printed together on one page with near professional-quality results. This development led to the widespread use of personal computers in publishing and, of course, the coining of a new phrase—"desktop publishing."

Before desktop publishing, book, magazine, and newspaper publishers used systems that cost in excess of one-half million dollars. People who didn't have this type of equipment had to literally cut out separate text and graphic elements and paste them onto a common page. This process was called (quite appropriately) "pasteup." Now, most pasteup is done electronically with desktop publishing software.

CAREERS

SALESPERSON · ELECTRICIAN · ASTRONAUT · MECHANIC · ENGINEER · PHYSICIST · DENTIST · FARMER · NURSE · DOCTOR · TEACHER · SURGEON · OPTOMETRIST · PILOT · PROFESSOR · SECRETARY · ARTIST

In the past, the only way to get a book published was through a professional book publisher. If no publisher needed or wanted your book, the public would probably never see it.

That's what happened to writers Wade and Cheryl Hudson. The Hudsons wrote several books, but couldn't find a publisher who wanted to print them. They were sure that the books would sell—so they took matters into their own hands. They published their books themselves with desktop publishing.

The Hudsons created their own company, called "Just Us Books," and have been publishing books successfully ever since!

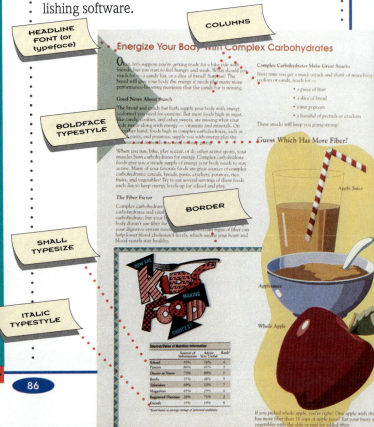

- HEADLINE FONT (or typeface)
- COLUMNS
- BOLDFACE TYPESTYLE
- BORDER
- SMALL TYPESIZE
- ITALIC TYPESTYLE

Word Processing with Desktop Publishing

> ## MULTI CULTURAL BYTE
>
> You may be surprised to know that Amy Tan, one of today's most talented authors, began her writing career working with word-processing and desktop-publishing software.
>
> Just a few years ago, Tan made a living by creating brochures for computer companies. This constant computer practice helped her build speed and agility on the word processor.
>
> Armed with the ability to work comfortably on the computer—and a strong writing talent—Tan was unstoppable.
>
> Today, Amy Tan is the author of two best-sellers: *The Joy Luck Club,* and *The Kitchen God's Wife!*

Today, text can either be created in a word-processing program or "scanned in," using an electronic scanner. The scanner converts pictures and text into images that can be manipulated on a computer. With a scanner, virtually any printed image can be copied into your document!

Once you have created or inserted text in your document, desktop publishing allows you to change the way it looks. Most DTP comes with different *fonts,* or *typefaces.* A font or typeface is a specific design for a whole set of text characters, including letters, numbers, and punctuation marks.

You can change both the way your text looks and the way it is read by combining fonts with different typesizes and typestyles. A *typesize* is the largeness or smallness of a character. A *typestyle* is a special look that is given to a character, such as boldface or italic. Big, bold headlines can be created by using a large typesize and a boldface typestyle. You can emphasize key points in your text with italics or an unusual font. Different fonts, sizes, and styles let readers know which words are more important than others!

DTP can also help you print text in columns. Instead of having long lines of text, you can have two or more columns. You also can have parts from two or more stories on the same page—just like a magazine or newspaper!

Special tools in most desktop-publishing programs allow you to add simple graphics to your text. You can divide copy with thick lines, set off a feature by placing it in a box, or illustrate statistics with a graph. You can even add a screen, or shading, to your box or graph. Whatever you choose, you'll find that graphics add interest to your printed page, making it easier to read.

In short, DTP helps you produce printed text that looks very professional. With graphics, headlines and columns, your work can look as good as your favorite magazine, newspaper, ad, or brochure!

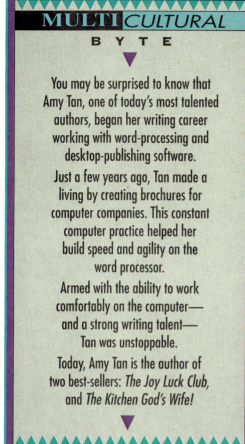

A sample of different graphic elements, typestyles, and fonts used in desktop publishing

★ Read All About It ★

Excerpted from *Home-Office Computing*
February, 1991
By Steve Morgenstern

Rules of Thumb for Making Readable, Attractive Pages

Knowing how to use desktop-publishing software is one thing. Knowing how to make your published materials interesting and easy-to-read is another.

As a contributing editor for several magazines, Steve Morgenstern knows a few tricks that may help you accomplish these goals. The following article details some of Morgenstern's "rules of thumb" for choosing and using type so that all your published materials are the best they can be!

Running a marathon across never-ending lines of text

Use a comfortable line length. Type set in overly narrow columns is tiresome to read—your eye has to jump back and forth every few words.

What I see more often in desktop-publishing projects, though, are lines that seem to go on forever. Getting through these wide-load columns of text is like asking your eyes to run a marathon—you're likely to stumble as you near the end of each line, lose your place in mid-paragraph, and just give up.

There is no hard-and-fast optimal line length, since the type size and design must be taken into account. However, there is a good rule of thumb: Most text faces work best when set with 55 to 60 characters (9 to 10 words) per line.

Minimize use of ALL CAPS. When all you had was a typewriter, hitting Shift Lock and banging away in all capitals was one of the few ways you could call attention to an important piece of text. With desktop publishing there are better devices, including larger type sizes and boldface or italic type. All-capital type, with all the letters the same height, tends to look squared off and blocky. That makes it both unattractive and hard to read, especially in extended settings. All caps are okay for short headlines, but even then I'd also try a bold typeface set in upper- and lowercase.

Continued on next page

Rules of Thumb for Making Readable, Attractive Pages

★ Read All About It ★

WRONG

Before word processors, there was really only one easy way to add emphasis to words—<u>by underlining them</u>! However, now that we can easily use italics, we'll never have to <u>underline</u> again!

RIGHT

Before word processors, there was really only one easy way to add emphasis to words—*by underlining them*! However, now that we can easily use italics, we'll never have to *underline* again!

Emphasizing text the old way and the new way

Never underline. Here's another holdover from typewriter days. Underlining looks amateurish in a desktop-published piece. There just isn't any elegant position for an underline—if it fits close to the bottom of the letters it can touch or cut through the descenders (the tails of the g, q, y, and so on). If the underline is low enough to clear the descenders, it's too far away from the word it's underscoring and hovers perilously close to the line below. You can achieve the same emphasis using italics.

Avoid long italic settings. Italics are often very attractive letterforms. . . . However, the way italics lean forward makes them hard to read in extended passages.

Italics are terrific for adding diversity to a layout when used in moderation, though. You'll often see italicized captions for illustrations, photographs, and charts. Introductory material is often set in italics.

Limit your type. The easiest way to achieve type harmony is to limit the number of typefaces you employ in each project. The rule of thumb says no more than two. I say, Start out by using just one typeface.

Sound boring? It doesn't have to be, since most typefaces give you bold and italic styles to play with in a choice of sizes.

Use contrasting type. Wait a minute—I just said you should strive for type harmony. Doesn't contrast contradict that?

Not at all. [A] common strategy is to use a serif typeface for basic text and a sans serif face for headlines and captions. Either way, the point is to create areas of darkness and

Continued on next page

Serif type

Times
Times Bold
Times Italic
Times Bold Italic
Garamond
Garamond Italic
Garamond Bold
Garamond Bold Italic

Helvetica
Helvetica Italic
Helvetica Bold
Helvetica Bold Italic
Helvetica Narrow
Helvetica Narrow Italic
Helvetica Narrow Bold
Helvetica Narrow Bold Italic
Univers
Univers Bold
Univers Italic
Univers Bold Italic

Sans serif type

WORD PROCESSING

Read All About It

light on the page—to create shapes that attract your reader's eye and encourage it to move around the page.

Space lines properly. Most desktop-publishing programs have a setting that automatically adds space between lines of type. This space is called leading (pronounced "ledding"), a holdover from the days when strips of lead were inserted between lines of movable type.

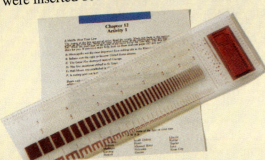

E-scale rulers—used to measure leading before desktop publishing

Generally the space automatically inserted by your page-layout program is 20 percent of the type height, conforming to another rule of thumb. That's a good place to start, but I urge you to experiment with line spacing on your own. The less space between lines, the darker the text block will appear. There will be times when you want that darker look to attract the reader's eye, such as text on a cutout coupon.

On the other hand, adding more space between lines lightens up a block of text. If you use a relatively wide column, added leading makes the longer lines less intimidating and easier to read.

When in doubt, ragged right. Virtually any desktop-publishing program lets you set justified type—that means it lines up at both the left and right margins. To justify text,

> Justified text lines up at both the left and right margins. To justify text, the program will add space between words and letters.
>
> ---
>
> The alternative is to align the left side and let lines end on the right side where the words break—that's called ragged right.

Justified (top)　　　Ragged right (bottom)

the program will add space between words, and sometimes between letters, and use a lot of hyphens.

The alternative is to align the left side and let lines end on the right side where the words break—that's called ragged right. Justified text has its advantages. It looks more formal and gives a sense of rectangular order to the page. Whenever I can, I stick with ragged right.

This choice is based on both aesthetics and convenience. With ragged right, the word spacing—the space between words—is consistent, so the lines of type look smooth and even on the page. In terms of convenience, a justified setting requires you to spend a lot more time policing the choices made by your program. For example, did it put hyphens in acceptable places? This intensive checking and manual adjustment is eliminated if you go with ragged right.

Experiment! I'm always impressed with the way a professional designer can visualize a page layout. I don't have that ability. But I do

Continued on next page

Rules of Thumb for Making Readable, Attractive Pages

★ READ ALL ABOUT IT ★

have a few rules of thumb to guide me in the right direction, and a desktop-publishing system that lets me quickly try out a variety of typographic options and judge their effectiveness based on actual printouts. With this combination of basic knowledge and computer technology, even those of us without formal training can produce attractive publications. ∎

YOU MAKE A DIFFERENCE

Each year, students from all over the United States take part in long-distance writing projects. These students don't live near each other, but they do "work" together.

➤ With the use of word processors, modems, and *telecommunications software*, students across the United States write to each other. Modems and telecommunications software use phone lines to connect word processors in one school to word processors in other schools.

➤ Using this technology and their own computer skills, students are making a difference! They create reports and newsletters about important issues facing kids today, such as the environment and product safety.

MODULE SUMMARY QUESTIONS

In order to check your comprehension of how you can use word processing and desktop publishing, you may wish to discuss the following ideas.

1. You have just learned about the world of word processing. Explain the benefits of a word processor. What are some of the special functions and special features that your word processor has?

2. In what ways can word processors help you in school? Think of some careers that require a knowledge of word processing. How would people in these careers use word processors?

3. Imagine that you and your classmates have been asked to create a brochure for the students in your school that tells about the danger of drugs. How could you use desktop publishing to accomplish your project? What "rules" would you keep in mind when designing your brochure?

MODULE 6
DATABASES

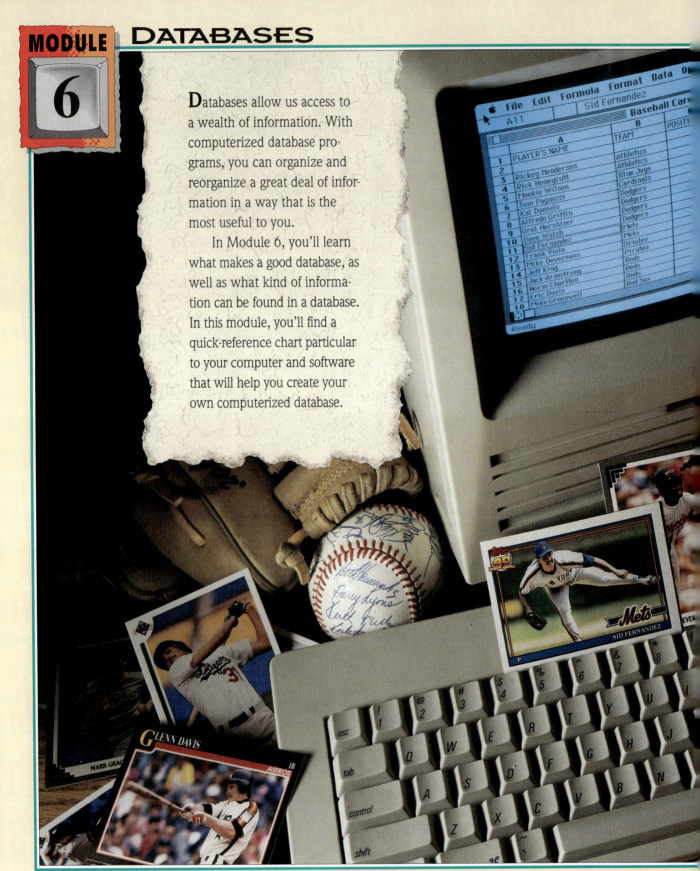

Databases allow us access to a wealth of information. With computerized database programs, you can organize and reorganize a great deal of information in a way that is the most useful to you.

In Module 6, you'll learn what makes a good database, as well as what kind of information can be found in a database. In this module, you'll find a quick-reference chart particular to your computer and software that will help you create your own computerized database.

What Is a Database?

WHAT IS A DATABASE?

Databases—the easy way to keep track of important dates

Have you ever collected baseball cards or cataloged the CDs in your collection, including the date you bought each one and the price you paid for it? Have you ever kept a list of the names and addresses of your friends and relatives, noting their birthdays? If so, you have the start to your own database without probably even knowing it! If you have collected information of any kind and kept some sort of list or file, then you have created a database. A database is a collection of individual facts that are stored in files.

When you flip through your baseball cards or CD collection, or scan through your list of friends' and relatives' birthdays, you are searching for specific information. For instance, you check your baseball card on Nolan Ryan to find out the number of strikeouts he pitched in 1990. You look through your music collection to find the latest CD by your favorite singer. When April rolls around, you look on your list of important dates so that you don't miss your grandmother's birthday.

If you have ten cards, CDs, or important dates on a list, then it is probably easy to find something. If you have thirty, it may take awhile. If you have much more than that, you may forget what you're looking for before you find it!

MODULE 6

What Is a Database?

Imagine getting the information you need by simply entering a command, or two, on your computer keyboard. Many people do this. They use *database management systems (DBMS)*—special software developed for record keeping—to create electronic files on their computers. Then, the computer does all the work of searching through the files to retrieve specific information. The data, or facts, are cross-referenced so that they may be used in many ways.

ORGANIZING AN ADDRESS BOOK

You might have an address book to keep track of your friends' names, addresses, and telephone numbers. Each individual name is one item of data. Each address and telephone number are additional data items. There is a designated space for each of these items.

In computer terms, these designated categories for specific data entries are called *fields*. Each category of data is always entered in its assigned field.

Together, all fields of data related to the same subject create a *record*. The entries in the address book that represent a single person—the name, address, and telephone number—form the record of data related to that person. There is a record for each person entered into the address book. When all of the individual records are collected together, they form a *data file*.

The address book is probably arranged by your friends' last names. This particular organization is useful because we usually look for names in that way, but it limits the ways in which you can use the data in the address book. For an example, think of a list of addresses of all the students in your grade at your school. Perhaps you have a school directory with such a list. If you wanted to find all the students who live in your zip code, you would need to look at every entry on the list because the list is organized alphabetically by name, not by zip code. If the same data were stored in a computerized database, however, you could sort the file into a numeric sequence based upon the zip codes. Then,

Updating handwritten records—a time-consuming and often messy chore

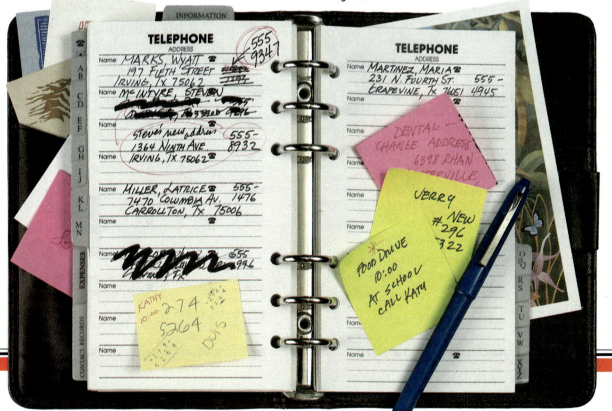

What Is a Database?

COMPUTERS THEN & NOW

In 1980, John Page invented the first easy data-management system called Personal Filing System (PFS), which ran on Apple II computers. Page developed it while working in his garage.

Page showed his program to two friends, Fred Gibbons and Janelle Bedke. The three tried to find a company willing to market the program. When they couldn't, they formed their own company called Software Publishing Corporation, which later became a multi-million dollar corporation.

all entries for the same zip code would be grouped together.

Electronically stored data can be organized in *any* useful way because an electronic file can be sequenced according to any of the fields. A listing of the records in the file, sequenced according to street names, might help if you were forming car pools.

One problem with writing information by hand is that it can be hard to add new information to the file. In the address book, you can add extra names as often as you like, if there is enough space for the new data. But what if you needed to add a name between two names that were already in your address book? Erasing and rewriting names is a lot of trouble, so you probably would write the new name wherever there is space—nearby, but not in the correct spot.

Because databases allow you to enter the new data easily, they also encourage the user to keep records up-to-date. Some databases also automatically insert new data so that it is correctly listed in the proper order between existing records.

The same considerations also apply to changing data. Adding new information to a page may be difficult, especially if there is no more room. However, adding or deleting a field in a database is not hard. For example, you might add a field to store your friends' birthdates, then use the database system to list all of your friends in an order based on their birthdates.

You may also want to update the data you have already entered. Making one or two corrections to entries can be done rather easily by hand or a computerized system, but what about major changes to many records? For example, nearly all of the Los Angeles area had, at one time, a 213 area code. The telephone company then added a new area code, changing the code for Pasadena to 818. Rather than looking up each friend's phone number who lived in Pasadena and correcting it, the database could correct the phone numbers. The computer would just need to know the new information and what information to replace it with. So, the database would search for all the people who lived in Pasadena and change their telephone numbers to the new area code.

While an address book is limited by the number of spots available on its pages, the size of a database is usually limited only by the amount of storage space available on the computer's disk. A database may contain literally hundreds of fields and millions of records.

No longer is there a concern about how the data is organized. The database program allows the reorganization of data in any way required. With a database program, you can make lists of data in almost any sequence or combination you can imagine. The use of databases has opened up a new way of looking at data.

CREATING A GOOD DATABASE

A good database has four important characteristics. Ask yourself the following questions when creating your own database.

1. **Is it complete?** The more complete a database is, the more likely it is to have the information that you need. For example, you'll find Dave Winfield's batting average only if you have his baseball card. You'll be able to check your friend's telephone number only if you've listed it in your address book.

2. **Can it be easily reorganized?** You might organize facts alphabetically, chronologically, or by topic. How you organize your database depends both on its content and how you are going to use it.

The more structured your database is, the easier it is to find information and to reorganize it. For example, if you've sorted your CDs by musical groups and added index tabs to your collection, you'll have little difficulty finding the CDs of your favorite group. If you've arranged the CDs alphabetically, you'll be able to quickly find all the groups that begin with "S." If you arrange the section chronologically, then you'll know what CDs were produced in 1992.

You can also reorganize your CD collection topically—with sections on rock, rap, country, and so on. Within each section, the CDs could be organized alphabetically by musical group. Then, you can turn to the rock section and easily find the CD that you are looking for.

3. **Is it up-to-date?** Your database can be accurate and complete only if it's up-to-date. You'll need to continually revise and expand the database to keep up with any sort of changes. For example, to have a complete collection of American League baseball cards, you must continually add cards with statistics about new players. When friends and neighbors move, you'll need to change their addresses and phone numbers, or when a baby is born into your family, you'll need to update your birthday list.

4. **Can it be used efficiently?** When a database is complete, well-organized, and up-to-date, there is a good chance that it can be used efficiently. You should be able to get the information that you need when you want it.

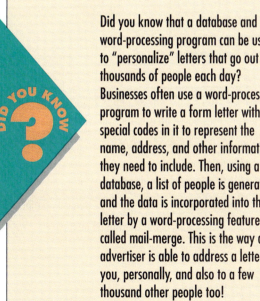

DID YOU KNOW? Did you know that a database and word-processing program can be used to "personalize" letters that go out to thousands of people each day? Businesses often use a word-processing program to write a form letter with special codes in it to represent the name, address, and other information they need to include. Then, using a database, a list of people is generated and the data is incorporated into the letter by a word-processing feature called mail-merge. This is the way an advertiser is able to address a letter to you, personally, and also to a few thousand other people too!

AppleWorks Quick-reference Chart for Your Apple II Computer

To use the *AppleWorks* database program with your Apple II computer you will need to know a number of commands. You may wish to make a copy of the following quick-reference chart and post it near your computer as a handy guide. This chart will help you to use your *AppleWorks* database program quickly and effectively without having to constantly refer to the documentation.

Here's how to use your quick-reference chart: the left-hand column lists several basic functions of *AppleWorks,* the center column provides a short explanation of these terms, and the right-hand column lists the key or keys to press in order to complete each function.

For more detailed explanations or additional commands, please refer to the documentation for the *AppleWorks* software.

APPLEWORKS DATABASE FUNCTIONS

Function	Explanation	Keystroke
Insert	Inserts records	⌘ + I
Edit/Cursor Switch	Switches between insert and replace cursors	⌘ + E
Delete	Erases records Erases character left of cursor Erases character at cursor	⌘ + D Delete ⌘ + Delete
Copy	Copies records	⌘ + C
Move	Moves records to a designated new position	⌘ + M
Find	Locates records based on user-defined criteria	⌘ + F
Record Selection	Lets you set record selection rules	⌘ + R
Save	Saves file to current disk Saves file to original drive/directory	⌘ + S ⌘ + Ctrl + S
Print	Prints the currently displayed report on paper (via a printer)	⌘ + P
Help	Gives you instructions about what to do next	Click cursor on ?

DeskMate Quick-reference Chart for Your IBM Computer

To use the *DeskMate* database program with your IBM computer you will need to know a number of commands. You may wish to make a copy of the following quick-reference chart and post it near your computer as a handy guide. This chart will help you to use your *DeskMate* database program quickly and effectively without having to constantly refer to the documentation.

Here's how to use your quick-reference chart: the left-hand column lists several basic functions of *DeskMate*, the center column provides a short explanation of these terms, and the right-hand column lists the key or keys to press in order to complete each function.

For more detailed explanations or additional commands, please refer to the documentation for the *DeskMate* software.

DESKMATE DATABASE FUNCTIONS

Function	Explanation	Keystroke
Copy layouts	Copies the current database format to a new file	F2 (Copy layouts...)
Copy	Copies the current record to a new record	F4 (Copy)
Cut	Removes highlighted record or field and stores it temporarily on the clipboard	F3 (Cut)
Paste	Inserts cut or copied field or record (from the clipboard) at the cursor location	F3 (Paste)
Sort	Sorts all records according to user-established order	F4 (Sort...)
Count	Counts the total number of records in a database	F4 (Count)
Find	Finds records based on user-defined criteria	F4 (Find)
Delete	Deletes a record	F4 (Delete...)
Add	Adds a new record	F4 (Add)
Form setup	Allows creation of or changes to a report layout	F2 (Form setup...)
Print record	Prints all the record information for a specific database record	F2 (Print record)
Print report	Prints a report based on format determined in Form setup	F2 (Print report...)
Exit	Exits from an address book	F2 (Exit)

DATABASES

ClarisWorks Quick-reference Chart for Your Macintosh Computer

To use the *ClarisWorks* database program with your Macintosh computer you will need to know a number of commands. You may wish to make a copy of the following quick-reference chart and post it near your computer as a handy guide. This chart will help you to use your *ClarisWorks* database program quickly and effectively without having to constantly refer to the documentation.

Here's how to use your quick-reference chart: the left-hand column lists several basic functions of *ClarisWorks,* the center column provides a short explanation of these terms, and the right-hand column lists the key or keys to press in order to complete each function.

For more detailed explanations or additional commands, please refer to the documentation for the *ClarisWorks* software.

CLARISWORKS DATABASE FUNCTIONS

Function	Explanation	Keystroke
Create a New Record	Creates a new, blank record	⌘ + R
Delete	Erases a selected field in a layout	In the layout, select the field and press Delete
Duplicate	Makes a copy of the selected record	⌘ + D
Find	Locates a specific record	Shift + ⌘ + F
Print	Prints the currently displayed record on paper (via a printer)	⌘ + P
Save	Saves file to current disk Saves file to original drive/directory	⌘ + S Shift + ⌘ + S
Close (record)	Allows user to exit file	⌘ + W
Cut	Extracts highlighted record or field and stores it temporarily on a clipboard	⌘ + X
Paste	Inserts cut or copied field, or record (from the clipboard) at the cursor location	⌘ + V

MODULE 6

Pizza Hut® Goes Online

Ivette has invited Gina to spend the night. After all, tomorrow is a school holiday and it would be fun to watch a movie and share a pizza tonight. Ivette dials the local Pizza Hut® to order her favorite—a large pepperoni pizza.

The phone barely starts to ring when Tina Clark, an energetic 16-year-old who works part-time for the store, picks it up. "Hello, Pizza Hut®. This is Tina. May I take your order, please?"

"Sure," replies Ivette, "this is Ivette at 555-9045. I'd like the same pizza I ordered last week, please."

Tina presses a few keys on the computerized cash register next to her phone. "Do you still live at 1425 Park Circle?" "Yes," Ivette replies.

As Tina completes the order, a form starts to appear on the printer next to the pizza counter. The order information shows the order number, type of pizza, and address of the person ordering the pizza.

Mark Pham, the Pizza Hut® driver, picks up the finished pizzas and their delivery tags. The store has several drivers and serves many neighborhoods in the city. To help make the drivers' routes more efficient, the computer groups together orders for the same neighborhoods. Mark's orders are all within a few blocks of each other.

Bob Adler, the manager of the local Pizza Hut®, explains: "We have four telephone lines and terminals hooked up to the main computer which is located in Wichita, Kansas. The computer connects us to a database that helps us run the store." For Pizza Hut®, the database includes facts about

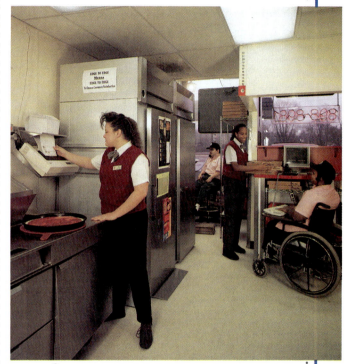

Pizza Hut® employees using computerized databases

their customers, pizza orders, supplies used to make the pizzas, the store's workers, and many other bits of information.

Keeping records manually takes a lot of effort and can lead to mistakes. For example, taking phone orders on an order pad takes from 90 to 120 seconds. The computer has reduced the amount of time per order to less than 60 seconds. It saves this time partly by relying upon data it has stored.

The database even remembers the customer's last order. That's what made it possible for Ivette to say, "I'd like the same pizza I ordered last week."

The first time Ivette called Pizza Hut®, her telephone number and address were stored in the computer along with a code to show the location of Ivette's house on a map of the store's service area. Since the computer already has Ivette's address stored, Tina doesn't have to record it again each time Ivette calls. This saves time and prevents mistakes. It means more orders can be taken in less time and gives the customer better service. On busy nights, all four telephone lines ring constantly. Adler says the computer makes it possible for employees to take as many as 240 orders and cook as many as 480 pizzas in an hour.

A database can help track the amount and use of supplies. Bob Adler gets a report on the amount of supplies that should have been used to make the pizzas ordered in his store. By comparing the computer report and the actual amount used, Adler can determine whether the right amount of ingredients was used. By keeping track of sales over the last few weeks, the computer can help forecast the amount of supplies Bob should order for the next week's sales.

When Tina, Mark, and the other employees in the store come to work they check in on the computer. The computer keeps track of the time employees work and prepares their paychecks. By comparing the volume of sales to the work force needed, the computer helps Bob schedule his crew so that there are just enough workers at the store to match the customers' calls.

Another helpful use of a database is that it can create sales information. For example, Pizza Hut® might distribute coupons to attract new customers. Then, the store could survey customer addresses to find out in which areas there are no, or few orders, and distribute coupons in these neighborhoods. Tracking orders from the new neighborhoods would tell the store how well the idea worked.

Today's business world demands up-to-date information. So much data can be collected that using all these facts is nearly impossible!

Pizza and computers—an unlikely but effective partnership

READ ALL ABOUT IT

From *Computerworld*
December 4, 1989
By Mitch Betts

Justice Aims Database at Gun Sales

The U.S. Department of Justice has decided to build a complete computerized database that lists convicted felons so that local firearms dealers throughout the country will be able to check out the criminal histories of gun buyers at the point of sale.

However, as Attorney General Richard L. Thornburgh put it in a letter to Congress late last month, the database "cannot be created overnight." First, the Federal Bureau of Investigation and state authorities will have to fully automate and standardize their criminal-history records and make the data much more accurate and complete.

Thornburgh said the FBI will be in charge of building an integrated database of convicted felons and establishing standards that states will be able to follow when reporting data. The Justice Department will dole out $27 million in grants during the next three years to help states comply with the FBI data standards.

A federal task force reported that there is a mixture of automated and manual criminal-history systems at the federal and state levels, and many of the automated systems show arrests but not convictions or other final dispositions. The task force estimated that only 40% to 60% of conviction records are automated.

"Right Chief, we're running the suspects through the computer right now."

"The lack of readily accessible conviction records is the greatest obstacle to an immediate and accurate felon identification system," Thornburgh said.

The eventual goal is to have local firearms dealers place a telephone call to a state police official who would then use a computer terminal to find out if the intended purchaser has a criminal record in the national database. If a felony record exists, the sale could not go through.

UNHAPPY

However, Thornburgh's decision did not please the interest group Handgun Control, Inc. because the screening system will not be implemented until some indefinite time in the future. In the meantime, Congress should

Continued on next page

Justice Aims Database at Gun Sales

★ Read All About It ★

enact legislation setting a seven-day waiting period before a purchase of a handgun, the group said in a statement.

Creation of a felon identification system was mandated by the Anti-Drug Abuse Act of 1988 in an amendment that was supported by the National Rifle Association (NRA) as an alternative to a waiting period.

The NRA supported Thornburgh's conclusions and said that the first order of business is to solve record-keeping problems. With existing systems, "checking for felons at the point of purchase is as accurate as a coin toss," said a statement by James Jay Baker, director of federal affairs at the NRA.

The point-of-sale system selected by Thornburgh is estimated to cost up to $44 million to develop and up to $70 million a year to operate. The attorney general chose the least costly of the technical options offered by the Task Force on Felon Identification in Firearm Sales, which also considered preapproval systems using smart cards, fingerprint scanning and biometric scanning. ■

MULTI CULTURAL BYTE

Thanks to computerized databases, civil service tests in some parts of the country will become more accessible. The computerized system replaces full-day, group testing. This new way of testing should attract more U.S. citizens with African American backgrounds in Denver. During a recent recruitment there, only about 12 percent of the people who signed up to take the test to become police officers were African Americans. It is believed that a convenient, computerized test will encourage more applicants, increasing the chances of recruiting more African Americans.

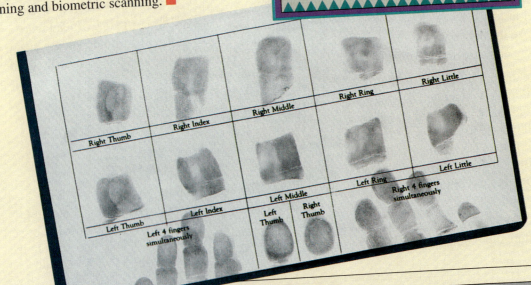

MODULE 6

104

ALTERNATIVE DATABASES

A computer is able to store more than just words. It is able to store pictures, video images, and sound. For instance, *National Geographic* has prepared a CD-ROM containing animations of animals in their native habitats using real animal sounds. CD-ROMs are coded to store data and images as well as sound. The computer treats a CD-ROM as a special type of disc. The computer is able to access the CD-ROM at any location. Other media that store databases include videotape and laserdiscs with sound and digitized images (pictures turned into coding that the computer can understand). With a database, the image and sound can be a powerful source of information.

The National Gallery of Art in Washington, DC, has an interesting and informative tour of art, but even a long visit to the museum could not match the information stored on the Gallery's videodisc. The videodisc contains all of the gallery's works, including some not usually on display. Along with the images are narrations of each artist's life and times, explanations of the paintings, and close-up views you could never see in the protected museum environment.

Using a database, you would be able to list all images containing a specific topic—say French Expressionists, for example. Then, you might locate all paintings by a particular artist, such as André Derain. With the lists, you could then view the images and listen to the sound track.

Certainly the use of computer databases with visual images is an exciting business trend. Real estate firms are using databases to show homes for sale. Some companies are keeping photographs of employees on file with their records. The possibilities are endless.

Touring The National Gallery of Art's videodisc selection of André Derain's works, including "Charing Cross Bridge" (pictured)

ONLINE CAREERS

Finding a new job or looking for the right career can be hard to do. However, *online* (done while connected to a computer) database searches can make doing this easier.

There are a number of online database services that collect job information (though they are not available everywhere nor for all jobs). Some universities have created these services for their students and graduates. Using a database system, the job-seeker is able to search the database for specific types of jobs or skills, company locations, or industries, and other related information. The database can contain sections for an applicant's name, address, and telephone number as well as previous work experience, prior employers, and special skills, such as programming and foreign languages.

One interesting reason to find and use some of these database services is to learn about different careers. For example, if you were interested in a career in medicine, you might search a database for medical personnel to learn about their employment requirements. Those interested in a computer career may learn which programming languages, hardware systems, and operating systems they'll need to know for certain jobs. This information will be helpful for you to determine what classes or experience you will need for a particular career or job that you are interested in.

C·A·R·E·E·R·S

SALESPERSON · ELECTRICIAN · ASTRONAUT · MECHANIC · ENGINEER · PHYSICIST · DENTIST · FARMER · ARTIST · SECRETARY · PROFESSOR · PILOT · OPTOMETRIST

In this Information Age, large amounts of data are available to the public and industries through thousands of databases. As this information increases, there will be a high demand for people who know how to custom-design database management systems (DBMSs) for specific kinds of organizations.

Carol Klitzner is a Database Administrator and has this to say about her job: "I feel like a master librarian, with a great database management system that I helped design. I enjoy knowing how all the data are organized, and I enjoy improving the system in ways that allow users to efficiently retrieve the data they need."

MODULE 6

106

★ READ ALL ABOUT IT ★

**Excerpted from *The Washington Post*
October 22, 1989
By John Burgess**

High Tech on the Range

Billy Perrin, owner of Hugo Livestock Commission Co.

HUGO, Okla. — Cattle are bought and sold daily at small markets scattered all over the Midwest. How much a cow fetches where means a lot to Billy Perrin because he runs one of the markets, Hugo Livestock Commission Co., which stands by the railroad tracks outside this small Farm Belt town. Newspapers, radio and telephone calls used to be his best hope of keeping up. Now he sits down at a desk in his cinder-block office and flips on a small video terminal.

Atop Perrin's roof sits a 30-inch antennae dish pointed at a satellite that broadcasts market reports on cattle as well as a host of other agricultural subjects. With a few commands at his terminal, Perrin can find out prices per pound at competing markets, how the average cost of raising a cow has changed today compared with yesterday and the government's latest outlook on the cattle business.

Computers are popping up in many corners of rural America these days. Farmers are using them to analyze futures markets, decide whether it's smarter to plant corn instead of wheat on those 100 fallow acres and select which dairy cows to sell as beef—all of them tasks traditionally done using gut instinct or long hours at the scratch pad.

The equipment tends to be simple by today's standards. But its use appears to be helping some farmers stay afloat in a business that in the last decade has become much more risky, much more competitive. Increasingly, today's farmer must function as strategic planner and futures analyst. Computers help accomplish that.

"It doesn't make any difference how good a crop you raise," said Burton Schubert, a wheat and milo producer who uses a personal computer in managing 2,500 acres in the Spearman, Tex., area. "If you don't watch those dollars and cents and tend to business, you're not going to be around very long."

A decade ago, pundits were predicting that computers would be standard equipment in virtually every farmhouse, but costs and resistance from older farmers slowed the spread of the machines. Many who did buy them couldn't figure out how to use them. "They became great paperweights," said Bob Coffman, managing editor of Oster Communications of Cedar Falls, Iowa, which runs a farm data network called Instant Update.

Today, experts estimate that, at most, 20 percent of America's commercial farms have

Continued on next page

★ Read All About It ★

computer equipment of some type, and the figure continues to grow. Farm-oriented software and electronic data companies that survived the rough periods of the past decade have brought prices down, made their products easier to use and are now settled down with more conservative expectations of their future.

Billy Perrin figures his satellite data system has made his market more popular with the local ranchers. They frequently stop in or phone Perrin for the latest numbers. If some market-moving federal report comes out on a Friday, the day when close to 1,800 cattle go on the block in Hugo, Perrin will walk back to the auction room and spread the word—that is, if the sellers, who are friends and neighbors from the surrounding counties, stand to get better prices. Otherwise, he keeps mum about what the system has told him.

"In rural America here, it allows us to have the same information you can receive at the terminal markets," said Perrin, referring to the big city destinations where most of the cattle eventually end up. The service is easy to use, Perrin said: "If the cowboys can do it . . . " he laughs, leaving the statement unfinished.

Perrin is one of 43,000-plus people, most of them farmers, who subscribe to the service, run by Data Transmission Network Corp. of Omaha. Perrin pays the most attention to cattle but there on his screen is row after row of data about corn, about pork bellies, about foreign currencies, about eggs. There are maps that show temperature and precipitation across the continent and ever-updated tip-sheets from the service's own reporters who share their thoughts on what the latest pricing shift means for the producer.

Perrin clearly enjoys using it. "A lot of times I'll come in early or come in late and spend an hour studying it," he said. "It's a world of information to digest." A good deal of what he sees, however, is mainly of academic interest. Prices in the cattle business, due to the difficulties of transport, tend to be

Continued on next page

Computers in rural America—providing farmers and ranchers access to databases for the latest updates on markets and weather

★ READ ALL ABOUT IT ★

determined more at a local level than do prices of, for example, grain.

Some farmers are installing data systems directly in their own homes, bringing in signals using satellite dishes, cable TV, FM radio frequencies or telephone lines. Many just scan the numbers on the screen and use it to decide on trades placed by phone with their brokers. Others exploit the fact that the numbers arrive in electronic form, storing them on a computer disk and then using them to assemble historical data or run calculations about the business. ■

YOU MAKE A DIFFERENCE

How could you and your classmates use a database to help the environment? You could make a database on recycling centers in your area for the residents of your community.

➤ Look in the telephone book, call your town hall, or look in your local newspaper to find out about the recycling centers near you. Find out the name, location, and operating hours of each service. You can use this information to create a database making separate fields for the materials, the locations, and rebates paid for recycled items. You may want to inform the residents of your community that you can provide them with information on recycling centers nearest to them.

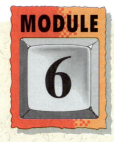

MODULE 6

MODULE SUMMARY QUESTIONS

In order to check your comprehension of databases, you may wish to discuss the following ideas.

1. How would you go about creating a good database for a comic book collection? What are the benefits of using a computerized database?

2. In what businesses might databases be helpful? What are the benefits to both the business and the consumer?

3. What kinds of information are available on a database?

MODULE 7

TELECOMMUNICATIONS

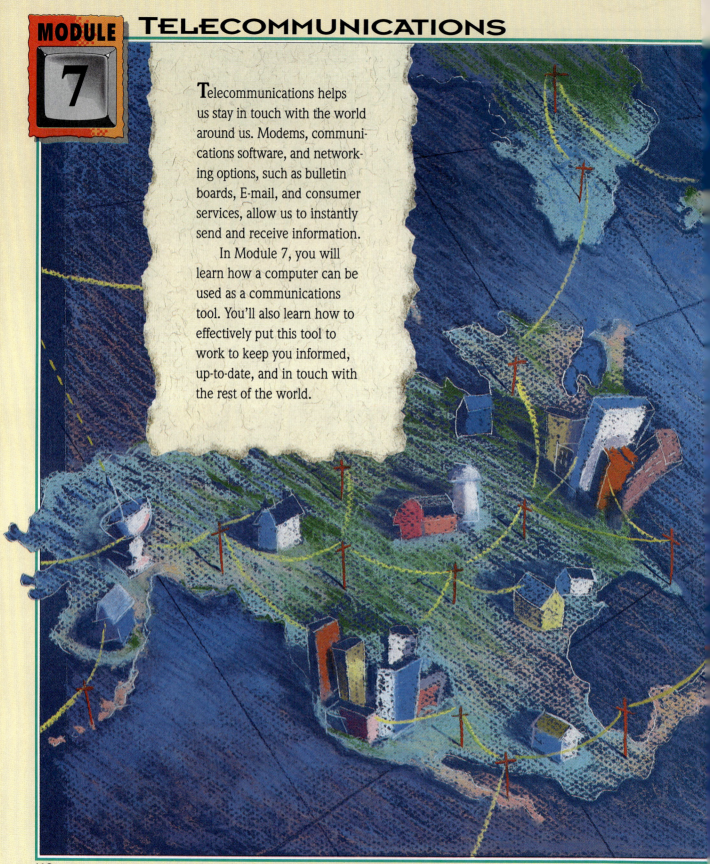

Telecommunications helps us stay in touch with the world around us. Modems, communications software, and networking options, such as bulletin boards, E-mail, and consumer services, allow us to instantly send and receive information.

In Module 7, you will learn how a computer can be used as a communications tool. You'll also learn how to effectively put this tool to work to keep you informed, up-to-date, and in touch with the rest of the world.

COMPUTERS AS COMMUNICATIONS TOOLS

When people share information, thoughts, and feelings with others, they're communicating. *Telecommunications* refers to the sending of information from one place to another using all forms of communications, such as video and telephone. This is how people from all over the world "talk" with one another. No matter where you live or work, it's possible to talk with a friend anywhere—thanks to telecommunications.

The telephone is the most commonly used telecommunications tool today. Most telephones are connected to one another by cables or wires (known as phone lines), or by satellites. But today, our way of telecommunicating is changing. Some telecommunications systems still use wires. However, many "wires" are actually made of glass, called fiber-optic cable. Fiber optics use light to improve the speed and sound quality of our long-distance communications.

Other modern telecommunications systems are wireless. Wireless systems often use satellites in space to send and receive information via radio waves, called microwaves. Many modern telecommunications systems combine the best features of both wire and wireless systems—with help from the computer, of course!

The computer is changing the world of telecommunications. It's helping make telecommunications faster and easier than ever before. Instead of communicating telephone-to-telephone, some people now communicate computer-to-computer. Like telephones, telegraphs, and fax machines (which send the information on printed pages over telephone lines), computers are usually connected to each other by cables, wires, or satellites. Unlike telephones, however, computers communicate over long distances in more ways than just through the spoken word!

People can instantly send and receive messages via computer. These messages can be text, graphics, sound, or all three. It's also possible to hear and see the person at the other end of the line (and what he or she is doing!) by using a computer connected to some additional equipment. This is called *video teleconferencing*.

Computers also enable us to communicate simultaneously with more than one person, each in a different location. Imagine sending to and receiving messages from people in Mexico City, Cairo, Hong Kong, and Berlin—all at the same time!

Many experts predict that soon people all around the globe will be linked to one another. Everyone, everywhere, will be part of a world-wide communications network. You'll be able to see, hear, send, and receive messages—and communicate in many other ways. How? In this module you'll learn more about using the computer as a telecommunications tool.

MULTI*CULTURAL* BYTE

Charles Kuen Kao was born in China and educated in England. Never heard of him? He's one of the electrical engineers who helped make fiber-optic telecommunications possible. For light to be sent along glass fibers—and to be used for telecommunications—the glass has to be very pure. If not, the light waves are distorted, making it impossible to transmit a signal. Kao helped discover a way to make glass fibers pure enough to carry light signals thousands of miles. Kao is credited with helping to make fiber-optic telecommunications a reality.

How the Computer Works as a Telecommunications Tool

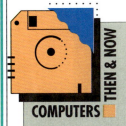

COMPUTERS THEN & NOW

When the modem was first invented, it was about the size of a small closet.

Today's modems are a lot smaller. Some are about the size of a telephone receiver. Others are part of a circuit board that fits into a computer.

Modems are still shrinking. Research is underway to develop a modem that is the size of a computer chip!

The modem changes information from your computer into signals that can be sent across phone lines. Think of a modem as a translator. Computers send out "digital" ("on/off" pulses) signals. Telephones use "analog" (continuous waves like sound waves) signals. A modem translates, or changes, the computer's digital signals into analog signals (modulation). These analog signals can then be sent across the telephone lines. The receiving computer's modem translates the audio tones back into signals that the computer can interpret (demodulation).

By now, you're probably wondering how computers "talk" with other computers. What do you need to make your computer a telecommunications tool? Keep reading to find out the answers to these and other questions.

A computer isn't ready for telecommunicating until two parts are added to it. The first is a piece of hardware called a modem. The second part is *communications software.* (In addition, all computers require a special communications *port,* or outlet, to perform telecommunications.) Once these two items are added, you're all set to become part of the telecommunications generation!

A modem is a hardware device that enables computers to communicate with each other by telephone. In other words, your computer uses telephone lines to communicate with other computers.

A modem (left), computer (center), and communications software (bottom center)

Telephone networks are constantly changing. Today, more and more telephone networks use digital signals than ever before. In the near future,

How the Computer Works as a Telecommunications Tool

Students in various parts of the world trading information through telecommunications

modems may be much smaller than they are today —or may not even be needed at all—since it is probable that telephones will make modems unnecessary.

Communications software lets your computer prepare and send information from your computer to the modem. It also lets your computer receive and understand the information it receives from the modem. In other words, it gives the computer and the modem instructions on how to work together.

Do you want to know how telecommunicating works? Here's how to send a message to some "pen pals" at home in Chicago.

First, make sure that the computer and modem are hooked up properly. Then, select the "enter message" function from your communications software. Type in the message—and proofread it for errors.

When you're sure your message is OK, dial your friends' computer-modem number. Use the "send message" function and begin sending your message to Chicago.

The modem translates your computer's digital message into a form that can be sent over the telephone lines—an analog message. Your message then travels over telephone lines, reaching your friends' modem in Chicago. Even a message from hundreds of miles away can be received in just seconds!

Their modem translates the analog message back into digital form, so that their computer can "read" it. They select the "read messages" function from their communications software program, and read your message!

A *host computer* is a mainframe computer used to telecommunicate. A host has special software which lets it share its resources with several clients. People who are connected to the host can work all at the same time, from different places.

For example, workers in Miami, San Diego, New York, and Houston can share a host's database in Chicago. Using their own computers and a modem, all workers can use the host computer to get the data they need to do their jobs. Although it seems like they're using the host computer at the same time, they're really taking turns.

MODULE 7

CREATING COMMUNITIES WITH TELECOMMUNICATIONS

A community is a group of people who share something in common, usually work, family, or interests. Computers do more than just help people with their work—computers help bring people together. Computers can help people become friends and feel like part of a community.

With computer-aided telecommunications, people no longer need to feel isolated or be alone. People who would never have met can meet. It doesn't matter where you live, what you look like, or who you are. You can share your ideas and feelings with anyone, anywhere. With friends from around the world, you can participate in solving the problems of our global community, such as recycling and the destruction of the world's rain forests, or you can just make new friends.

By using the computer for telecommunications, people from all over the world may become members of one global community, or "village." How? Well, nowadays the barriers to communication are being torn down quickly. Computers are helping us break down these walls and build new connections between people from different countries.

The idea of the global village is that everyone around the world can feel that he or she lives in the same place. When you stop to think about it, our "village" is the planet Earth. Earth is a home we all share. Being part of a global village means that people can use the computer and telecommunications to share information at school or at work—together—as well as to share other parts of their lives with one another.

Using a computer, special telecommunications software, and a modem, it's possible to send and receive messages to anyone from anywhere on Earth. And, in the not-too-distant future, we may all be linked to one another by computer.

For this to happen, however, we have to solve some problems first. For example, not everyone speaks the same language. How can we all communicate with each other without a translator, or without learning every language? Well, in the future, there may be software that will help your computer translate any language quickly. Think of this software as a kind of "language" modem!

Another problem is the cost of telecommunications hardware and software. Today, prices are coming down because people are learning how to make more efficient and less expensive computers and telecommunications equipment. In the future, it's likely that the computer, or some combination of the computer with other technologies, will become our most important tool—for work, for school, and for personal communications, too.

The global village is beginning to happen already. The limits and boundaries of our world are shrinking because distance is no longer an issue, thanks to the computer, television, telephone, fax machine, and our ability to telecommunicate.

How, do you think, will you and I use telecommunications to speed contact with our friends and family around the world? What telecommunications options will become available, and which will you choose? How exciting to be able to answer questions like these in our lifetime!

COMPUTER NETWORKS

In addition to allowing us to access a modem, communications software lets us hook up to, or communicate on, different networks. A network is a number of computers linked together, usually through a powerful central computer, so that the users can work and communicate with one another. Networks help people communicate with others and share files or information—or even equipment, such as printers and terminals.

In general, there are two types of networks. *Wide-area networks* (WANs) are connected through phone lines and modems, allowing one computer to "speak" with another computer a great distance away. The second type of network is a *local-area network* (LAN). Local-area networks connect their computers or terminals directly, by means of cables or wires. LANs are usually located in the same building—or even in the same room.

A computer can belong to one or hundreds of networks—or to none at all. An example of a network that is both LAN and WAN is one that allows users to send messages to different computers in the same building *and* to other computers across the country.

In schools, a networked computer classroom offers additional benefits to students and teachers. By having a number of microcomputers networked to one "teacher station," a teacher can easily work with individual students or with groups of students. The teacher's computer is connected to the student terminals. By being networked, the students and their teacher can communicate back and forth by computer.

The networks you, your school, or a business installs depend on many factors. Cost, ease of use, and speed are three factors; however, the most important factor in setting up a network is determining the type of work you want the network to do for you.

TYPE OF NETWORK	CONNECTED BY	PURPOSE
(Wide-area Network)	Phone lines, Modems	Allows computers to communicate over a long distance
(Local-area Network)	Wires, Cables	Allows computers to communicate within the same room or building

You MAKE A DIFFERENCE

Students at the Aldrin School in Schaumburg, IL, found out how they could make a difference when they joined a group of over 10,000 schools nationwide. As members of Kids Network, they telecommunicate with students all over the country about science-based issues, like the environment, water purification, and life in the United States. Surveys and studies are completed using all means of telecommunications—from phone, to fax, to modem, to information networks. You, too, can make a difference by using a WAN.

MODULE 7

NETWORKING OPTIONS

There are a number of different types of online computer networks for you to choose from: electronic mail, *bulletin boards, databanks,* and others. Here are a number of networking options, and a description of the benefits and services each provides the users.

Electronic mail   Electronic mail, or "E-mail," for short, is one way of sending and

```
CompuServe Mail   Main Menu

1 READ mail, 1 message pending

2 COMPOSE a new message
3 UPLOAD a message
4 USE a file from PER area

5 ADDRESS Book
6 SET options

!_
```
E-mail: one use for computer networks

receiving messages electronically. Anyone who is part of an E-mail network can send and receive private messages.

An E-mail network can be set up just for your school. To send a message to one person on an E-mail network, you need to address your message to that person. The E-mail system places the message in the recipient's "mailbox." He or she can read the message at any time—and then send you a return message.

Bulletin boards   Often, we want to send messages to everyone on our E-mail network or to post information for general access. To send a separate message to each person's mailbox would be awfully time consuming. To accomplish this task more efficiently, why not use an electronic bulletin board? An E-mail bulletin board works like a bulletin board at your school or in any office. People place messages on the bulletin board for everyone to see.

Each E-mail bulletin board section has a heading. The heading helps people decide which bulletin boards they want to read—and which ones they don't. For example, bulletin boards might be headed "General Messages," "Video Games," "Sports," or "Environment."

If you're interested in video games, you can read any message that appears on the video-games bulletin board. Or, if you want to send a message to people who share an interest in video games, just

```
CompuServe                          TOP
 1 Member Assistance (FREE)
 2 Find a Topic (FREE)
 3 Communications/Bulletin Bds.
 4 News/Weather/Sports
 5 Travel
 6 The Electronic MALL/Shopping
 7 Money Matters/Markets
 8 Entertainment/Games
 9 Hobbies/Lifestyles/Education
10 Reference
11 Computers/Technology
12 Business/Other Interests
```
Accessing different bulletin boards for different interests

place a message—by E-mail—on the video-games bulletin board.

Timesharing   Special software and a modem will let you telecommunicate with mainframe computers to do all sorts of things. For example, if you want to get information from a local university library, you can use your modem and communications software to help you communicate with the library's mainframe computer. Once you're connected, you can search for information about any topic you want.

Of course, you're probably not the only person using the library's mainframe, but don't worry! A mainframe computer is powerful enough to let many people use it at the same time. This type of sharing is called *timesharing.*

Networking Options

CompuServe: one of the many available consumer-services networks

Did you know that the initials *EFT* stand for **e**lectronic **f**unds **t**ransfer? Do you know what an *automatic teller machine* (ATM) is? In everyday language, it means long-distance banking.

EFT is a financial transaction that originates at a terminal and transfers money from one account to another. Banks are connected electronically to cash machines—or to PCs in people's homes. The bank uses mainframe computers to make sure that the EFT system works properly— and to make sure that everyone's account balances! It helps people bank 24 hours a day, away from home.

Consumer-services networks

Consumer-services networks connect computers to banks, stores, government offices, and more. Some consumer-services networks only provide you with information by letting you read what's on your computer screen. (For example, one online network lets you call up a specific city and find out what the weather forecast is for that day.)

Other consumer-services networks give you information *and* let you send data, too. For example, you might want to become a member of a travel-services network. This way, you and your friends can research the cost of plane tickets to different parts of the world, and receive this information.

You can send information on this travel network, too. Did you know that you can actually make a reservation on some airlines, and even buy a ticket, using your computer? You can do all these things. How come?

"Our next speaker will talk on the subject of 'the pitfalls of electronic funds transfer systems'."

Because you're part of an online computer network.

Consumer-services networks may allow each one of us to

MODULE 7

Networking Options

shop for everything from home—yes, even cars, food, clothes, computer equipment, and more. What do you think? Would this improve your life? If so, how?

Databanks Databanks are networks that let computers share large amounts of database information. Most databanks allow you to read or receive information, but not to send or add new information unless you have a special approval code.

An example of a databank would be a computerized listing of treatments, symptoms, diseases, and medicines. If you were able to access a medical databank, you would be able to search for any medical subject you wanted. Databank networks are a big help for people who need to find specific information quickly.

Teleconferences *Teleconferences* allow two or more people to communicate at the same time. Many businesspeople, teachers, lawyers, and politicians depend on teleconferencing to get their work done. Teleconferencing can often save time and money. People no longer have to travel long distances to share information with each other. They just have to set a time to hold a teleconference and—presto—they can have a long-distance meeting! Some

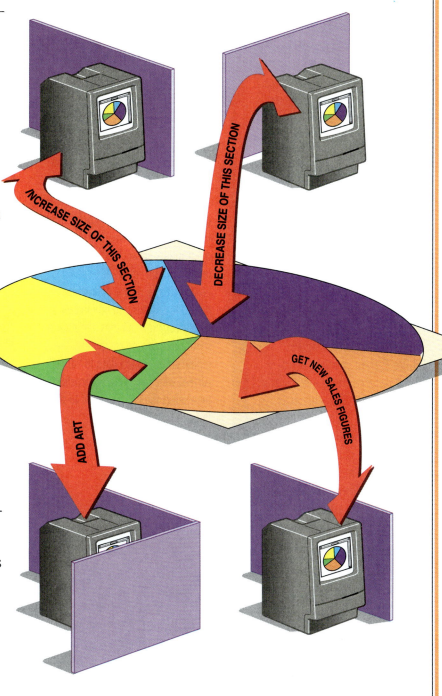

Combining many people's ideas into one document through teleconferencing

TELECOMMUNICATIONS

Networking Options

teleconferences allow people to see and hear each other. Other teleconferences allow people to hear each other's voices and see graphics via computer terminals.

Today, another type of teleconferencing is becoming popular. Using a teleconferencing network, two or more people can link their computers to a network—and each can send and receive both graphics and text messages at the same time!

Teleconferencing with computers can also take place at different times. Like E-mail, people send and receive messages over a network whenever it is convenient for them to do so. Many businesspeople depend on this type of teleconferencing. It allows more freedom for everyone to "meet" at a time that's best for him or her.

A growing use of computer teleconferencing is working on documents at the same time from different places. For example, scientists in California, Texas, and New York can use a teleconferencing network to work on an environmental study together.

The document appears on each scientist's computer terminal. Each scientist can make changes in the document on his or her computer. These changes then appear on all of the other scientists' terminals.

If the scientists all agree with the changes, their study is complete. If they disagree with any change and want to make more changes, they can then do so. Changes can be made until everyone agrees that the study is complete.

Soon, students from across the country may use teleconferences the same way that scientists do. Students can use teleconferencing to write newsletters, magazines, and reports on topics that matter most to them, such as the environment, sports, or weekend activities.

Today, it takes time and money to set up these different networks. You have to add different communications software, modems, and other special equipment to your computer. In the future, each computer may contain all the hardware and software needed to telecommunicate.

What networks do students at your school use? Do you know anyone who uses a network at school or work? Ask around your community, too. Most likely, your public library, city hall, police station, and telephone company use networks to do business—and to make your life easier.

SALESPERSON • ELECTRICIAN • ASTRONAUT • MECHANIC • ENGINEER • PHYSICIST • DENTIST • FARMER • NURSE • DOCTOR • TEACHER • SURGEON • OPTOMETRIST • PILOT • PROFESSOR • SECRETARY • ARTIST

C·A·R·E·E·R·S

Do you notice how often the weather changes? To stay on top of these changes, more and more forecasters depend on computers for up-to-the-minute weather information.

Weather forecasters are able to get this information quickly because they are part of a weather telecommunications network. Monitors—many of them robots and satellites—constantly record data across the United States and other countries. Every few minutes, the data is sent to mainframe computers. These mainframes use the data to "draw" current weather maps. Forecasters then select the maps needed to show the weather in your area!

MODULE 7

SCHOOLS AND TELECOMMUNICATIONS

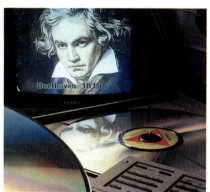

Combining images, sounds, and text onto a videodisc

More and more schools are taking part in long-distance learning. To learn how, read how students in Katie and Manuel's Spanish class used telecommunications to "travel" to Europe.

We just visited Madrid, Spain—and we never left our school! How? Our school is part of a long-distance learning network.

This network helps us "travel" all over the world. To "go" to Spain, we used a school computer and modem, a cordless telephone, a VCR and monitor—and a small satellite dish. We were connected to 10 other schools, too.

While we watched a video about Hispanic culture, we were able to talk to some students and teachers by telephone in Spanish or English. At the same time, we could also send and receive messages by computer to other schools and teachers—also using Spanish or English.

We had a great trip! It seemed like we were in the same room, not in separate classrooms miles apart. Best of all, we learned about Spain and America as a team. We were able to ask questions to other students and help answer each other's questions—together.

We've taken many other field trips this year. We've "visited" a NASA control center, a science museum, and the bottom of the Pacific Ocean. All our trips have been fun—and a great learning experience.

In other classes, we've used telecommunications to learn about math and science. Several schools in our district take these classes with us at the same time. Often, we learn with one lead teacher, guiding us as we watch on the monitor.

If the teacher asks a question or gives us a problem to solve, we can use our computers to send in an answer or solution. The lead instructor's computer can then show several answers and solutions for everyone to see. Sometimes, our answer is the best and it's the one everyone sees!

We've also been using *interactive videodiscs* to learn about social studies. An interactive videodisc stores lots of information about certain topics and can be accessed and controlled by a computer. The information includes images, sounds, and text.

Using a computer, special software, and a videodisc on American history, we're learning what life was like in the 1930s. The videodisc lets us move from pictures to words to sounds.

Because we use telecommunications equipment and a host computer, each school doesn't have to own its own videodiscs, and more than one school can even use them at the same time. We can talk about the images we see and the sounds we hear, and help each other understand what life was really like in the United States almost 70 years ago.

What's great about long-distance learning is that it lets students and teachers from schools in the city, the suburbs, and rural areas learn together. We also like it because we're making new friends!

★ READ ALL ABOUT IT ★

Excerpted from The Boston Herald
September 12, 1990
By Linda Hayes Tischler

Classroom TV Brings in World

The anchorman was droning on about the usual governmental wrangling, but for Allison Rossi the morning newscast was pretty exciting stuff.

"Hey, I understand that!" said the Watertown High School senior with surprise.

It wasn't a sudden revelation of the mysteries of the consumer price index or an insight into how the CLT tax rollback referendum will affect the state that had the teen so energized.

Rossi had been listening to a broadcast of the news from Paris—in French—delivered to Watertown High via satellite.

"Six years of French have finally paid off!" she said.

The daily news—in French, in Greek, in Chinese, Polish, Arabic and 10 other languages—now will be available to Watertown and 50 other school systems in the state as part of their membership in the Mass LearnPike, a satellite-based broadcast network. But the news will be only a fraction of the programming these schools will be able to pluck from the heavens. With a dish on the roof, and TVs and VCRs in the classroom, schools will be able to tap into learning channels from as far away as Texas and Oklahoma that offer advanced placement courses in English and history, as well as enrichment courses in everything from coastal ecology to Flamenco dancing.

Tomorrow the Mass LearnPike will officially open with a link-up between the Soviet space exhibit at the Museum of Science and junior and senior high school students from network member schools around the commonwealth.

The video telecast, which will originate at the museum, will allow students to ask questions of the museum staff who will demonstrate such things as weightlessness, and Soviet rocket scientists, who will be on hand for the occasion.

A satellite dish, used to bring in information from around the world

★ READ ALL ABOUT IT ★

Excerpted from Teaching and Computers
By Dr. Barbara Kurshan,
Beverly Hunter, and Suzanne Bazak

Today's Software, Tomorrow's Children's Workstation

What is a "Children's Workstation"? It's what we hope will be the elementary school computer of the future, with software that is fully-integrated, easy-to-use, and powerful enough to support learners not only in acquiring basic skills but also in solving problems, developing critical thinking skills, communicating ideas, and working collaboratively on multi-disciplinary projects.

GENERAL FEATURES
Friendly interface   Easy integration

Suitable user interface and integration of functions are important in any workstation, but are especially critical for young children. The interface features we looked for include iconic menus *(Explore-a-Story)*; input with keyboard, tablet, and/or mouse *(The Newsroom)*; simple screen layout with only a few choices provided on the screen *(Kidwriter)*; uniform screens, menu selection devices, and function access *(AppleWorks, Eight-in-One, The Children's Writing and Publishing Center)*; a filing system with student directories and subdirectories *(A+)*; and sound and voice output *(My Words, Talking Textwriter)*. In terms of integration, we looked for integration of tools accessed from a main menu *(Kid Talk)*; messaging among users and functions *(Bank Street Writer III)*; integration of guides to systematic thinking and problem solving *(SemCalc, Homework Helper Math or Writing)*; and a built-in calculator across functions *(Math Problem Solving Courseware)*. In addition, to facilitate use of the Children's Workstation, some keyboarding activities should be included in the form of a "type" program to introduce the keyboard and other input devices at the workstation.

In general, a Children's Workstation should be simple enough for children to use yet sophisticated enough to be used by the teacher for instructional design and classroom planning tasks.

COMMUNICATIONS
Both local area networking and telecommunications ability
Structure for collaborative learning   Shared databases

Local area networking and telecommunications support are essential to our Children's Workstation. In addition to the convenience and range both kinds of networking provide, they can support collaborative learning through messaging among students, teachers, and administrators and through use of shared databases. They also add power to instructional management.

Only one of the existing programs reviewed was designed to take this kind of advantage of local area networks. *Bank Street Writer III with E-mail* has a built-in feature to be used with an Apple Talk Network, allowing students to write, send, and receive "mail" to and from other students and teachers.

There is also at least one existing program which makes good use of telecommunications for access to information networks and bulletin board systems. *Kids Network* provides for telecommunications among schools involved in its network, and has an easy-to-use communications interface for uploading and downloading messages and database information. In addition, a new version of this front-end interface will provide other tool capabilities such as word processing and graphics. ■

Telecommuting

TELECOMMUTING

Most adults you know have to commute to work, right? They go on foot, by bike, car, or use public transportation to get to their jobs each day. School hallways may get crowded in-between classes, but can you imagine having to spend two or more hours a day just to get there? Unfortunately, many people do just that.

One way people can beat the rush-hour commute is by *telecommuting.* Telecommuting means working from home, using a computer, a modem, and special telecommunications software to stay in touch with the office. Once your home computer is linked to the computer in your office, you become part of an office network. And, as long as you can plug into a telephone line, it's possible to telecommute to work from thousands of miles away! After an assignment is complete, the worker "sends" it to the office, using the modem and the phone lines instead of the freeways or rail lines.

Today, many different jobs can be done while telecommuting. Some writers and journalists, for example, don't have a corporate office to go to each day. They work by telecommuting. Some salespeople work far from their company's offices. Often, they, too, stay in touch with their offices by telecommuting. Some adults have to stay home to take care of children or aging parents. Telecommuting provides these people with the opportunity to meet their personal obligations while still contributing at work.

There are environmental benefits to telecommuting, too. Rush-hour traffic can be reduced and pollution can be cut down, just to name a few. Best of all, telecommuting allows people to work and live wherever they choose—anywhere on earth or, maybe, in space! In the future, more and more people may be joining the ranks of the telecommuters.

Avoiding the rush-hour traffic crunch through telecommuting

WORKING AROUND THE WORLD

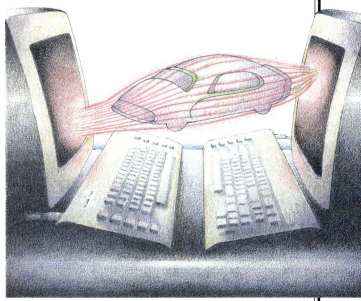

Working together across long distances to accomplish business goals

Many businesses use telecommunications to work around the world. How does telecommunicating help a car company build cars? Well, to design and build a car takes teamwork. Today, a number of the largest automobile manufacturers have plants and offices in different countries around the world. This helps them take advantage of technical expertise, facilities, raw materials, and lower-cost labor, which might not be located all in one place.

How do employees of a car company with plants and offices in the United States, Mexico, and Japan work together? They're connected to each other by a long-distance computer network.

A teleconference lets the teams of engineers from Japan, Mexico, and the United States talk, plan, and work together on a new car design. Each team has a microcomputer with a modem and special telecommunications software. Since the computers are connected to each other, they can look at different images of car designs on their computer screens. They can also look at the same image at the same time. Satellites are also used to send messages back and forth.

Each team's computer is also connected to a host computer located in Japan. The host computer gives the teams' computers the power to work together from anywhere. It also helps them share resources, such as special car-design software. Each team can work on the design alone—or as part of a bigger team!

After their teleconference, the teams communicate via E-mail. They can send and receive messages anytime that's convenient. When the time comes to start building a model of the car, the ability to telecommunicate helps everyone continue working as a team. If major problems come up, teams can set up a teleconference to find a solution together. If there are minor revisions, teams can communicate through E-mail.

Without telecommunications, revising the model would have taken days—and cost a lot more money. Engineers would have had to fly to one central location to meet and work together. By telecommunicating, teams from each country know exactly how the project is going, without ever leaving home.

Telecommunications helps this car company save time and money. By working as a team, the engineers were able to efficiently design and build the model for a new car. Best of all, telecommunications helped them build a new car—one that looks and drives great!

Using an Online Information Service

Online services, such as *Prodigy, CompuServe,* and *Dialog,* provide information as well as entertainment in a database format. There are also many specialized online information services that doctors, engineers, and other professionals use. Lawyers often use *Nexis* or *Lexis* to search for cases and points of law.

Let's take an imaginary trip through *Prodigy* to see how an online information service works. Connecting to *Prodigy* requires a computer, modem, telephone line, and *Prodigy* communications software. When you begin to access *Prodigy,* your computer will dial a local telephone number to connect with the *Prodigy* computer. A message asks you to enter your user identification and password. The ID number shows on the screen, but the password is hidden to prevent unauthorized users from copying it.

Now you're ready to begin using *Prodigy.* Let's say you decide to spice up a report on Paris by looking up today's weather in that city. Clicking on WEATHER takes you to another menu that offers choices of information on the weather. You select the one that lets you find the weather for foreign cities, then you indicate Paris. The screen then displays a current weather report for Paris, France.

You find the information that you need, but the whole process can be shortened by using a more exact entry. By entering just the word

Accessing the weather in France with the touch of a button

Using an Online Information Service

WEATHER, the computer does not know the specific information that you want. You need to give the computer more detailed information. If you entered W PARIS instead, the weather report for Paris would have appeared immediately.

Let's say that you need to work on a report for current events. You can use *Prodigy* to help you. *Prodigy* updates the news frequently throughout the day. Given a certain command, it will show reports on the screen. Sometimes a heading for a related topic will appear on the screen that explains some detail about the topic of the news report. You can call up the heading for more information.

This power of relating information in a database is one of the primary reasons database searches can outperform a manual search. It is not difficult to find related topics when looking in books, magazines, or newspapers, but it is time-consuming to flip from one source to another, keeping all the page numbers straight, and so on. A database can do this automatically. The time saved by online database searching also attracts the busy person who must have information but who cannot afford the time it takes to locate it manually.

You might want to save the information you find on the database service. Sometimes the service will provide a way for you to print the information on your printer by pressing an appropriate key on the keyboard. However, you might want to make an electronic copy of the information to include with your report, which you are creating with a word-processing program.

The technique of making a copy of information from one computer to another is called *downloading*. It is not always possible to download, or even to print, information from online services. Often these services pay license fees for the right to transmit the information over their service. The license may not give the database service the right to let you, or any user, copy the information.

MODULE 7

MODULE SUMMARY QUESTIONS

In order to check your comprehension of how computers are used in telecommunications, you may wish to discuss the following ideas.

1. What is telecommunications, and what equipment is needed to telecommunicate using a computer?

2. Name five reasons you and your family might have for using a consumer-services network.

3. Imagine that you wanted to find out more about current events for a social studies project you are doing. Which networking options might you consider: E-mail, bulletin boards, databanks, consumer-services networks, or teleconferencing?

MODULE 8

SPREADSHEETS

Computers can be used for much more than simply calculating numbers. With spreadsheet software, we are able to organize thousands of numbers into information that can be easily understood. In addition, spreadsheets allow us to transform numerical information into useful visuals such as charts and graphs.

In Module 8, you will learn what a spreadsheet is, how it works, and when it should be used. Before you know it, you'll realize that using spreadsheets is as simple as 1–2–3.

WHAT IS A

Have you ever wanted something, but couldn't figure out how to pay for it? With a spreadsheet to help you organize your budget, you could lay out a plan for purchasing the item. The spreadsheet would show you how much you would have to save each month before you could afford it. Best of all, the spreadsheet could help you manage all these numbers more quickly and easily than you could with a pencil and paper.

For example, in the window at Bob's Bike Shop is a mountain bike that you want to buy. This bike features 21 speeds, knobby tires, quick-release wheels, push-button shifting, upright handlebars, and is painted green and purple. Unfortunately, the bike costs $240.00. How are you going to pay for it?

With a pencil, paper, and a calculator, you sit down to figure out how you can pay for the bike. You list the items on which you normally spend your allowance—movies, tapes or CDs, and other items—and decide which items you can do without.

The list might look like the one below:

Usual Monthly Expenses

Entertainment	$15.00
Food	$40.00
CDs	$25.00
Clothes	$20.00
Other	$10.00

What you have created is the same tool people have used for centuries to figure out problems—a worksheet. It allows you to arrange numbers in a logical system of *rows* and *columns* so that you can "see" the problem and figure out how to solve it. Computer worksheets, called spreadsheets, simplify "number processing."

To buy the mountain bike, you will have to cut your current expenses. Your mom agrees to lend you the $240.00, but you have to pay her back in three months. You decide to save $5.00 a week and to earn $15.00 a week by babysitting, petsitting, and mowing lawns in your neighborhood. By paying your mom back at a rate of $20.00 a week, you expect to be able to pay off your loan in three months.

If you had used an electronic spreadsheet, your budget could look something like the one illustrated on the next page. There are many reasons to use electronic spreadsheets, but some reasons are more important than others. For starters, arranging information in rows and columns can help you organize your thoughts when solving a problem. For instance, in the example, we put your entire monthly expenses for three months on one sheet of paper. You could see where it was being spent and how you could cut back to save enough money to buy the bike.

Spreadsheets can also make sense of hundreds of numbers by allowing you to summarize them in totals. Looking at just one category—or even several categories—in our example doesn't really present the whole picture. But by looking at the totals, which were created by using a simple spreadsheet formula called SUM, you can see that $240.00 is available to be spent on the bike over the next three months.

SPREADSHEET?

By focusing on the big numbers—the totals—we can make the small numbers fit our plans.

If we did this exercise on an electronic spreadsheet, we would create one formula that totaled a column. Then, we would copy the formula across the page so that the totals for each column were shown at the bottom of each column. If we watched the computer total the numbers, we would be astonished at how fast the numbers were being processed.

Using an electronic spreadsheet can help you make calculations easier and faster. If a number in your handwritten worksheet changes, you have to spend time refiguring everything over again. With the ability to recalculate numbers quickly, electronic spreadsheets perform that operation for you quickly. Also, if you find an error, you can input the correction and print it again.

Spreadsheets offer you convenience, accuracy, and speed. Once you get the hang of it, using spreadsheets to handle numbers will be easier than sharpening a pencil!

REVISED MONTHLY EXPENSES			
A	**B**	**C**	**D**
	Jan.	Feb.	March
Available $	110	110	110
Expenses:			
Entertainment	15	15	15
Food	40	40	40
CDs	15	15	15
Clothes	10	10	10
Other	10	10	10
Left Over $	20	20	20
Earnings	60	60	60
Total Savings	80	160	240

A budget spreadsheet showing how the bicycle loan can be repaid

HOW SPREADSHEETS WORK

All spreadsheets follow a basic design of rows and columns. Each column (vertical) is assigned a letter—A, B, C, AA, BB, CC, AAA, BBB, CCC, and so on. Each row (horizontal) is assigned a number—1, 2, 3, and so on. Each point where a column and row intersect is called a *cell*. The cell's position on the spreadsheet is labeled according to its corresponding column and row—Column A, Row 1 (A1), Column B, Row 2 (B2).

To reach a specific cell, or an address, use the cursor keys or a mouse. The computer will indicate which cell you are in by placing a boldface border around it or by highlighting it. The contents of the cell will also appear on a line at the top or on the bottom of the screen, called a *status line* or *formula line*.

Spreadsheets use *standard formulas* to calculate numbers that are in various cells. The user creates simple mathematical equations which use these standard formulas. An equation tells the program to use a formula to perform a calculation on the contents of certain cells. These formulas may also contain special spreadsheet functions. These functions are special commands that you enter in spreadsheet cells, either alone or within formulas. When the computer comes to a specific function within a formula, it automatically performs a designated mathematical task.

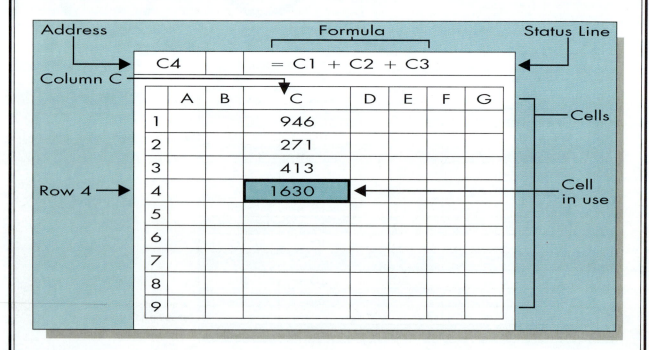

The parts of a typical spreadsheet

Calculating and recalculating numbers before computerized spreadsheets

Spreadsheets may contain numerous formulas that, in turn, contain several functions. However, some basic formulas are common to most spreadsheet programs. SUM is one of the most basic formulas used in spreadsheets. It produces the sum of the numbers contained in a selected group of cells. For instance, the equation SUM(A1:A5) would total the contents of cells A1 through A5.

Some other common spreadsheet formulas include: AVG (average), which finds the average of the numbers in a selected group of cells; MAX (maximum), which selects the maximum, or highest, number within a group of cells; MIN (minimum), which selects the minimum, or lowest, number within a group of cells; and ROUND (rounding), which rounds numbers to a specified number of decimal places.

If you use a spreadsheet formula to set up an equation, any change in the figures of the equation will change the total of the equation. You only have to change the figures—the computer will recalculate the answer.

One of the most important features of spreadsheets is that you can copy formulas from one cell to another, and the computer will store those formulas in the new cells. There's no need for tedious retyping of formulas to copy them from one address to another—the computer does it for you!

With a spreadsheet, figures can be changed instantly—with only a few keystrokes. This is especially helpful for "what-if" scenarios. If you wonder "what-if" a formula were applied to a different amount, all you have to do is enter the new number. The computer places this new number into a *variable,* or location within the computer's memory. The computer will apply your old formulas to the number contained in this variable, giving you a new answer.

WORKING WITH SPREADSHEETS

Let's see how you can use a spreadsheet to help you calculate information. Imagine that you're planning to work at a concession stand this summer selling lemonade. You know that you can expect higher drink sales when the weather is hot.

Making some estimates, you calculate how many gallons of lemonade you will sell based on the past three years' average summer temperature—87 degrees. You decide that you can probably sell 870 gallons, or 10 gallons for every degree of temperature. But what if it's hotter or colder than 87 degrees? You will want to create additional scenarios that reflect possible temperature changes so you can decide whether the concession stand will be worth your time.

Since spreadsheets can produce several types of graphs (including bar, pie, and line), you can create a bar graph showing all the possibilities. First, select the spreadsheet cells to be included—in this case, you only want to plot the temperatures and the number of additional gallons you expect to sell as the weather gets hotter. Remember that for each degree of increase in temperature, you expect to sell 10 additional gallons of lemonade.

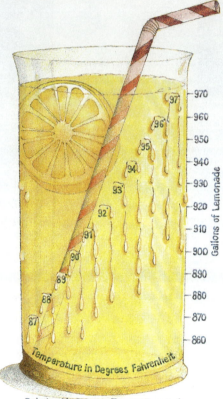

Relationship Between Temperature and Lemonade Sales

Second, select the CHART or PLOT command to create our graph. In this case, we choose a column graph. Each bar shows the number of gallons sold at a specific increase in temperature.

When completed, the graph tells us that a hotter-than-average summer will mean an extreme increase in beverage sales (assuming our estimate of a 10-gallon increase in sales per degree is accurate). In fact, if temperatures stay over 97 degrees, you could turn quite a profit!

When you enter dollar figures into a spreadsheet, you don't have to type a dollar sign in front of the dollar amount. Spreadsheets have features that allow you to specify how numbers are treated—as dollars, dates, percentages, and so on. If you define a cell for dollars, with two decimal places, the program will round the number off to two decimal places, even if more exist.

You can also format dates so that they appear in month-day-year order, in year-month-day order, or so that only the year or the month is displayed. Spreadsheets offer a wide range of format choices and you should take advantage of them to make your work more presentable.

The History of Spreadsheet Programs

The first electronic spreadsheet program for personal computers, *VisiCalc,* or "visible calculator," was produced in 1978 for the Apple II. Written by Dan Bricklin and Bob Frankston, *VisiCalc* was designed to make the calculations that businesses use in making decisions easier—and the program did just that.

Bricklin and Frankston created a program that did for numbers what word processors did for words. Based on the fact that spreadsheets are the second most widely used computer programs, you could say these two inventors were successful. While spreadsheet features have grown over the years, Bricklin and Frankston's basic design has remained relatively unchanged. The concept of rows and columns used in *VisiCalc* is the same for every spreadsheet program now on the market.

After *VisiCalc,* a major revision of the spreadsheet concept came in 1983 with the introduction of *Lotus 1–2–3.* It added *graphing* to spreadsheets as a standard feature. With *1–2–3,* in addition to displaying rows and columns of numbers, you could also prepare graphs—visual aids—based on those numbers.

In 1985, Microsoft introduced *Excel* for the Macintosh, which added several innovative features to spreadsheets. Designed for Apple's Macintosh, and later used with MS-DOS computers, *Excel* was the first spreadsheet to take advantage of a *graphical user interface,* also called a "GUI" (GOO ee). You could have many spreadsheets in separate *windows* on the screen at the same time. Edit commands are displayed across windows, making it possible to easily move data and formulas between windows and, thus, between documents. You could even have many graphs on the screen in separate windows.

Another feature that *Excel* utilized was *macros*—where one function combines the results of many. Macros save time by allowing repetitive commands to be combined into a few simple keystrokes. A macro can be created, for example, that selects a column, changes the format of cells in that column, and sorts the cells in ascending or descending order. Once the macro has been created, a repeated action can be accomplished with just a single command, to run the macro.

COMPUTERS — THEN & NOW

In 1642, the French mathematician and philosopher Blaise Pascal developed one of the first calculating machines, called the Pascaline. Although it could perform only addition and subtraction and was expensive to repair, accountants were concerned that they might be replaced by this technology.

Over the years, accountants have adapted to advances in technology to perform their work faster and more efficiently. Many accountants today could not do their work without the benefits of computers and spreadsheets.

The History of Spreadsheet Programs

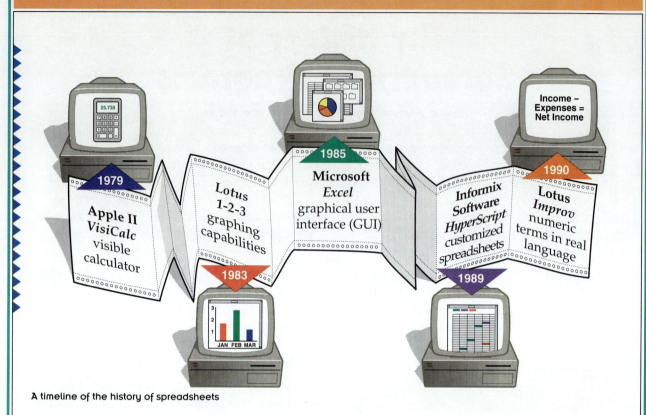

A timeline of the history of spreadsheets

A further development of spreadsheets was the inclusion of *scripting* languages that allow you to create customized applications. *Wingz,* introduced in 1989 by Informix Software, added the language *HyperScript* that allowed you to create elaborate scripts for spreadsheets.

Modern spreadsheet languages can also be used to create interfaces (devices that allow the user to work with the software). For instance, *HyperScript* can create a custom menu that makes the spreadsheet program look like another type of software. If you want to create an application that tracks a collection of baseball cards, you can design an interface that looks like a baseball card—complete with a picture of Nolan Ryan. The rows and columns are still in the background but data for them is entered on the baseball card. This is a much easier way to view and work with this information.

DID YOU KNOW?

Did you know that macros make it much easier and faster to use most modern spreadsheets? Macros record a procedure, somewhat like a tape recorder records sound. When the exact same procedure needs to be repeated, the macro will allow the computer to "play back" the procedure automatically.

To continue using the macro, all you have to do is enter a single command each time. If the procedure is done frequently or regularly, you can save a lot of time.

MODULE 8

The History of Spreadsheet Programs

In 1990, Lotus introduced *Improv* for the NeXT computer, and it may well change spreadsheets forever. Spreadsheets created with *Improv* use traditional rows and columns, but they use words in describing and addressing them. Instead of A1−A2=A3, an Improv formula might read Income−Expenses=Net Income, a much easier way of describing numbers.

Which brings us to the final point in the evolution of spreadsheets—the output. Although spreadsheets are manipulated on the computer screen, they are almost always output to paper, to a page-layout program, or to a word processor.

Because of this, most modern spreadsheets offer a variety of formatting options, including the use of fonts and other typographical elements to make both graphs and numbers look good on the printed page.

MULTICULTURAL BYTE

English is considered to be the language of spreadsheets in the United States, but these spreadsheet programs are also popular overseas. In fact, Lotus Development Corporation has announced that it will translate a version of the spreadsheet into Russian.

More than half of Lotus Development Corporation's 1990 sales came from international sales, due largely to the popularity of its *Lotus 1-2-3* spreadsheet program.

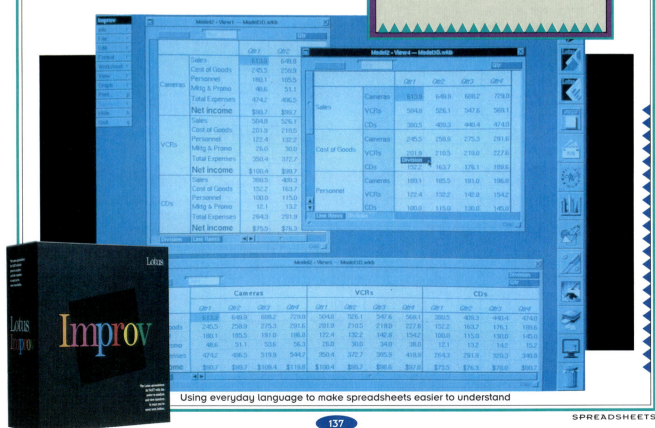

Using everyday language to make spreadsheets easier to understand

HOW IS A SPREADSHEET CREATED?

	A	B	C	D
1		Hits	At-Bats	Average
2	Game One	1	3	.333
3	Game Two	2	4	.500
4	Game Three	0	2	.000
5				
6	Total	3	9	.333
7	Average	1	3	.333

Figuring batting averages with a spreadsheet program

Do you play softball or baseball in the summer? By entering your hits and at-bats in rows for each game, you can figure out your batting average. For instance, you put the number of hits in column B and the number of times you went up to bat in column C.

Let's say that in the first game, you batted three times and got one hit. You enter these numbers in row 2. In your second game, you batted four times and got two hits. You enter these numbers in row 3. In your third game, you batted twice and had no hits. You enter these numbers in row 4.

Your batting average is the number of hits divided by the number of times at bat. So, in cell D2, you enter the formula B2/C2 to arrive at your average for the game. Then, you copy that formula down into cells D3 and D4 to figure your batting average for the second and third games. If you look at D3, for instance, you see that the formula has changed to B3/C3 because the formula was created in relation to its surrounding cells. D4 is now B4/C4.

This formula tells you your batting average for each game, but you really want to know how you did during the entire season. First, you create a row that totals hits and at-bats in each column using the SUM formula for your application, to add cells B2 through B4 and cells C2 through C4. This formula would tell you that you had three hits in nine times at bat. You could then copy the formula in D4 to D6 to get your batting average for the season (.333).

What if we were calculating the results for 30 or 40 games during the season? As long as the information entered in columns B and C is correct, the results returned in column D will be correct. However, in order for a column of numbers to be calculated correctly using SUM or AVG, all of the cells need to be included. In other words, to add the numbers in B2 through B32 your formula might be SUM (B2:B32). (Check your spreadsheet documentation for the correct formula for your computer.)

You MAKE A DIFFERENCE

At Portage Path School in Akron, Ohio, sixth-graders are using spreadsheets to manage an experimental school store. These students record the money that comes in, calculate income and expenses, and create graphs comparing each day's profits. "Keeping all the store sales, inventory, and costs on the computer is like having a friend give you the answers," says Heidi, one of the sixth-graders who works at the store. Does your school have a store? If so, why not try using a computer and a spreadsheet program to help manage it?

WHEN SHOULD A SPREADSHEET BE USED?

People use electronic spreadsheets to make everyday tasks easier.

For instance, your teacher may use a spreadsheet to enter your test scores and your homework grades. At the end of the grading period, the spreadsheet will calculate your average grade.

The local grocer may use a spreadsheet to track inventory and to decide what items and how many of them to stock in the store. This inventory spreadsheet can be printed and used to place orders with suppliers.

A baseball or softball coach can look at statistics that players have accumulated during the season to determine ways to help the team win games. If a certain player doesn't bat well against left-handed pitchers, the coach might decide to send in another hitter whenever that player faces a left-handed pitcher.

Think of an electronic spreadsheet as a word processor for numbers. Organizing numbers into rows and cells allows you to create information in a logical way that can be understood by others, much like languages. By using the language of spreadsheets to communicate, businesses and individuals can make decisions about their futures.

Since spreadsheets are basically math programs, you could use one to check your math homework. Although you still need to know how to calculate results without a computer, entering the numbers in a spreadsheet after you've completed your homework can tell you if an answer is correct. In addition, the experience of creating the formulas should teach you about mathematics.

You can use a spreadsheet any time a problem involves a lot of numbers that you can arrange in rows and columns. For example, if you're tracking numbers over weeks or months, then a spreadsheet will almost certainly make the job easier. All you have to do is assign columns for each week or month. If what you're tracking will have numbers that change often, then a spreadsheet would make it much easier than erasing or crossing out your numbers on paper.

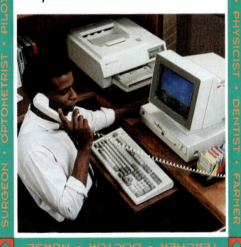

CAREERS

SALESPERSON • ELECTRICIAN • ASTRONAUT • MECHANIC • ENGINEER • PHYSICIST • DENTIST • FARMER • NURSE • DOCTOR • TEACHER • SURGEON • OPTOMETRIST • PILOT • PROFESSOR • SECRETARY • ARTIST

A business analyst is someone who studies how a business works and develops a solution to any problems it may have.

A business analyst can use a spreadsheet to prepare "what-if" situations. A business analyst's education usually includes courses in accounting, finance, management and information management systems.

SPREADSHEETS

★ READ ALL ABOUT IT ★

**Excerpted from *The Washington Post*
By John Burgess**

High Tech on the Range

"Moooving" the cattle industry into the computer age

In Module 6, Databases, *you read the beginning of this informative article. In that portion of the article, Burgess told how Oklahoma businessman Billy Perrin uses computer databases at his livestock market to stay up-to-date on market prices and other important information. On the pages that follow, you will read how spreadsheets also help Perrin run his business effectively.*

. . . . Perrin has made other forays into computers. Until this February, he hired a half dozen or more clerks on sale day to handle the flood of paperwork. Typically, it would take them 2-1/2 hours after the sale ended to finish all the documents that allow buyers to leave with their cattle. Then the clerks would settle down for a few more hours to balance the books, carrying them bleary-eyed into early Saturday morning.

Continued on next page

READ ALL ABOUT IT

The entire job now takes about 45 minutes after the sale's close, using software and a network of PCs Perrin leases for $695 a month from Auction Computer Services Inc. of DeKalb, Tex. The clerks who lost the $4-an-hour work aren't happy with the new arrangement, but Perrin is. He figures he's paying less and getting more accurate documentation. Plus he can offer his customers a year-end printout of all their activity for tax purposes.

Customers like the speed, he said, but what they like best is his computerized scale. A cow steps on it just before entering the auction room. It takes 50 measurements in 4 seconds (the movement of the animal prevents taking a single accurate count), averages them and flashes the number on an electronic board that buyers and sellers can see. It takes the guesswork out of a scale and is replacing an institution in cattle country, the weighing of a skittish animal standing on a primitive scale.

A few miles south of Hugo, in what is probably the most common application on farms, rancher Donald Jack Leslie has been using a PC just as would any other small business: as a bookkeeping aide. Whenever he spends money on gas for the pickup or feed for the cattle, he enters it into a $1,200 PC that he keeps in his study. When he makes money baling hay for a neighbor or selling a calf, he enters those numbers too. The accounts stay straight, Leslie said, and allow him to keep a minute-to-minute grip on his ranch's finances.

His is a "cow-calf" business, consisting of herds of mother cows that produce a stream of calves for sale to other ranches. Living on scattered pastures that he owns or leases, the business can present some challenging accounting problems, some of which he now answers with a few commands to the computer. How much has he spent on feed for each cow this

Calculating the right amount of feed per animal—another use of spreadsheets on the farm

Continued on next page

Read All About It

year? What was the figure in the same period last year? Leslie said the computer helped him figure out that his feed was costing $30 per cow more than the handbooks say it should. He switched feed brands and the cows now eat for less.

Leslie used to use "a ledger sheet about 10 miles long," pencilling in line items and then trying to add them up by hand. It used to take him, he estimates, 40 hours of busywork just to get his papers ready for the accountant at income tax time. Now it's in the machine, waiting to be printed out. The system also pleases his banker, a crucial partner in all farm operations. "The better your books are," Leslie said, "the easier it is to get a loan."

Farmers also are using advanced software to plan the season ahead. "Crop simulation" programs let a farmer play complex "what-if" games before they put a single seed in the ground. A package developed by Datasphere Computer Systems of Portland, Ore., prompts farmers to type in such data as rainfall, soil conditions and fertilizer on a prospective field to try to forecast the yield and impact on the farmer's bottom line. All of this is possible with a pen and scratch pad, but people tend to run out of steam before too many options can be explored.

Grain producer Joe Reinart said a crop simulation program he runs on a PC helped him discover a certain type of sorghum he was growing was costing him more than he could sell it for. He cut back. "It's sure increased the profitability of the farm to know which crops make money," said Reinart, a resident of Stratford, Tex., whose fields are scattered around three counties.

Gary Nixon, who runs a ranch outside Paris, Tex., is another cattleman who is getting on board with computers. His business is to buy calves and raise them until they're ready for sale to a feed lot, the final stop before the packing house.

His business challenge is to buy calves that will grow as fast as possible at the lowest cost.

When he buys a calf now, he gives it a number, which will be used to identify it to the computer. Records on its initial weight, purchase price, cost per pound, ultimate selling weight and other variables are entered into a PC, which analyzes the data and displays them as charts or graphs.

Computers cropping up on farms across America

Continued on next page

READ ALL ABOUT IT

"The next time we're up at a sale and see one," said his son, Raymond, "we've got a good idea of how that calf might perform."

Similar software is available that is tailored specifically to dairy cows, hogs or other animals.

A dairy system made by Red Wing Business Systems of Red Wing, Minn., for instance, keeps up with each cow's particulars like a big company's personnel system would, advising farmers on how many cows are lactating, how many are pregnant, which are due for an exam by the vet. By tracking the milk production of each cow, it helps the farmer cull those that aren't pulling their weight.

Leslie and Nixon would never be using computers were it not for Raymond. He went away to Texas A&M University after high school and got interested in computers.

When he returned home, he began writing programs, ever growing in complexity. Now his software helps run his father's farm, as well as Leslie's.

People like Raymond Nixon are in short supply in most rural communities, however.

Many farmers, especially older ones, need coaxing to get them near computers and they need a lot of support afterward.

Without them, they stick with pencils and shoeboxes stuffed with receipts.

"The average age of producers in this county is 55," pointed out Billy Perrin. "They refuse to change."

But a turnover is continuing as the younger generation attends college, which use more computers, and come home to take over the family farm.

Today's young farmers experiencing the benefits of computers

Here and there, farmers who did make the switch are making a side business of helping others do the same.

Grain producer Reinart, for instance, for a fee will buy and install a PC at a farm, customize software and teach the owners how to use it.

About half a dozen neighbors have availed themselves of his services.

Not surprisingly, he's a computer lover: "It's just as important a piece of equipment as a combine or tractor."

SPREADSHEETS
ARE THEY ALL THE SAME?

Most spreadsheet programs are organized in exactly the same way: numbers label horizontal rows and letters identify vertical columns. Rows and columns form a grid and each box within the grid is a cell, which has an address identified by the corresponding number and letter: A1, A2, B1, B2, etc. You enter information, such as words, numbers, and formulas on a line called the status line or formula line.

Spreadsheets can sort, shuffle, and manage information. But, features offered by modern spreadsheets differ as much from *VisiCalc,* the first electronic spreadsheet, as today's desktop computers differ in size and function from the first computers.

Finding a spreadsheet that manages data well, including words, can be important. Some spreadsheets allow limited word processing and desktop-publishing functions when called upon to organize words with graphics. Graphs have probably done more to change the way we think about numbers than any other type of innovation. Whatever program you choose at least should be able to prepare simple charts and graphs. However, some spreadsheets can create complex graphs such as three-dimensional (3-D) graphs. Usually, data is plotted horizontally and vertically. Three-dimensional charts allow you to plot depth, adding another dimension.

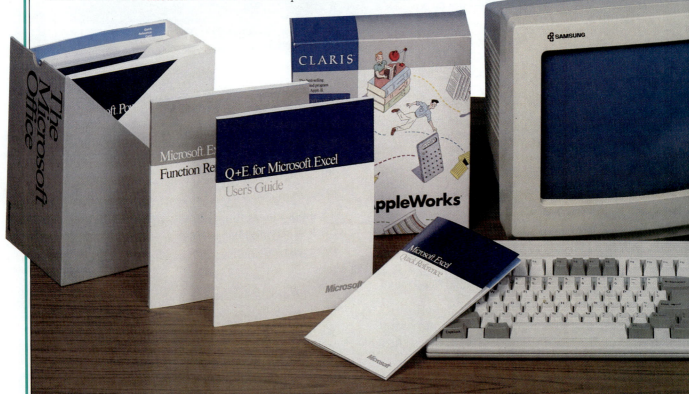

A sample of the many available spreadsheet software packages

Spreadsheets—Are They All the Same?

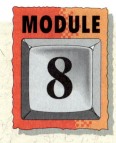

MODULE 8
MODULE SUMMARY QUESTIONS

DID YOU KNOW?

Did you know that one part of your computer may be a calculator? Many computers have an "extended" keyboard that contains a numeric keypad that makes putting numbers into a spreadsheet faster because all numbers are grouped together. On most keyboards, when the "number lock" is not engaged, these buttons function as cursor keys. By engaging the number lock (Num Lock) function on your computer, you are able to use this separate keypad with the calculator that is built into your software. (If you look at the "5" key on the keypad, you will usually notice a bump. This bump helps your fingers quickly find numbers on the keypad.)

In order to check your comprehension of spreadsheets, you may wish to discuss the following ideas.

1. What are three common uses for spreadsheets?
2. What is one advantage of using a spreadsheet for calculations rather than using a pencil and paper?
3. What is one way teachers could use spreadsheets to keep track of students' performance in a particular subject?

SPREADSHEETS

MODULE 9
PROGRAMMING

Did you ever wonder how computers know what to do? Every computer must be programmed, or given a set of instructions, to do the functions we need it to do.

In Module 9, you will learn about some different types of programming and how to use hypermedia. You'll read how your programming software can help you write your own adventures, keep track of collections, and write reports. You'll even learn how you, too, can create your own program.

BOBBY BONILLA
Bobby Bonilla is an outfielder for the Mets. In 1991, he signed a 29-million-dollar contract— at the time, the largest contract for a professional athlete in team sports.

SHEA STADIUM
Shea Stadium is located in Queens, the largest borough in New York City. Shea Stadium was the first to introduce moveable seating in 1964. The stadium seats over 50,000 people.

BASEBALL TEAMS
New York City has two major-league baseball teams— the NY Yankees (of the American League) and the NY Mets (of the National League). The Yankees play in Yankee Stadium in the Bronx. The Mets play in Shea Stadium in Queens.

SPORTS

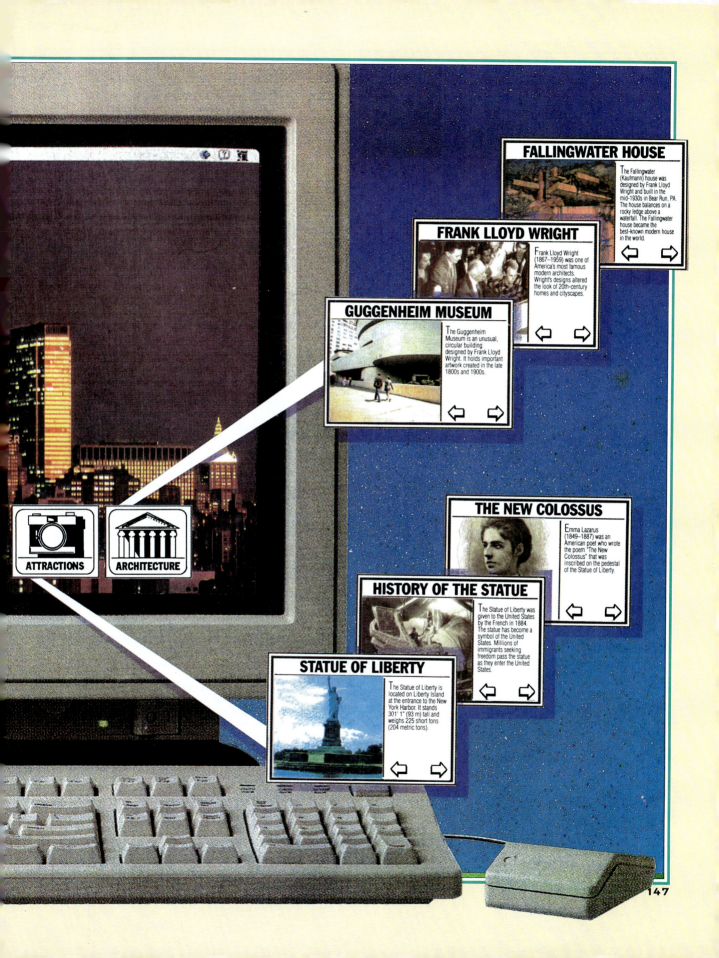

A New Generation of Programmers

So, there's this new generation of kids that are growing up who have had computers in their environment and can imagine solutions using computers and things to do with computers that those of us who are at the ripe old age of 35 have a little more difficulty imagining.

Those kids are all going to go and be creative. And I hope they do great things that will benefit society as a whole by taking this technology and making it useful, because it is not going to be done by one or two people.

These kids will hit the work force in large numbers sometime in the nineties . . . there will suddenly be a rush of great new things that are happening . . . a big change. And these are the kids that are going to write the great software of the nineties. . . .

Excerpted from "On the Next (Human) Generation" by Bill Joy, Byte, Sept. 1990

The quotation above tells how one person views the impact you can make on society in the next several years. "Me—make an impact?" you ask. You bet!! Young adults of today are more comfortable with using computers than most of their parents were in their youth. In fact, many of their parents never even used a computer until recently.

The new generation—creating programs to shape our future

"What do I need to know?" you ask again. Well, you need to know how to make a computer perform specific tasks. This is called *programming*, the topic of Module 9.

How You and the Computer Solve Problems

Imagine that you are looking at your math homework. Today's lesson covered the calculation of proportions. Your homework includes thirty problems on how to calculate proportions. There are questions such as, "You have learned that 98 out of 100 students in your school have at least one television in their home. How many televisions would you expect to find in a town of 5,000 people?"

How would you go about answering this type of question? What is it that you would have to know, and what would you have to do?

First, you would have to know how to solve the problem. Step-by-step instructions would help you to identify the important parts of the problem. You might reword the problem in a very general way, for example, "A is to B as C is to D." This statement identifies four specific facts in the problem—A, B, C, and D. You need three of the facts to find the fourth. For the example, the sentence would read, "98 is to 100 as C is to 5,000." Here, C is the unknown item you need to calculate. You can put this into an equation: $C = (98 \times 5{,}000) / 100$. The more general equation is $C = (A \times D) / B$. With this general solution for the problems of proportion, you can solve each of the thirty questions you were assigned.

Let us review what you would do to answer the homework questions. First, you create a *procedure,* the step-by-step rules for solving the problem. Next, you find the facts to be used in solving the problem and record them in the proper part of the equation. Then, following your procedure, you solve the problem by calculating the answer. Finally, you write down the answer.

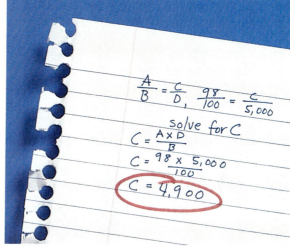

Using a step-by-step procedure to solve a problem with pencil and paper

Guess what! You've just acted as a computer would to solve the same problem! When you looked at the homework problem to see how it would be solved, and then decided in which sequence each step had to be done, you were creating a procedure. A computer program is nothing more than a procedure which includes both instructions and the order in which they are to be done.

To use the computer to solve the proportion problem, for example, you would input the values for A, B, and D. The computer would store these values as data in its memory, then follow the instructions, also stored as a program in its memory, in order to calculate C and then print out the answer.

Programming the computer is the way people give the machine its instructions. A programming language is used to communicate to the computer the specific tasks to be done, including the sequence in which they are to be completed. This set of steps in a specific order, such as the instructions in a program, is called an *algorithm.* To create a program, the programmer must first have a complete understanding of the problem to be solved by the computer. A number of tools and techniques have been developed to help software designers create good programs to solve problems.

Flowcharts are one of the tools used by programmers. A flowchart is a diagram used to plan a program, showing each task to be completed as well as that task's relationship to other tasks. By following a flowchart, programmers can construct a program that correctly completes the task. Flowcharts help programmers organize the steps of their programs. But, the flowcharts for complex programs can sometimes be complicated themselves!

Structured design techniques help programmers create software programs more easily. One technique is called *top-down design.* Using this technique, a program is planned by starting at the "top," with the most general task. The program is divided into modules. Each program module performs a single task—such as reading data input, calculating an answer, or presenting output—which is needed to accomplish a larger task. In top-down design, the modules are coded from the most general task to the most specific task. By concentrating on each function, one at a time, the programmer is able to make certain the program code works correctly. Also, when changes have to be made to the program later on, modular design reduces the chance for errors.

Taking the concept of modules a bit further, a module can be thought of as a piece of program code representing a specific activity. One of the newest techniques, called *Object-Oriented Programming* (OOP), is based on this concept. A library of preprogrammed *objects* (small amounts of code which perform a particular function) is used to construct an application. An object has three characteristics: an interface (way of communicating), data, and operations. Programmers construct programs by selecting objects that provide the features needed to accomplish an applications program's functions.

The difference between OOP and modular programming in Pascal is that the individual modules of code in a normal Pascal program cannot run independently from the rest of the program. If you insert a module, you need to to change other parts of the program. On the other hand, OOP is similar to the component designs of cars and appliances. If a part breaks, it can be pulled out and replaced with a new part. Each part is designed to perform a specific function and interface with the rest of the car or appliance.

OOP modules are now available for Pascal and other languages. They come on disk —you just copy them into your program, set up the communication links, and the module is ready to go!

CAREERS

SALESPERSON · ELECTRICIAN · ASTRONAUT · MECHANIC · ENGINEER · PHYSICIST · DENTIST · FARMER · TEACHER · DOCTOR · NURSE · SURGEON · OPTOMETRIST · PILOT · PROFESSOR · SECRETARY · ARTIST

Tom Rettig, once the costar of a 1970s television show that featured a collie named Lassie, is now a computer consultant. After retiring from Hollywood, at age 15, Rettig tried a number of jobs before discovering he had a talent for programming. He taught himself the dBASE database management system and went to work for Ashton-Tate, the developers of dBASE. He now has his own computer consulting business for developing customer software. Rettig also writes books that help others use dBASE.

✯ READ ALL ABOUT IT ✯

**Excerpted from *PC Novice*
October, 1991
By Gretchen Boehr**

HOW DO YOU CREATE SOFTWARE?
The Art of Programming

If you've ever stood spellbound by the colorful array of software packages at the local computer store, you're probably not alone. The diskettes inside those boxes bring the magic of a new program home to your computer. Just pop in the installation diskettes and behold! Even if you're a computer beginner, you've probably suspected that it's more than magic. And guess what, you're right! Making software doesn't require an eye of newt, a lock of ogre hair or even a single buzzard egg.

We're going to take a closer look at programming, programmers and the creation of a software product. You'll soon learn more about what went into those wonderful software products you can't seem to live without!

Like many things, software comes in different categories: spreadsheets calculate numbers; databases organize data; and communications software sends and receives information. With word processing programs you can type documents while desktop publishing software helps you create publications. Integrated software usually includes a spreadsheet, database and word processing program. But regardless of species, someone somewhere wrote your software (and programmed your computer).

Choosing from the vast array of software packages available in most computer stores

WHAT IS PROGRAMMING?

When you program something, you give that object instructions it needs to carry out a function. The list of instructions is known as a "program." Computer programming involves writing instructions and giving them to the computer so it knows how to complete a particular task. These instructions are programs. The software packages you buy at the store are programs that have been stored on diskettes so you can give them to your computer. One note about the words "program" (noun) and "software": a software product is a program. In common usage many people will refer to a software package as a "software program," but technically that's kind of redundant.

Programmers are translators between what you want your computer to do and what it understands. A programmer takes your request like "display the words I type" and translates it into code the computer can comprehend.

Tom Reeve, development manager for the entry business unit in the Microsoft Corp. applications division, said programming is like writing a long list of instructions.

Continued on next page

How Do You Create Software?

★ READ ALL ABOUT IT ★

"Basically when you write a program the size of *Microsoft Works* you are writing a very detailed instruction manual about the size of a Dickens' novel," Reeve said. *(Microsoft Works is a popular integrated software package.)*

When writing a program you need to use a special language, one the computer understands. And it doesn't understand much, just electronic impulses like on and off. (Sounds like an average light bulb, doesn't it?) In computer language 1 stands for on and 0 for off. For example, when you press a key on your keyboard, the computer processes a series of 1's and 0's (electronic impulses) that represent that letter or character.

LINGUISTICS OF MAN AND MACHINE

In the early years of computing, you had to be a programmer to just use a computer. The first programmable computers were created after 1940. They came about partly because of World War II as the United States Defense Department needed computer technology for greater precision in anti-aircraft logistics and ballistics.

Back then the only way to program a computer was with machine language. This involves controlling the thousands of electronic on-off switches inside the computer. Machine language is referred to as binary code because it's made up of the binary digits 1 (on) and 0 (off).

Reeve of Microsoft said any instruction the computer executes is stored in machine language. "The CPU can execute certain functions and it gets those instructions out of memory. The instructions are represented by a few primitive machine language instructions, just 1's and 0's stored in RAM," Reeve said. The CPU, or central processing unit, is the microchip which acts as your computer's brain. Instructions stored in RAM (random-access memory) are from your software program.

A computer can easily understand machine language because it's the most basic programming possible, Reeve said. But it's difficult for people. In order to use machine language a programmer must understand the inner workings of the computer.

Assembler or assembly language is one step up from machine language. It allows programmers to write a more English-like code. Instead of just binary numbers (1 and 0), assembler allows programmers to use digits 0 through 9 and letters A through F.

Programming languages that are even closer to English are called high-level languages. Some of the common high-level languages are COBOL (common business oriented language), Pascal (named after the French mathematician Blaise Pascal) and BASIC (beginner's all-purpose symbolic instruction code). High-level languages use short phrases like "Go To 10," "Input A" or "IF A$ = D THEN 10." Though easier for the programmer, high-level languages don't make sense to the computer without some type of translator. A software program called an interpreter or compiler translates the high-level code into machine language.

Since your computer has to take time to translate these high-level instructions, it takes longer for it to read them. So programs written in assembler operate faster. (The computer needs to interpret instructions written in assembler, but this language is close to machine language so it's fairly quick.) Instructions written directly in machine language are

Continued on next page

MODULE 9

★ Read All About It ★

the fastest. Machine language is still used for some programming including instructions stored inside your computer. The instructions programmed on the ROM (read-only memory) chips enable the computer to start up and retrieve information from a diskette or operating system. An operating system (like DOS, which stands for disk operating system) controls the operation of your computer.

CREATIVE PROCESS

Before a software program is ready to venture out into the real world it goes through a cycle of design, prototyping and testing. Erik McBeth is a product advisor in the support services department at Ashton-Tate. The company manufactures *dBase* software, a popular database program. McBeth said creating a program involves brainstorming, researching existing software and then defining goals. But it's also a very creative process, McBeth said.

"I'll sit down and just brainstorm, talk about everything I want it to do. Then I'll go through and start a feasibility study, nothing real complicated but I'll just go through and see those things that I can sort of tie together. The things that are just too wild I'll throw out," McBeth said.

At many software companies programming teams, ranging from three to 30 or more programmers, work on each product. McBeth said when working on large programs like dBASE, each programmer is assigned a certain area. "You would generally have an area that you would specialize in dBASE, maybe the part of dBASE that handles opening the file or displaying data," McBeth said. Typically programmers work on a high-end computer like a 386 or 486 connected to a network. As they develop the software, it's stored on the network.

Before the project begins, programming teams and other departments in the software company spend hours of extensive research. As well as researching products currently on the market, programmers analyze feedback from user groups. David Anderson, project manager of spreadsheet development at Borland International, said this research gives programmers ideas for new products. "It's important to make sure you're not going to reinvent the wheel," he said. Borland manufactures the popular *Paradox* database program.

Reeve said during focus groups conducted by Microsoft they ask people what they like and dislike about products. "We find out what features they feel are important or not, what tasks they're really trying to solve that the products either can or have trouble helping them with. And then we incorporate feedback from the focus groups into our design," Reeve said.

A meeting of the minds—working together to create innovative programs for an ever-changing world

Continued on next page

How Do You Create Software?

★ Read All About It ★

After they've compiled and analyzed their research, the programmers are ready to start creating. Reeve said before it begins, the programming team defines exactly what they want the program to do. "When you get down to implementing you realize that you have to take things one step at a time. So by having a fairly clear plan of what features you would like to incorporate in the product and the overall structure you want to present to the user, you have a starting point, a foundation to build on," Reeve said. Once the program's structure has been determined they begin designing the software, he said.

"At that point you know what you want it to look like. You know the basic approach you want to take. You basically have a rough sketch of all the components and then you start going," Reeve said. Now the programmer is ready to write the individual blocks of code necessary to make the program run.

Sometimes a program is designed in sequence from beginning to end and sometimes not, McBeth said. "It's a personal taste. Recently I designed a program that had some menus and different screens and so forth for a utility that is going to be used here in support. Initially I kind of had an idea of what the screens were going to look like and designed it, but then I went back and improved on it. A lot of times I'll do that; just like in writing, I'll get my rough draft and then I'll go back and add the bells and whistles and optimize the code," he said. (A utility program basically performs "housekeeping" tasks on your computer.)

PROGRAMMING: THE FINAL FRONTIER

Hopefully this article gave you some insight into the world of programming. It's certainly an ever-changing industry that will no doubt progress rapidly in the next few years.

In the near future you might find yourself writing programs within one of your commercial software programs. Macros are tools you can use in many programs to automate certain functions. They are really miniature programs. For example, in a word processing application you could program a macro to type messages for you. The growing popularity of macros is one way in which programming is becoming easier for the end-user.

As you learn more about your computer you may develop an interest and, eventually, a knack for programming. On the other hand, you may find you're happy just staying with those "magical" shrink-wrapped software packages. You can take it as far as you want to go. ■

MULTI CULTURAL BYTE

Mathematician Seymour Papert has been a pioneer in connecting computers to education. More than 25 years ago, Papert realized that computers had a great potential for making a difference in our culture. So, in 1968, he created the programming language Logo to help kids master the computer.

Today, Logo is in at least one third of American elementary classrooms as well as in classrooms in Latin America and the Soviet Union.

Papert has developed a number of projects to educate students in cities, such as Boston, where a typical inner-city school is made up of 30 percent African American students and 30 percent Hispanic American students. Papert's goal is to build a computer culture within the school which has "roots in the general culture."

MODULE 9 — 154

WHAT IS HYPERTEXT?

Do you find that when you're thinking about something, it sometimes reminds you of something else? Your mind jumps to a new fact or piece of information. Then, perhaps it jumps again, to something else.

Hypertext is a method of programming that is based on the idea of linking associated data. It's designed to mirror the brain's ability to store and retrieve information. The brain links information based on relationships contained within the information itself. Linking using a hypertext program refers to the action of clicking on a word that retrieves a new screen or window of text. This text provides more information on the word that was clicked on.

Linking can lead to unexpected connections. For example, if you looked up steam cooking in a hypertext program, you might find steamed clams along with references to Chinese cooking. Looking up Chinese cooking might lead to Chinese culture. That may lead to the Ming dynasty, which could lead to porcelain. Porcelain could link to pottery, leading to clay, leading to mineral deposits, and so on. This ability to associate information is the true power behind hypertext.

The underlying concepts of hypertext were presented as long ago as 1945 in an *Atlantic Monthly* article by Vanovar Bush. More recently, Ted Nelson has been recognized for his contributions to hypertext programming. Nelson is still working on a project called Xanadu that he began in 1960.

One of the most important concepts in Xanadu is that information would take new forms. For one thing, it would be nonsequential (not one-after-another, or not in a list). Many books are made up of sequential information. You are forced to move through the information in a certain order. For example, you wouldn't understand the material if you read the third paragraph, then the first, then the sixth, then the fifth, and so on. However, presenting the information on a computer in hypertext you are able to skip around but follow a path leading to related concepts based on your choices, needs, and interests.

Another key idea, called transclusion by Nelson, is that a piece of information can be in two or more places at once. Suppose that you copy a quotation from a book to add to your report. When you copy the quotation (taking it out of the context of the book), you lose the connection to the remainder of the text in which you found the quotation. However, if you were creating a hypertext report on a computer, you could link the quotation in your report to the original in the book allowing the quote to be read in its original context while also becoming part of your report.

HYPERMEDIA

Hypermedia is similar to hypertext. Like hypertext, hypermedia programs make associations between related concepts. Hypermedia programs present the information using other mediums in addition to text. In hypermedia, when you click on a word to find out more about it, new information is presented in a picture, an animation, a video clip, or a sound.

Hypermedia programs include Apple Computer's *HyperCard*, IBM's *LinkWay*, and Techware's *TutorTech*. Try a hypermedia program that is available for your computer.

A LOOK AT

The first hypermedia program was developed by Apple Computer. *HyperCard* is the most well-known example of hypermedia and hypertext. Since it is so widely available, let's use *HyperCard* to explain hypermedia programming.

CARDS, FIELDS, AND STACKS

First, the goal of *HyperCard* is to allow you to store information on electronic "index *cards*" and to be able to easily retrieve that information. Individual cards do have somewhat the appearance of paper index cards. The information stored on each card may take the form of text, graphics and, in some cases, sound.

Information stored on the cards is usually placed in fields, which are categories of information. If your card were to contain the names and addresses of your friends, there would be separate fields for each friend's name, street address, city, state, and zip code. Fields help to organize and to classify information. Each one of your friends would have his or her own card full of information. Taken all together, the cards form a stack.

Cards may also contain tools, called buttons, which make it easy to link information in the card stack or represent an action for the individual card. A button is either a graphic that looks like a type of button that you'd find on electronic equipment or another type of graphic symbol. You "press" a button by pointing to it with a mouse. *HyperCard* provides a number of button graphics, called icons, from which to choose, or you can create your own buttons.

LINKING CARDS

Card stacks are created in a sequential order, so it is easy to think of a stack as having a top and bottom card with several cards in between. In use, though, stacks are more like an endless ring of cards. As you move from one card to the next through the stack, it is as if you place the top card at the bottom each time you move to a new card. Immediately after the last card in the stack, the first card reappears. Two arrow buttons, facing "forward" and "back," are generally provided for this type of movement through the stack.

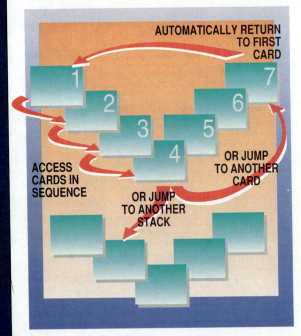

Jumping from card to card and stack to stack to access information

MODULE 9 — 156

HYPERCARD

COMPUTERS THEN & NOW

An early use of hypertext was using it to provide "help" in software programs. Computer users could click on a command and a help screen would appear explaining the command. *HyperCard* provided early examples of hypermedia where programs used text, graphics, animation, and sound to present information about some topic. The most common use of hypermedia programming today is for authoring programs that are able to link text, graphics, animation, and sound.

A button can also "jump" to another card in the stack without going in sequence. In hypertext programs, linking cards can develop associations between cards. For example, if some of the people listed in the address book were also members of the soccer team, a button might permit jumping from one team member's card to another without having to look at the cards of people who are not members of the soccer team.

Another button on the card might link it to associated stacks. An associated stack is a group of cards that depends on the main stack of cards to make sense. For example, the soccer players in the stack might be linked to a subroutine stack that shows their playing positions and game statistics.

It is also possible to link separate stacks of cards. Say, for example, that there are separate stacks of player cards for each team in the soccer league. By pressing a button linking the team stacks, you would be able to see player information contained in the other team's stack. Likewise, a button on a card in the second team's stack would return you to the first stack. This movement between cards and stacks is called *traversing* a stack.

DID YOU KNOW?

Did you know that calculators can do a lot of what the computers in your classroom can do? You might think that one of the differences between your computer and a calculator is that your computer can be programmed. But, advanced calculators can also be programmed. The real difference is that calculators only deal with numbers; modern computers can handle alphanumeric data—letters and numbers—as well as sound, graphics, animation, and video.

AUTHORING A HYPERMEDIA PROGRAM

Authoring a hypermedia program will be a new experience since it is a new form of creating programs for the computer. Hypermedia authors,

A Look at HyperCard

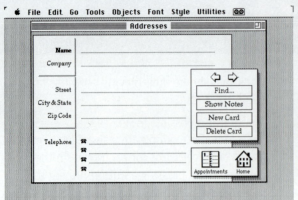

Creating hypermedia fields

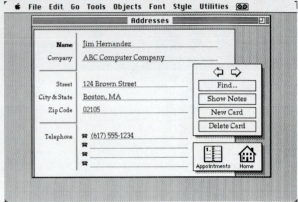

Supplying entries for each field

like other programmers, begin by planning what they want the program to do and then develop the steps needed to make it work. However, the next step in authoring is unlike writing any other program in languages such as BASIC or Pascal.

The hypermedia author does not write in languages such as BASIC or Pascal, nor does the author write computer code to implement the plan for the program. Rather, the author creates a program by linking together objects using tools provided in the hypermedia program. In *HyperCard,* the objects are called cards, fields, buttons, backgrounds, and stacks. Let's look at an example of how these objects would be linked together to create a *HyperCard* program, or stack, which keeps a list of addresses. The following example explains the major steps involved in creating an address stack. However, if you wish to create this stack on the computer, you will need to refer to the documentation for your program for details on using specific commands.

To start the stack, return to the "Home Stack" in *HyperCard,* and select the "Preferences" option in the "Home" menu. Then, select the "Authoring" user level. Now, you are set to create a new stack. Select the "New Stack" option from the "File" menu. You will be asked to give your address stack a name. What will you call your stack? Once you name your stack, *HyperCard* will automatically save all changes that you make on it. When you create a stack, the first card in the stack is automatically created. A card is equivalent to one computer screen. The card consists of two layers, a *foreground* and a *background.*

FOREGROUNDS AND BACKGROUNDS

Think of a card as having two layers on which graphics, fields, and buttons can be placed. Imagine the top layer, the foreground, as being printed on a transparent surface, like glass, through which you can see the background. The background is the layer that seems "farther" from the viewer. Backgrounds allow several similar cards to share the same (repeated) information. Every card has a background, but its background may be shared with another card.

A stack can have as many backgrounds as it has cards but, almost always, some of its cards will share backgrounds. Those shared backgrounds mean that a stack will not have as many *types* of backgrounds as it has cards.

When you look at a card on the screen, you see a combination of both layers because you can see the background through the top layer. However, if any elements on the top layer are positioned over elements of the background, those background elements will be "covered up" and you will not see them. Also, when you create backgrounds, you can make any background object invisible, if you wish, by assigning a "transparent style" to it when it's created.

Select the "Background" option in the "Edit" menu. Note how the menu bar has dashes around the edges indicating you are viewing only the background on the screen. In normal use, backgrounds usually contain things that apply to several related cards such as names of fields that are the same on each card. In our example stack, the field names might be: Name, Address, and Phone Number. Using the "Text" tool in the "Tools" menu, type the field names on the left side of the first card leaving plenty of space between the names. Select the "Browse Tool" in the "Tools" menu when you finish typing.

Using Button-tool options to create a button

ADDING FIELDS

You can add the fields to the background next to each name by using the "New Field" option in the "Objects" menu. With the "File Tool" in the "Tool" menu, you can select the style of field you want, position the field on the screen, and change its size and shape. To do this correctly will take some planning, so, before you actually create any fields, it's best to write down on paper all of the fields you expect to create and their contents. The best designs for fields are those which work in a usual or expected way. For example, an address book is generally completed in the order of name, address, city, state, zip code, and telephone number. If you put the telephone numbers first, that would not be the usual order for an address book. Information that is not in the order that people expect it to be can often lead to errors when it is entered.

ADDING BUTTONS TO THE CARD

Placing buttons on the card is the first step toward making a *HyperCard* stack really work. The first buttons to add to the card are the left- and right-facing arrows that will take you to the next card or previous card. Select the "New Button" option in the "Objects" menu. With the "Button Tool" in the "Tool" menu, you can select the style of button you want, position the button on the screen and change its size and shape. You can also select an icon for the button, in this case the right and left arrows. Finally, the "Button Tool" has an option that links the button to another card. In this stack, the right arrow will point to the next card and the left arrow will point to the previous card.

Other buttons can also be added for special purposes, such as linking the cards of soccer team members. Each button is created in a similar

way by first selecting the appropriate type of button, then adding linking instructions. You are able to select from ready-made icons for buttons, but are also able to draw special buttons or use fancy graphic images. Practically anything can be a button if properly created. For example, the button for the team could be a soccer ball that you draw with the paint tools. Buttons can also be copied from one card to another. In this way, different cards in a stack could share similar functions.

ADDING NEW CARDS

With the newly created card structure, you are now ready to enter data on the cards. Select the "Foreground" option in the "Edit" menu. This action takes *HyperCard* out of background mode and lets you see the foreground and background layers of the card. Select the "Browse Tool" from the "Tools" menu. Enter the data into each field on the card. When the first card is complete, add another card to the stack by selecting the "New Card" option on the "Edit" menu. Fill in the information on the second card. Finally, use the "Button Tool" to have the right/left arrow buttons link the cards together. Repeating this process, you will be able to complete the address book stack.

HYPERTALK

If all the *HyperCard* stack did was speed the reference of information from one card to another, it would be powerful and useful, but it would be rather limiting. Working with data often requires a program that is able to follow logic, or sequences of instruction.

To use the full power of *HyperCard* requires learning how to use HyperTalk, *HyperCard's* programming language. HyperTalk consists of just over 40 commands. The commands are simple words, such as "answer," "choose," "click," "print," and "write," that can be used to construct sentences to give specific commands. The command sentences form a script, or a collection of instructions. As an example, to place the current date into a field, HyperTalk's commands are:

```
on openCard
   put the date into field1
end openCard
```

Notice the terms, "on openCard" and "end openCard." These are called events. Events are used to specify when an action takes place. So, when the example card is opened, which is a computer term for the moment the information on the card becomes available, the date will be placed into the first field on the card.

Let's take a look at another script—this one for doing some calculations when a field is closed. A field is closed by clicking the mouse on another field, or by pressing the enter key.

```
on closeField
   get value of line 2 of field 3
   put it into amount
   multiply amount by .06
   put amount into line 3 of field 3
   put value of line 2 of field 3 into holdit
   add amount to holdit
   put holdit into line 4 of field 3
end closeField
```

Many other things can be done using the functions and commands, of course, and these illustrations are simple examples. *HyperCard*, with its HyperTalk capabilities, is a powerful and thoroughly modern way to control the flow of information with a computer. Like anything new, however, learning to do it well takes practice and patience.

WHAT CAN YOU DO WITH HYPERMEDIA PROGRAMMING?

N ow you're ready to use your hypermedia program, whether it be *LinkWay, TutorTech,* or *HyperCard*. Read on to discover what you can do with hypermedia.

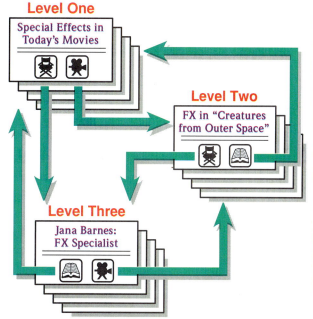

Exploring several levels of information on special effects

CHOOSE YOUR OWN ADVENTURE

Hypermedia programs can help you to write stories that allow you to choose your own adventures. This is easy to do with hypermedia programs. You begin your story on one card. When you come to a point where the story could go in more than one direction, you add buttons. The buttons allow the reader to choose the direction he or she wants to go with the story. One button might send the reader to a card where the hero saves a dog. If a different button is pushed, the hero fails. Push a third button and...here comes the train. You decide where the third button leads. You can use this technique to branch to other cards several times, giving your story many possible outcomes.

PRESENTING A REPORT

Let's say that you have a report to do on special effects (often called FX) in new films. Your teacher says that you can turn in your report on a disk if you want to use a hypermedia program.

Hypermedia programs let you organize your material in several levels. The first (or highest) level might be your basic report. In this basic report, you might write about various kinds of FX being used in today's films. This information might occupy several different cards. The second level could be a set of cards with more detailed descriptions of the FX used in each individual film. The third level might give information about the individual people who created the FX.

When your teacher reviews your presentation, buttons at all levels would allow him or her to move around through the information, along paths between related topics. When your teacher is reading about Jana Barnes, Hollywood FX specialist, she can "press" a button to go directly to a card that tells about the movie where Barnes' recent work appeared. Or your teacher could press a different button to go to a card in the first level of your report that compares Barnes' creations to those of Saul Petra, an FX man whose work is similar to Barnes'. Because hypermedia programs offer the freedom of moving around through documents like

SEASHELLS BY THE SEASHORE

Do you have a lot of information to keep track of? How about that big seashell collection?

Let's say that you've collected a lot of shells on vacations. You've checked out books from the library and identified almost all of your shells. You know their names, what kind of creatures lived in them, all the places in the world where each type can be found, and the places where you actually found each one. Your collection is getting so big that you're having trouble deciding how to organize it. Do you put this large conch shell with other large shells or with other shells from St. Petersburg, Florida, where you found it? Or do you put it with other conch shells or with other shells of the same color?

How about using a hypermedia program? You could put information about each different shell on a card and even include a picture of the shell. You could link the cards together with buttons for type of shell, size, location where each was found, and any other categories you choose. Then, for example, you could browse through the information on all your conch shells one day and, on another day, all the information on this, your teacher could review your report in any of several different ways.

You MAKE A DIFFERENCE

At 15 years of age, Christopher Lees used his computer skills to work for doctors. How did someone at his age use a computer to help professionals in the medical field?

> During one summer, Christopher was working on Saturdays as a volunteer at a hospital pharmacy. An employee of the pharmacy learned that Christopher knew a lot about computers. The employee asked him to set up a small database to track the use of a certain heart medication.

> "That's how I got my foot in the door," Christopher said, "and the word spread." A doctor heard about Christopher's programming talents and asked him to write a computer program for his office. Then, that doctor recommended him to others and, before long, Christopher had set up 10 systems!

your bivalves (shells with two matching sides). Some other time you might browse through all the shells you have found on the Pacific coast.

As you collect more shells, you can add them to your hypermedia "collection." As for the actual shells? Put them away in boxes, each with its own identifying (ID) number. The ID number for each shell would be on its information card in your hypermedia program. This way, when you locate a shell in your hypermedia program that you want to take a look at, you can quickly find the shell, by its number, in your collection.

CHARGE IT!

Would you like to be the brains behind an innovative idea at your school store?

Let's suppose you have accounts set up for various students in the school store. You want to keep a running balance for each student, showing the total amount owed. You guessed it—you can use your hypermedia program to keep the records!

The calculating features of the program allow you to have a card for each student with a button that adds the current charge to the total amount owed. Another button can subtract payments from

What Can You Do with Hypermedia Programming?

MODULE 9

MODULE SUMMARY QUESTIONS

Keeping track of student purchases with a hypermedia program

the total owed, so that the balance always stays accurate. What if a student tries to charge more than the allowed limit? How about adding a button that adds current charges to a field called "past due"? And perhaps creating another button that adds a penalty to the past-due amount by multiplying that amount by a percentage.

Whether you're writing a report or a story, organizing a collection, or operating a school store, a hypermedia program, including IBM's *LinkWay,* Apple's *Tutor-Tech,* and Macintosh's *HyperCard,* can be applied. *LinkWay* and *Tutor-Tech* have functions very similar to those in *HyperCard. LinkWay* and *Tutor-Tech* use pages in the same way that *HyperCard* uses cards. These pages are linked together into stacks. But, no matter which hypermedia program you are using you're sure to discover all the possibilities it has to offer.

In order to check your comprehension of computer programming, you may wish to discuss the following ideas.

1. A computer cannot work by itself. It must be told what to do by people—it must be given instructions. What do we call these instructions?

2. The idea of hypertext is based on the way the human brain works. How do we recall facts and information with our brains?

3. What does OOP stand for? How does it work?

4. On your coat, a button holds fabric together. What does a "button" do in *HyperCard?*

MODULE 10
THE HISTORY OF COMPUTERS

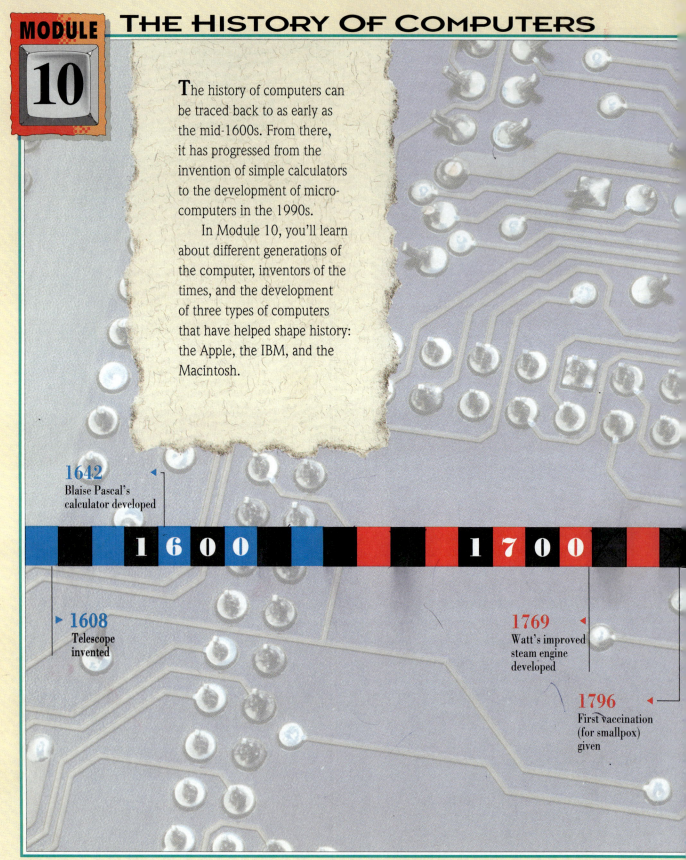

The history of computers can be traced back to as early as the mid-1600s. From there, it has progressed from the invention of simple calculators to the development of microcomputers in the 1990s.

In Module 10, you'll learn about different generations of the computer, inventors of the times, and the development of three types of computers that have helped shape history: the Apple, the IBM, and the Macintosh.

1642
Blaise Pascal's calculator developed

1600 — **1700**

1608
Telescope invented

1769
Watt's improved steam engine developed

1796
First vaccination (for smallpox) given

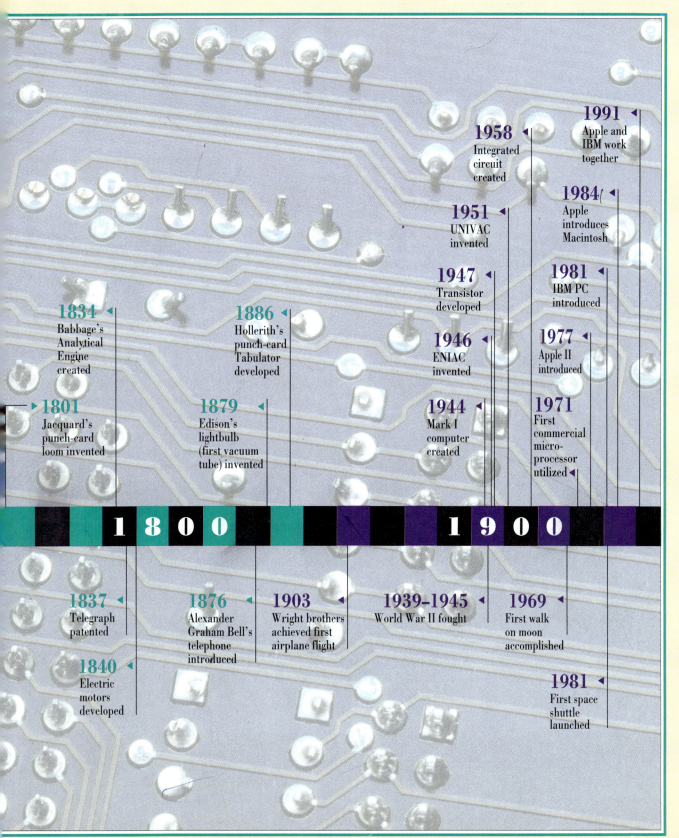

THE AGE OF THE COMPUTER

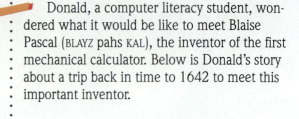

Donald, a computer literacy student, wondered what it would be like to meet Blaise Pascal (BLAYZ pahs KAL), the inventor of the first mechanical calculator. Below is Donald's story about a trip back in time to 1642 to meet this important inventor.

MY JOURNEY INTO THE HISTORY OF COMPUTERS

My invention was almost ready. Using computer-aided-design software, I drew up the plans and built a time machine. I wanted to travel back in time to talk with the inventor of the mechanical calculating machine, the Pascaline. This early device helped people think about new ways machines could do work. It eventually led to the invention of the modern computer!

So, I set my machine for the early 1600s and got ready to take off for parts unknown. I landed somewhere in France. The year was 1642. The person I hoped to meet was 19-year-old Blaise Pascal. I had read about his invention—the first mechanical calculator—in a history book. Now, here I was standing before him in his workshop.

"*Bonjour, Monsieur Pascal,*" I began. "I'm interested in learning about Pascaline, your newest invention. Would you tell me how it works?"

"Certainly," he replied. "My invention looks simple, but it can solve complex math problems. It uses a device called a gear, which is a special wheel with 'grooves' (also called teeth or notches). The grooves in each gear help it to lock onto and turn another gear. All the gears are connected this way. If you rotate one of the wheels in a certain way, you can figure sums. Watch as I add two numbers."

COMPUTERS THEN & NOW

The term *calculator* comes from the Latin word "calculus," which means "pebble." After people graduated from counting on their fingers and toes, they used tiny stones to keep tallies. These pebbles were inserted into the flat grooves of a counting board. This board was divided into columns representing ones, tens, hundreds, and so on.

In Roman times, this invention allowed merchants to perform complex calculations when selling their merchandise—much like today's cash registers!

Throughout history, inventions have directly changed the way we have lived our lives and done our jobs. Today, we live in the Information Age, a new period in history, made possible by a very important invention—the computer. Today's computers help us write, perform complex calculations, and communicate over long distances. However, the earliest computers were little more than simple calculators.

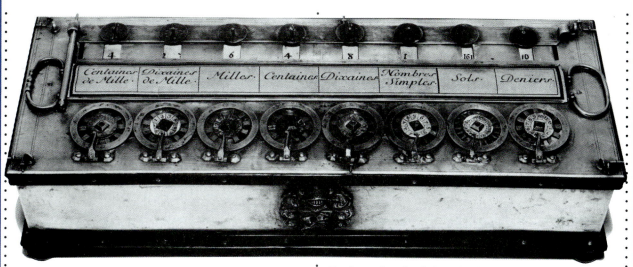

I stared while he added 2,356 and 1,755. Some gears represented tens, others hundreds, a few thousands, and so on. He had to turn each gear the right number of notches to produce the correct answer: 4,111.

"That's great!" I said. "Can your machine also subtract?"

The Pascaline, the first mechanical calculator

"It has problems subtracting large numbers," he admitted. "The gears have to rotate in the opposite way, and I can't quite get them to work correctly."

"What seems to be the problem?" I asked.

"The biggest problem is that it takes us several days to make just one gear," he answered. "It's hard to work with metal. We aren't very good at it, yet. Soon, I hope to find the solution."

"Well, Mr. Pascal, I think your mechanical calculator is awesome," I said. "I, too, hope to invent a great machine someday. Can you give me some advice?"

"Let me think . . . ," he said thoughtfully. "Yes, I can. The best advice is to believe in yourself and your own ideas."

I told him, *"Merci beaucoup,"* and strapped myself back into the time machine. As I traveled home, I thought about the invention I had just seen. I knew Pascal never got it to work right. Yet, it helped other inventors build better mechanical calculators and set the stage for the development of the modern computer.

By using my personal computer—an invention inspired by Pascal's idea—maybe someday I will be able to design a machine that will be just as important to our world as his mechanical calculator.

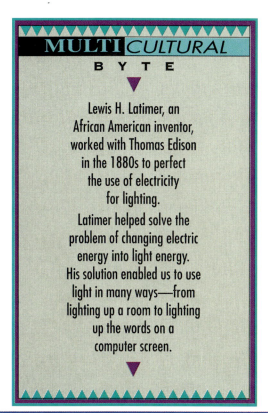

MULTI CULTURAL BYTE

Lewis H. Latimer, an African American inventor, worked with Thomas Edison in the 1880s to perfect the use of electricity for lighting.

Latimer helped solve the problem of changing electric energy into light energy. His solution enabled us to use light in many ways—from lighting up a room to lighting up the words on a computer screen.

THE ANALYTICAL ENGINE THAT COULD
(A One-act Play)

Charles Babbage was a nineteenth century English inventor. Historians call him the grandfather of the modern computer. Like today's computers, Charles's invention couldn't work without a program, which is a set of instructions that tell it what to do.

Lady Ada Augusta Lovelace, daughter of the English poet Lord Byron, helped Babbage program his steam-powered mechanical computer, known as the Analytical Engine. Get to know Charles Babbage and Lady Ada better by acting out the following one-act play.

CHARACTERS

Lady Ada Augusta Lovelace
Charles Babbage
Narrator

SETTING

It is the early 1830s in England. The action begins outside the laboratory of Charles Babbage, the famous inventor. Lady Ada Augusta Lovelace, Charles's assistant, sets the stage for the audience. Throughout this one-act play, the Narrator stands stage left.

LADY ADA *(speaking to the audience)*: I'm about to walk into Charles Babbage's workshop. Do you know Mr. Babbage? He's a dear friend of mine and, I dare say, a genius. His Analytical Engine could change the world.

I'm Lady Ada Augusta Lovelace. My job is to prepare a written set of instructions for Charles's Analytical Engine. Once the machine has these instructions, it will be able to work with any numbers that others might give it. In some ways, I believe that instructions help machines think intelligently, almost like a human brain.

(Lady Ada turns to face the laboratory door. She knocks, but enters without waiting for a response. Charles is already at work.)

LADY ADA: Good morning, Charles. I'm very excited about working on the engine today. I was up late last night, thinking of a good way to make it understand my instructions.

BABBAGE: Let's hear your idea, then!

(Charles smiles. Ada's ideas appear to bring new life to his tired face.)

LADY ADA: Do you remember reading about Joseph Jacquard's (ja KAHRDZ) loom? His machine followed instructions to weave cloth. Your machine will have to follow instructions, too—if it is to work right. Mr. Jacquard's loom worked from punch cards. Each card told the loom what to do—step-by-step.

BABBAGE: Do you intend to use a series of punch cards to instruct my engine?

LADY ADA: Exactly. Now, let's get started.

NARRATOR: Lady Ada and Charles began work on a set of instructions for the engine, using punch cards to convey information. They wanted the machine to learn how to add.

LADY ADA: To design a program, we must know the exact sequence of steps it takes to reach the answer.

NARRATOR: Figuring out a step-by-step process that would instruct the machine to add two numbers took Lady Ada and Charles several weeks! It took even longer to get these instructions on punch cards.

BABBAGE *(doubtfully):* I think we're stuck. How will

The Analytical Engine that Could

Charles Babbage's Analytical Engine

the engine read these cards? Perhaps we should use a different system?

LADY ADA: Charles, if there were a better way to program our machine, we would have thought of it. Cards are the best tools we have.

BABBAGE: Yes, Ada, you're right. If I could only make sure my engine followed your rules to the letter.

NARRATOR *(as Charles and Ada perform the actions described):* Eventually, Charles devised a mechanical system to "read" the cards. He made the engine work by punching holes in the cards. Each hole turned a gear (or series of gears) in the machine. The engine would do whatever the holes on the cards instructed.

LADY ADA: You know, Charles, your engine is only as good as its program. If the program has an error, the engine will make a mistake.

BABBAGE: We must keep testing our programs. The more problems the engine can solve, the better it will be. I hope we can program the machine to do all sorts of work.

LADY ADA: I think we can—we're a great team!

NARRATOR: Lady Ada Lovelace and Charles Babbage worked together for about 10 years. She prepared instructions that directed the engine to do many things. Charles kept trying to improve his machine design. The Analytical Engine was never a great success, but it showed people that a mechanical device could solve problems—as long as it had programs to follow!

★ READ ALL ABOUT IT ★

Excerpted from *Computerworld*
July 7, 1991
By Ron Condon

Babbage's Difference Engine Launched—142 Years Later

LONDON—More than 140 years after it was designed, Charles Babbage's Difference Engine finally cranked laboriously into action last week at London's Science Museum.

The museum, which strictly followed Victorian methods of manufacturing (with the help of some computer-aided design), has proved that the designs would have worked, ending years of doubt over whether the Victorian inventor's ideas for automated calculation could ever be put into practice.

The Difference Engine No. 2 was designed between 1847 and 1849 as a refinement of an earlier design that Babbage had abandoned.

Now with an $810,000 sponsorship from Hewlett-Packard Co., Unisys Corp., Rank Xerox, International Computers Ltd. and Siemens-Nixdorf, along with $405,000 from the museum's own coffers, the machine has finally been assembled.

It weighs three tons, measures 7 ft. high, 11 ft. long and 18 in. deep and contains 4,000 parts. It is cranked manually with a handle and, according to Doron Swade, the museum's senior curator for computing, can handle seventh-order polynomials to 30 places—"no mean feat even by today's standards," Swade said.

As for Babbage's more ambitious Analytical Engine, a true precursor of the programmable computer with "if-then" logic and stored programs, the museum estimates that it would need $1.62 million to tackle the project. ■

HOLLERITH— An Inventor Founds IBM

Herman Hollerith was another important inventor of the late 1800s. He, too, helped make modern computers possible. In 1880, Hollerith worked for the United States Census Bureau. At that time, it took only a few months to collect census data from the entire country—however, it took up to nine years to add all the figures and interpret the results.

Hollerith invented a machine to speed up the calculation process. In the beginning, his invention used tape to keep records. But it took too much time to locate a piece of data once the tape was rolled up.

Then, Hollerith borrowed the idea of punch cards. Unlike Babbage, he used cards only to record data. His machine, called a "Tabulator," relied upon a stored program to do the tabulating (adding). It was the world's first automatic data processor. It was also one of the first machines powered by battery-supplied electricity.

Hollerith's invention was a great success. It proved that a machine could be programmed to work automatically. Users only had to feed in data and the Tabulator would do most of the work!

In the early 1900s, Hollerith went on to start his own company. In 1924, it would become the International Business Machines Corporation, better known today as IBM.

First-generation Computers
INVENTIONS THAT CHANGED THE WORLD

A *generation* refers to a stage of improvement in the development of a product. People often use the term "generation" when talking about computers. A generation of computers is a group of computers that are able to perform certain closely related functions. So far, there have been several generations of computers.

You may recall reading in Module 1 about some of the first-generation computers. Each one is associated with the work of great inventors. Here's the scoop on the best and the brightest of these inventors and the products they created.

HOWARD AIKEN: THE MARK I

Like other inventors, Howard Aiken thought he had a great idea. As a math professor at Harvard University, he was frustrated by how much time he wasted while solving complex math problems. So, Aiken spent several years with a team of men and women working on the construction of the ASCC (Automatic Sequence Controlled Calculator), better known as the "Mark I."

When the machine was finished in 1944, it was an amazing sight. Composed of 750,000 parts and 500 miles (804.5 km) of wiring, it weighed five tons (4.5 t). Unlike today's tiny desktop computers, Mark I stood 51 feet (15.5 m) long, 8 feet (2.4 m) high, and 2 feet (.6 m) deep. Yet, it could solve three simple problems in a second, multiply two 23-digit numbers in four seconds, and do six month's worth of manual calculations in a single day! Mark I was the fastest calculator invented up to that time.

J. PRESPER ECKERT AND JOHN MAUCHLY: ENIAC AND UNIVAC

In 1943—the middle of World War II—the United States Army had a problem. It needed a machine to help military personnel make complex calculations involving supply schedules, aircraft design, and the paths explosive shells must take to reach their targets. The more help the Army could obtain, the better the chance of Allied victory.

J. Presper Eckert and John Mauchly believed they could invent a computer—a high-speed electronic calculator—to provide faster, more accurate data processing. Their answer was ENIAC, shorthand for *E*lectronic *N*umerical *I*ntegrator *A*nd *C*alculator. The machine was unveiled in 1946. Instead

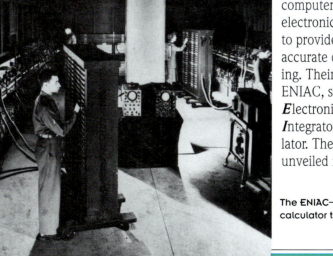

The ENIAC—the first electronic calculator to use vacuum tubes

First-generation Computers

YOU MAKE A DIFFERENCE

Do you ever have ideas about machines you would like to invent? If so, a patent can help you protect your invention, once it is developed. A patent identifies the owner of an invention. It prevents other people from using or copying an invention without permission.

- A patent holder controls all revenues earned through the use of the invention. Without a patent, anyone could duplicate, sell, or use an invention without permission.
- If you're interested in patents, or have an invention of your own you'd like to protect, write for more information to:
- Office of Information
  United States Patent Office
  Washington, DC 20231

of using 750,000 parts, like the Mark I, ENIAC relied upon nearly 18,000 *vacuum tubes* to store and process data electronically.

ENIAC worked hundreds of times faster than the Mark I. Still, it was not a friendly-looking machine. The computer was so large that it filled an entire room. Operators were able to input data by switching the wires around on a huge device called a plugboard. Legend was that the lights of Philadelphia dimmed every time the computer was turned on.

In 1946, Mauchly and Eckert went on to form the Electronic Control Corporation. This was one of the first commercial computer companies. In 1951, they created UNIVAC (***Univ**ersal **A**uto-matic **C**omputer).

Many models of the UNIVAC were made and sold to businesses. Therefore, it was the first commercial computer. UNIVAC was also the first computer to use magnetic tape for input instead of punched tape or cards.

JOHN VON NEUMANN: STORED-PROGRAM COMPUTERS

When Eckert and Mauchly tried to improve ENIAC's design in the late 1940s, they sought assistance from a brilliant mathematician named John von Neumann.

Von Neumann was a respected Hungarian scientist. He came to the United States in 1930 to teach at Princeton University. In the early 1940s, he spent most of his time as a consultant to the top-secret "Manhattan Project," the United States' effort to develop the first atomic bomb.

Von Neumann believed that ENIAC could work faster if it were modified. He came up with the idea for a central processing unit (or CPU). The CPU coded programs as numbers so they could be stored in the computer's memory with other data.

Since the CPU stored both the computer's programs *and* data in its memory, data processing took place at a much faster rate than ever before.

First-generation Computers

GRACE MURRAY HOPPER: COMPILERS AND COBOL

Navy Captain Grace Hopper worked as a programmer on the Mark I computer and its successor, the Mark II. Later on, she was a member of the UNIVAC team. Most historians credit her with being the inventor of a very important computer program called a *compiler*.

A compiler allows a programmer to use a language that can be translated into machine language. Before compilers, programmers had to write every program in machine language, a slow and tedious process. The invention of the compiler helped speed up data processing significantly.

Hopper also invented one of the first computer programming languages, called COBOL (***CO***mmon ***B***usiness ***O***riented ***L***anguage). A programming language helps programmers write computer instructions in terms the computer can understand. With a standardized computer language like COBOL, more people were able to write computer programs. The language is still in use today.

DID YOU KNOW?

Did you know that problems in computer hardware or software are often called *bugs?* A computer bug prevents the computer from working properly. Until the bug is fixed, work cannot continue.

How did the "bug" get its name? Well, Grace Hopper was working on the Mark II when it suddenly broke down. After searching for several days, she found the source of the problem. A moth had gotten stuck between two relays, breaking the electrical connection. Once she removed the bug, the computer operated just fine.

Since that day, if anything goes wrong with a computer, people say the computer has a "bug."

Second-generation Computers
THE DAWN OF MODERN COMPUTING

A new age of computing began a few years after World War II. Before then, the world of computing was dominated by central processors housed in colossal mainframe computers. The mainframes of the 1940s and 1950s were imposing machines with many knobs, vacuum tubes, flashing lights, and wires. They cost a lot of money to buy and even more money to maintain.

Companies kept mainframes locked in sterile, air-conditioned isolation. Nobody could get into the computer room without a pass. Average American citizens never came into contact with these gigantic electronic brains.

Most people thought mainframes were too big and expensive for small businesses to own. However, the invention of the *transistor* in 1947 made it possible to produce smaller, more accessible data-processing machines. By 1960, these "minicomputers" had become popular among smaller businesses as well as large corporations.

Transistors, compact electronic devices that control the flow of current without the use of a vacuum, were more reliable than vacuum tubes. They were smaller, less expensive to make, and worked faster. Minicomputers built in the early 1960s by companies like Digital Equipment Corporation (DEC) and Data General incorporated this new transistor technology.

Although DEC's PDP minicomputers and IBM's System/360 mainframe series were still large and cumbersome by today's "micro" standards, they were considered technological marvels. For example, DEC's PDP-1 shipped in four six-foot (1.8 m) cabinets, weighing 250 pounds (113.5 kg) each. Yet, it was lighter in weight and more economical than a mainframe. Companies could purchase a PDP-1 for about $120,000. Some mainframes had cost almost 10 times that amount.

Transistors—much smaller and less expensive than vacuum tubes

In 1965, when DEC introduced its dazzling PDP-8, the computer was about the same size as a small refrigerator and cost only $18,000. DEC could make the PDP-8 that small because the computer used integrated-circuit (IC) technology rather than just transistors. ICs consisted of tiny chips that held several transistors. These technological miracles ushered in the third generation of computers.

Third-generation Computers
THE SHRINKING OF THE MODERN COMPUTER

The development of the integrated circuit revolutionized the world of computers. An IC is a miniature electronic circuit etched on a piece of silicon about the same size in diameter as a pencil eraser. A single IC could take the place of thousands of transistors—and one transistor already did the work of 40 vacuum tubes.

Integrated circuits not only made third-generation computers smaller than earlier models, they also made them more reliable and more powerful. Because they were so tiny, integrated circuits could be mass-produced at a low cost. This decreased the price and increased the availability of computers dramatically. Thousands of businesses that had been unable to afford the bulky, second-generation computers now were able to take advantage of modern technology.

This widespread use of the computer in the business world started another important trend. Businesses created a growing demand for general-purpose computers—machines that could do a variety of tasks. Prior to this, most early models had been special-purpose computers that were designed for solving complex problems. Today, both general-purpose and special-purpose computers are commonplace.

Fourth-generation Computers
COMPUTERS GET PERSONAL

With the invention of the microprocessor, or "computer on a chip," computers became smaller and more affordable. However, it wasn't until the 1970s that people began buying computers for personal use.

Early personal computers (PCs) were weird-looking homemade machines, assembled from jumbled piles of chips, switches, integrated circuits, and circuit boards. These electronic gadgets were often put together on garage workbenches, kitchen tables, and bedroom desks. They were designed for fun, rather than work.

One of the earliest personal computers to achieve national popularity was called the Altair 8800. In 1975, computer enthusiasts could purchase the Altair kit, consisting of a circuit board and a metal box that housed its power supply. To get this contraption to work, hobbyists had to purchase a central processing unit (CPU) and circuit-board cards for the keyboard and video display. These electronic gadgets attached to connectors on the circuit board. Software consisted of programs written on paper tape.

The Altair 8800 was very popular with the do-it-yourself crowd. However, MITS, the company responsible for Altair's main components and software, didn't win favor with businesspeople or average folks. The Altair kit soon disappeared from hobby store shelves, but it will always be remembered as the first personal computer.

During the 1980s and early 90s, dramatic improvements were made in computer technology. On pages 176–178, you'll read about the development of Apple, IBM, and Macintosh computers—three leaders in the PC industry.

THE STORY OF APPLE COMPUTERS

While Altair may have been the first personal computer, it took a couple of innovative businessmen and a computer known as the Apple II to make PCs popular tools for work, play, and school.

Steve Wozniak and Steve Jobs thought everyone should be able to own a computer. They believed that computers should be fun to use and easy to buy. Their commitment to this idea led them to found one of the world's most popular lines of desktop PCs—Apple computers.

The corporation officially got its start in 1975. That year, the Altair computer kit hit the market. When Wozniak discovered he couldn't afford one of the computers, he decided to build his own. This homemade model became the prototype for the Apple I.

Wozniak's Apple I was very basic. It was intended for hobbyists. It had no case, memory, or power supply. It even lacked a monitor. To obtain a video display, you had to hook it up to a TV.

Like the Altair, the Apple I used chips as the main component. Unlike the Altair, however, Wozniak's Apple I had a very inexpensive microprocessor (CPU). It could be purchased at hobby stores for only $20—much less than the $370 that the Altair's CPU had cost.

Wozniak and Jobs formed a partnership in 1976. Wozniak worked on engineering and design, while Jobs concentrated on marketing. It was Jobs's idea to name their company "Apple Computer." Some say this name was chosen because Jobs knew that "Apple" would appear before "Atari" on any alphabetically arranged computer list. Others say Jobs went with the name "Apple" because it was the name of the Beatles' record label or because he had worked in the Oregon apple orchards.

In the beginning, the main problem the two inventors faced was money. To cut costs, they set up operations in Jobs's garage. Working together, they produced several Apple Is for sale at a local computer store. The machines sold quickly because they were reliable and quite inexpensive. As a result of their initial success, Jobs and Wozniak were able to borrow more money and attract investors. With enough capital to experiment, Wozniak built an improved computer. In 1977, the company introduced the Apple II.

This new computer was not a hobbyist's toy. It arrived fully assembled in an attractive, light-colored plastic case. The package included a keyboard and power supply, but users still had to add a TV or monitor. Yet it was easy to operate, faster than the Apple I, and great for operating a number of exciting programs—including video games!

The Apple II had many wonderful features. Wozniak gave it color and graphics capabilities, a speaker for sound, and internal slots for special cards that connected to monitors, printers, and disk drives. Best of all, he designed it to be small enough to fit on an ordinary desktop.

While this computer was primitive by today's standards, it met with instant acceptance. Jobs and Wozniak moved the company out of Jobs's garage and into its own building. Jobs and Wozniak were well on their way to becoming millionaires.

IBM—THE PC INVADES THE BUSINESS WORLD

In 1981, four years after the introduction of the Apple II, IBM (International Business Machines) came out with its first personal computer. Until the arrival of the IBM PC, people primarily thought of personal computers as toys. This attitude changed when IBM entered the picture.

IBM commanded respect and admiration in the business world as a maker of large-size mainframes and smaller minicomputers. The company was also known for its terrific typewriters. IBM's decision to make personal computers would prove to be one of the most important events in the history of personal computing.

Companies like Apple, Commodore, Tandy, and Atari all made popular personal computers in the late 1970s, but each machine required its own special software. Programs written for an Apple II wouldn't work on a Commodore VIC-20, Tandy TRS-80, or any other computer. Similarly, hardware devices like monitors, printers, and disk drives purchased for a Commodore Pet wouldn't operate on an Atari 400/800 or any other machine.

When IBM brought its own PC to the market in 1981, a new standard was born. People who were afraid to buy an Apple or a Commodore because these machines couldn't communicate with their expensive IBM mainframes now had a personal computer that was compatible, meaning that it could communicate with their computers. While other computer manufacturers made sure that only their software and hardware would work on their equipment, "Big Blue" (a nickname for IBM) made the technical design details for its personal computer available to anyone.

As a result, software developers could easily write programs for the IBM PC, while hardware manufacturers could make copies ("clones") of the machine or develop new add-on equipment. The IBM PC quickly became the most popular personal computer. Historians say that, by 1984, three out of every four PCs sold had the IBM label.

Remarkably, IBM's 1983 venture into the home computer market did not fare as well. The little machine known as the "IBM PC Junior" (nicknamed "Peanut"), was much less powerful than the original IBM PC. True, it was more affordable, but it also had only half the PC's memory capability. As a result, many programs that ran on the IBM PC would not work on the Junior. Because of widespread dissatisfaction, IBM stopped making the machine in 1984.

The IBM PC, however, continued to appeal to a wide audience. Children liked it because it had fun games and enjoyable software for school. Families liked it because it helped them organize and keep holiday mailing lists, calculate household budgets, and type error-free letters. Businesses liked it because it allowed ordinary office personnel to perform jobs that once required mainframes and highly specialized technical help. IBM's personal computer, just like the Apple II, put data-processing power into the hands of ordinary people.

Fourth-generation Computers

Macintosh—Computing Becomes Less Complicated

The market for desktop PCs grew in the early 1980s. IBM PCs achieved popularity with business types, while Apple IIs won favor in the classroom. Steve Jobs and Steve Wozniak tried to build better and more powerful computers. Two efforts, however, called the Apple III and Lisa, were failures.

In 1984, Apple came out with another revolutionary machine—the Macintosh. The "Mac" had several features that made it very popular with people new to computing. Unlike many other PCs of the time, it came bundled with two software packages: MacWrite for word processing and MacPaint for graphics. It also had a "mouse." By moving the mouse on a tabletop, users could easily control the computer without touching the keyboard.

When people started up one of the early microcomputers, they were often greeted by a flashing prompt such as >. To get the machine to do something, users had to type in special commands. People who didn't know much about computing were often frightened by how much they thought they had to learn to get the machine to work.

To make computers easier to use, Apple developed a graphical user interface (GUI) for the Macintosh. A GUI allows a computer user to point to pictures or items on a menu to perform certain functions. This meant that when you turned on a Macintosh, you saw recognizable objects like file folders, trash cans, and push buttons. Instead of having to memorize commands, you merely selected options from menu lists or used the mouse to click on pictures representing program choices.

The Mac's GUI provided a visual way to manipulate data. People knew instinctively that to organize their electronic desktop they needed only to place related files in a folder, or to remove unwanted files by dragging them into the trash can. Even beginners felt comfortable with the machine. Instead of requiring 20 or 30 hours of training to learn how to use an Apple II or an IBM PC, Mac users could be up and operating in 20 or 30 minutes.

Apple, the company that two men started in a garage, has had a major impact on personal computing. For one thing, as a result of Macintosh's success, Microsoft, the world's largest software company, developed the "Windows" graphical user interface for IBM PCs and compatibles. One can only wonder what new and exciting surprises Apple has planned for the personal computers of the 21st century.

Making computing easier through the use of a graphical user interface

MODULE 10

The NeXT Step

In 1985, Steve Jobs left Apple Computer to start a new computer company called NeXT. He wanted to develop and market powerful personal computers for colleges and universities. People wondered what these new machines would look like. Jobs had to promise Apple that NeXT computers would neither use the Macintosh operating system nor run any Macintosh software.

Steve Jobs

In October 1988, Jobs introduced the first-generation NeXT machine. As everyone expected, it was a very impressive piece of technology. NeXT offered many innovative features, including a UNIX-based graphical user interface with realistic 3-D icons (pictures). Built-in sound capabilities allowed users to record or play back their voice and other special audio effects.

Unfortunately, NeXT was expensive, compared to other personal computers. In addition, the machine had a limited software library. As a result, sales were initially meager.

In September 1990, Jobs unveiled a new, more powerful NeXT computer. Prices were still high (though somewhat more affordable), but this time the machine had software. Industry analysts agreed that NeXT represented state-of-the-art technology, however NeXT would have a long way to go to be as popular as Macintosh.

Future Generations—

What Can We Expect?

In just a few decades, computers have progressed through four generations of technology. As we head into future generations, what changes can we expect to see? That may be a hard question to answer. If we've learned anything from the past, it is that the world of computers is full of surprises!

We can make a few predictions, however, based on recent events. For instance, Apple Computer and IBM were rivals for most of the 1980s and early 1990s. But the two corporations have now joined forces to combine their expertise. Together, these industry giants hope to create a new computer—better than either Apple's "Mac" or IBM's PS/2. The product of this merger will definitely have a major effect on the world of computers.

In addition to creating a new computer, Apple and IBM are also working together to make their existing computers more compatible. If they are successful, a freer exchange of information and technology will be possible. With more people experimenting within a common format, changes and innovations will occur quickly, causing technology to grow at a phenomenal rate.

The IBM/Apple joint venture is just one event that is destined to have a long-range effect on computer technology. Today, major changes are occurring in the world of computers on a daily basis. To be sure, future generations of computers will provide us with greater capability and greater convenience—and lots of surprises!

GENERATIONS PAST AND PRESENT

Computers have changed a lot since Babbage first worked with punch cards. Each generation of computers produced a new type of machine. Here is a summary of the important milestones that distinguish one computer generation from another.

FIRST-GENERATION COMPUTERS

First-generation computers were developed in the 1940s and early 1950s. These early machines used vacuum tubes as switches, instead of mechanical gears or electromechanical relays. Computers like ENIAC and UNIVAC were very large, difficult to operate, and hard to program. Still, they were the fastest calculating machines invented up to that time.

SECOND-GENERATION COMPUTERS

Second-generation computers were much faster and more powerful than their predecessors. They used transistors instead of tubes. Transistors handle the flow of electricity like vacuum tubes, but take up much less room. They also can perform as many as a million operations per second.

The first transistor was invented in 1947. When it was perfected in the mid-1950s, it made possible a new class of computers.

THIRD-GENERATION COMPUTERS

The invention of the miniature integrated circuit (IC) in 1958 heralded the dawn of modern computer history. In the beginning, a silicon chip held only a single electronic transistor. ICs developed in the 1960s and 1970s could hold thousands of transistors and perform many functions.

COMPUTER GENERATIONS

GENERATION	DATE	TECHNOLOGY	PRODUCTS
1	1946–mid-1950s	Vacuum tubes	ENIAC, UNIVAC
2	mid-1950s–1964	Transistors	IBM System/360 DEC PDP-1
3	1964–mid-1970s	Integrated circuits	Minicomputers developed (DEC PDP-8)
4	mid-1970s–1990s	Microprocessors	Microcomputers developed (PCs, laptops, etc.)

In the 1940s, the vacuum tube colossus called ENIAC stood two stories high, and weighed 30 tons (27.2 t). Computers with integrated circuits were no larger than a small refrigerator. What's more, the new computers could accomplish the same tasks as the older vacuum-tube and transistor models, but much more quickly and cheaply.

FOURTH-GENERATION COMPUTERS

The 1970s brought us a new generation of computers. These computers were controlled by an innovative IC chip—the microprocessor. Computers with microprocessors were small enough to fit on a desktop.

Remember the enormous sizes of the Mark I and ENIAC? Imagine shrinking these two machines to the size of a pencil eraser—and imagine that eraser now being even more powerful than both of those computers combined. That's how powerful the microprocessor is in comparison to those early giants.

In reality, the microprocessor is a tiny computer. When several microprocessors are combined in the same PC, you have a very powerful machine. Because of its small size and extraordinary power, the microprocessor has made possible the world of personal computing.

C·A·R·E·E·R·S

Today's computer scientists and inventors are creating a new type of machine—the *micromachine*. Using the idea of microprocessors, inventors have developed tiny machines—smaller than the width of human hair—that are being used as "sensors" that perform a variety of tasks, including collecting information, triggering air bags in cars, and directing robots.

Are you interested in a career as a computer scientist or inventor? What inventions do you think the world will need 10 or 20 years from now?

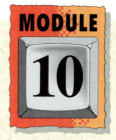

MODULE 10

MODULE SUMMARY QUESTIONS

In order to check your comprehension of the history of computers, you may wish to discuss the following ideas.

1. Which invention do you think was most important in the development of computers? Why?

2. Improvements in technology led to the invention of smaller, more efficient, and increasingly more powerful computers. Why are modern computers so much smaller than the earliest models?

3. What is meant by a "generation" of computers? Computer technology has progressed through four of these generations. Give a brief description of each.

Module 11
Ethics and Privacy

Today, millions of people use computers. This, in turn, affects millions of others. With so many people involved, the rules of computer ethics and privacy are constantly changing.

Fortunately, there are some basic, unchanging rules that we can follow to ensure that we do not violate others' rights.

In Module 11, you will learn basic guidelines for respecting others' privacy, obeying copyright laws, and protecting yourself and your computer from unethical computer users.

WHAT IS ETHICS?

"Do unto others as you would have them do unto you."
—*The Golden Rule*

"The golden rule is that there is no golden rule."
—Bernard Shaw, *Maxims for Revolutionists*

Webster's Dictionary defines *ethics* as "a set of moral principles or values." But, like the golden rule, ethics are continually being redefined in today's information society.

Technological advances in computers have made possible things that weren't even imagined 10 years ago. Although instruction manuals have taught us how to utilize this new technology, its proper moral and ethical use has been left entirely up to us. It is every individual's duty to use computers wisely and responsibly. If individuals don't act responsibly, everyone suffers.

How can one person's unethical use of a computer hurt someone else? Imagine that, one night, someone breaks into your room. The burglar goes through your diary and reads your most private thoughts. The next day at school, you walk into your classroom and see your picture on the bulletin board with all your secrets posted for everyone to see. Chances are, you wouldn't like that very much. You probably would feel that your privacy had been violated.

Somewhere in the world, during virtually any moment of the day, someone is breaking into a person's electronic "diaries," or files, and stealing secrets. Somewhere else, a person is making copies of software that someone has spent months—or years—creating. Still elsewhere, a vandal sits in front of the computer screen creating a program that can destroy your software and, possibly, your computer.

Electronic burglary—an ethical dilemma

Is it right to damage or steal another person's electronic "property"? Is it all right for someone to browse through your private files, publishing them for the world to see? Is there anything you can do about this invasion of privacy?

The answer to the last question is an emphatic "YES"! Just follow the golden rule of computing—*Do unto others' computers as you would have them do unto yours.* You wouldn't want someone to steal your property, so don't steal theirs—and that includes making illegal copies of games and programs.

If you look up to *hackers*—people who use their computer skills to break into other people's private computer systems and browse through their electronic files—imagine how you would feel if it were your files they were going through. Think it would be fun to create a program that destroys work that someone has worked on for days? Imagine having to spend a week putting your computer back together because someone had a little "fun" creating a computer *virus*—destructive code capable of damaging software or scrambling your hard drive.

The ability to use a computer can give you an edge over other people in many aspects of life, including school, business, and your career. However, this advantage brings with it certain responsibilities. It is up to you to use your computer knowledge in a way that doesn't deprive others of their rights.

The Fine Print—Who Owns the Software You Just Bought?

Fresh out of the computer store, you rush home to try out your new computer game. As you rip the shrink-wrap off the package, you barely notice the tiny writing on the disk envelopes. Without thinking, you remove the disks and toss the envelopes aside.

One by one, you insert the program's 10 disks into your disk drive, immediately making backup copies in case your original disks fail. At long last, you boot up the program. A nice graphic of the game logo pops up on the screen, but since it isn't part of the game, you basically ignore it.

In these few brief moments, you have overlooked some important information about your new software. For instance, if you had taken the time to read the fine print, you might have noticed that you really don't own the software at all. All you own is the plastic and metal that make up the disks, and the paper on which the manual is printed. The game maker owns the *copyright* on the program—and the ideas contained in it. That person (or company) has let you know this by printing on the package a © symbol, or the word "Copyright," a year, and his or her name.

When you purchase a computer program, the publisher simply grants you a license to use that product. Just because you own the disk doesn't mean you own the software. It's like a book. If you buy a copy of Robert Louis Stevenson's *Treasure Island,* you can't turn it in as your own work for an English assignment. If you did, you would be plagiarizing (stealing) and would surely receive a failing grade.

However, a failing grade is nothing compared to the trouble you could face if you duplicate software for others' use or pass it off as your own work. In fact, you could face up to $10,000 in criminal fines, a year in jail, and up to $50,000 in civil penalties for each copy you give away.

Reading important copyright information—the first step toward being a responsible computer user

185

ETHICS AND PRIVACY

The Fine Print—Who Owns the Software You Just Bought?

But, don't panic. The key phrase here is "for every copy you give away." Simply backing up your disks isn't illegal. Under the Copyright Act of 1976, the United States Congress included a *fair use* provision that allows you to make a copy of software as long as it is strictly for backup purposes in the event of media failure. In other words, you can make a backup copy for yourself, but you can't give the program to your friends.

There are basically four different types of software—and it might be a good idea to become familiar with them so you don't use them illegally. *Commercial* products are copyrighted and are purchased from a software store, mail-order house, or computer dealer. They include full documentation and usually offer some technical-support telephone numbers. *Shareware* programs are copyrighted, but allow you to try them out before buying them from the author. If you like a program, you send money; if you don't, you erase it from your disks.

The remaining two types of software don't cost you a thing. *Freeware* programs, such as James W. Walker's *PrintAid*, are copyrighted and distributed freely in the hope that someone will find them useful. *Public-domain software* is not copyrighted, and is usually basic, functional software that is used almost universally. This is given away freely because most people already own it, in some capacity, anyway. This type of software has been common in the past, but authors like to protect their work, so few of today's computer programs are released into the public domain.

When using a copyrighted program, you are usually required to abide by the terms of a special license. Licenses generally spell out what you can and can't do with a program. When you open an envelope containing computer disks, you agree to abide by the rules of the license printed on it.

Some licenses grant you the right to copy software onto a single computer. Anyone who wishes to use the program must use that computer. A single-user license may give you the right to copy the program to other computers, but the program can be used only by you. Both of these types of licenses are designed to protect the copyright owner from having his or her program illegally duplicated. Since you only bought one copy of the program, you can only use one copy at any given time.

Some licenses are less restrictive, however. A site license allows software to be used by anyone on any computer at a given site or location. Your school may have a site license for programs used on school computers. A network license allows a program to be networked to a number of computers through a central file server. One of the main benefits of site and network licenses is that they are generally less expensive to purchase than several individual copies of the program.

However, even with the availability of licenses, some people continue to copy and use disks illegally.

You MAKE A DIFFERENCE

When he was just 17 years old, Ray Lau, an Asian American, was exchanging large amounts of data with a friend using modems.

Seeking a way to speed up the transfer of files, Lau wrote the program *StuffIt*, which compresses computer files by more than 50 percent. As a shareware program, *StuffIt* became the most popular file compression utility for the Macintosh. It was eventually sold to Aladin software, and has accumulated more than 100,000 users over time.

MODULE 11

The Fine Print—Who Owns the Software You Just Bought?

Toll-free help lines—personal assistance for computer users

Therefore, some publishers have added hidden codes to their software to force users to comply. For instance, only one copy of a program with serial number 12345 can be used on a network at one time. If a network license of the program is purchased, the serial number is removed and the disk can then be copied for other users.

Two similar coding schemes are *copy protection* and password protection. Copy protection requires you to have the original disk handy to run a program. Password protection requires you to use the manual to answer certain questions before you can run a program. Both have been used by publishers to deter users from distributing unauthorized copies of software. However, their use has dwindled in recent years.

With all of these rules and regulations, you may think that software users are the only ones who have to practice ethical conduct. This is far from true! The people who provide the software that you purchase also must act responsibly.

Included in the fine print of most software licenses are warranty statements that explain a publisher's duty to you, the user of the program. The warranty may say that the product will perform the functions that the written materials say it will. If you get a bad disk, the company will usually replace it within 90 days or some other period of time after purchase.

Many companies try to place major limits on their responsibilities to you, however. If a product causes your computer to go up in smoke, the

ETHICS AND PRIVACY

company might not willingly pay for the disaster—even if their program was directly responsible. The good news is that the company has probably spent months or years perfecting the program so that nothing too outrageous happens. In any event, most warranties limit the amount of damages you can claim. Usually, the maximum is a refund of the purchase price or the cost of repairing or replacing the software.

There are exceptions to this limit, however. Your state may have a law that prevents companies from excluding or limiting warranties. For example, the company may have to extend your refund period beyond the standard 90 days, or it may have to replace any computer hardware that has been damaged by its program.

Once you get a software package home, you need to be able to figure out how to make it perform all of the functions that it has been programmed to perform. Otherwise, you will have wasted your money. Unfortunately, many people fail to consider whether or not the software manufacturer provides any help in this area. A good rule of thumb is to buy products from companies that have strong technical-support programs that help consumers figure out how to use their programs. Many offer toll-free services that allow you to call and ask questions without running up a huge phone bill.

Good software companies also improve and enhance their products over time. Therefore, it's a good idea to purchase software from companies that offer free minor upgrades and reasonably priced major upgrades. Although these upgrades are usually limited to 90 days or a year from the date of purchase, they can save you a lot of money. Without them, you will need to purchase a whole new program every time the company adds features or eliminates bugs. By looking for liberal upgrade policies, you don't end up paying companies to fix bad products.

As the software industry has matured, publishers have realized that responsible conduct keeps their customers happy. In turn, happy customers come back to that company for newer and better products. As the consumer, you have both the responsibilities of using software ethically and seeking out software companies who practice good ethics. Remember, you have the power of the pocketbook—use it wisely!

COMPUTERS THEN & NOW

After passing copyright laws in 1909, Congress did not revise or expand them for more than 65 years!

By the time lawmakers passed the Copyright Act of 1976, the world had changed dramatically.

Between 1909 and 1976, radio, television, and photocopying machines were all invented, allowing original material to be seen and used by others. New copyright laws were desperately needed.

Similarly, the invention of the personal computer and the fax machine has brought even more demands on copyright laws since 1976. No doubt, lawmakers have their work cut out for them as they change the copyright rules of the future to meet our ever-changing needs.

READ ALL ABOUT IT

From the pages of *Computerworld*
June 17, 1991
By Michael Fitzgerald

Open Up—This Is the Software Police!

Using copyrighted software illegally—an act that can result in federal prosecution

One day last March, Snap-on Tools Corp. Chairman Marion Gregory completed an afternoon meeting and walked into the lobby of the firm's headquarters.

Gregory stopped dead in his tracks at the sight of three armed federal marshals and four other somber-looking men appeared ready to do battle with drug lords.

The stunned Gregory asked Snap-on's internal legal counsel who the visitors were.

"The Software Publishers Association," the counsel said.

The experience following was painful for Snap-on as the SPA conducted a full-scale audit of Snap-on's personal computers, looking for pirated software.

"It was a pretty grim couple of days," said a Snap-on spokesman, who related the Gregory story. During a 2½-week period, Snap-on's internal auditors joined its microcomputer managers and other departments to dig out purchase orders, invoices and manuals that proved Snap-on had paid for all of its software.

Ultimately, the SPA recanted its charge against the Fortune 500 company. But many

Continued on next page

Read All About It

of the approximately 70 companies that have been raided by the SPA end up paying thousands of dollars in fines.

Users who have been through an SPA raid say the experience is alarming. Representatives generally announce themselves to the top executive in the firm and ask that all work being done on personal computers at the time be stopped immediately.

"They adamantly requested an on-site inspection of the software, and we had two choices: We could either cooperate, or they would line people up against the wall and go look at the computers that way," said a source at a New York publishing firm that was raided by the SPA early last year.

Users added that SPA representatives have dealt with them fairly, and many said that in the end, they were relieved that the raid had forced company management to take piracy seriously.

"It was a company policy to distribute software freely and have only one license copy," said Michael Fitzpatrick, computer technician

Did You Know?

Did you know that the Software Publishers Association only performs a surprise raid when it appears unlikely that a company will cooperate in an investigation? In fact, SPA representatives spend much of their time working with businesses to help them obtain licenses and avoid breaking the law.

As a result of the SPA's work, software piracy is now being reported more often, which results in a decrease in the crime. Many companies even call the SPA's "Anti-piracy Hotline" to ask for help with their own piracy problems.

If you would like to know more about the SPA, or would like to receive free literature about the legal and illegal use of software, call the Anti-piracy Hotline at 1-800-388-PIR8 (1-800-388-7478).

Keeping detailed records of software and license purchases to prove legal ownership

Continued on next page

★ READ ALL ABOUT IT ★

at Versatron Corp., an aerospace design firm in Healdsburg, Calif. Fitzpatrick said he disagreed with the policy and had recommended to company management that they license all pirated software.

ANYONE LISTENING?

The recommendations fell on deaf ears, and Versatron was raided last December by a team of seven federal marshals and SPA representatives.

Paying the price for software piracy

The auditors strode in and told Versatron employees to save their work and immediately step away from their PCs. They then audited each of the company's 30 PCs, a process that took most of the day.

"They were real hard-nosed when they came in," Fitzpatrick said. "They weren't rude, but they were certainly pushy. After a couple of hours, when they saw we weren't trying to cover up, they lightened up."

Versatron ended up paying a $60,000 fine and was required to buy copies of Autodesk, Inc.'s Autocad, Lotus Development Corp.'s 1-2-3 and Manuscript, Ashton-Tate Corp.'s dBASE, and other software at full retail price. Fitzpatrick said he has no regrets that the SPA raided his firm. "I'm glad they did," he said.

During a raid, federal marshals watch as SPA representatives check each hard drive using an SPA product called Spaudit [CW, Dec. 10, 1990]. They print out lists of the .EXE files on each hard drive.

Then the SPA puts together a list of its findings and challenges the company to prove that it owns the software on its hard drives. "We do our best to work with management under the circumstances," an SPA spokeswoman said. "We are not there to be disruptive or adversarial in any way."

No hardware or software is impounded or restricted—although a suit is filed against the company accusing it of violating copyright laws, and an injunction is installed that forbids the company from removing programs from its hard drives or erasing the drives.

Not all of those contacted by *Computerworld* said they knew their companies were violating copyright laws, but several said they did. Fitzpatrick said his board of directors had even asked him what he thought the chances were of being raided. "I gave it a one-in-10 chance," he said. ■

FOCUSING ON INFORMATION, ACCURACY, AND PRIVACY

Computer information has evolved from simple bits and bytes into a mass of information about virtually every person in America. This explosion in electronic information has brought with it new moral and ethical responsibilities for all computer users.

Gaining access to personal records through a social security number

You may be surprised to know that, somewhere, someone has access to detailed files about you. These files have been stored away in a computer database, ready to call up at a second's notice. People rely on these files to make judgments and decisions about you. Since the contents of these files can have such a dramatic impact on your life, you can see that it is important to control the accuracy of the information and the number of people who have access to it.

Your entry into computerized files may have begun as early as the day your parent or guardian applied for your social security number. The information on that application was entered into a file that will follow you the rest of your life.

When you are paid for working, the government takes part of that pay in the form of taxes. Your social security number allows the IRS to keep a computerized record of all the money you have earned and how much of it you owe to them. Allowing this detailed financial information to fall into the wrong hands could prove disastrous for you. Therefore, the IRS has a huge ethical responsibility to ensure that this doesn't happen.

At school, your grades and attendance records are probably kept in a computer database. If you miss a day of class, the principal can call up your records and see exactly how many days you have been absent. When you receive a grade on a test, the teacher may enter it into a computer so he or she can calculate grades at the end of the semester.

The school takes ethical responsibility for these records—and that's probably why you can't access them! Barring all students from the database helps ensure that some prankster will not enter the file and change your grades to "F"s.

But altering information isn't the only unethical use of computerized information. Simply reading a private file can be unethical. This is often true of medical records. Your doctor probably has detailed, computerized information about each time you have visited his or her office. This file lists the nature of your visit, any ailments, and any medications or treatments that were prescribed.

It is unethical for your doctor to allow others to read your medical records without your permission. History has shown that revealing this kind of information can result in job discrimination and other unfair practices. Therefore, it is standard practice for doctors to keep your records confidential unless you request that they be forwarded to another doctor, a health insurance agency, or some other third party.

You must also grant permission for a third party to read your credit report. A credit report is a record of how you pay every bill—whether it was paid in full, partially paid, paid late, or not paid at

Focusing on Information, Accuracy, and Privacy

C·A·R·E·E·R·S

SALESPERSON · ELECTRICIAN · ASTRONAUT · MECHANIC · ENGINEER · PHYSICIST · DENTIST · FARMER · NURSE · DOCTOR · TEACHER · SURGEON · OPTOMETRIST · PILOT · PROFESSOR · SECRETARY · ARTIST

For an interesting career, you may want to consider a job in computer security. With the public's increased ability to access private electronic files, the market for computer security professionals is growing every day!

Many firms in this country offer security consulting and other services to help companies keep hackers out of their private information. Some companies spend in excess of $1 million annually for these services.

On the other hand, many companies are finding that the best way to ensure confidentiality is by making sure their employees are well trained. This could lead to a boom in security training careers throughout the 1990s.

Certain other personal records are not private, however. The information can be accessed by a number of different people who can use it in ways that directly affect your life.

For example, when you get your driver's license, several items about you are entered into a database. These include your date of birth, height, weight, eye color, and social security number. Later, any traffic tickets you receive or accidents you are involved in become part of your driving record. If you are pulled over for a traffic violation, a police officer will check this information to see if you have any unpaid tickets, an invalid license, or any other signs of illegal conduct. Insurance companies also use this information to decide what kind of driver you are and to assign a risk factor that determines how much you pay for insurance.

The fact that insurance companies and others can tap into this type of personal information brings up a question of ethics. Is your information strictly your own property? How can you keep unauthorized parties from gaining access? The computer age has made it hard to answer these questions.

all. When you apply for a loan or a credit card, you sign a form that permits banks and others to use your social security number to review your credit report. If your record is good and your income is sufficient, you'll probably get the loan; if not, you'll be turned down as a "bad risk"—which will also be noted on your credit report.

Calling in a driver's license number to check for possible violations

ETHICS AND PRIVACY

Before computers, records were kept on paper in filing cabinets. Once a record was filed, it might never be looked at again unless a problem arose. Then, it was pulled from the file and viewed by someone at that location who was specifically authorized to look at it. Today, however, computers and modems make it possible to access computerized records from virtually anywhere in the world. In some cases, all it takes is a touch-tone phone.

Password protection can limit access to computer databases, but information thieves often break these codes and access files without anyone knowing it. Because these files can contain credit card numbers and other vital information, breaking into other people's computer records is illegal—and punishable by a prison sentence.

Today, many records are originally entered into a computer with no written record kept anywhere. Some paper records, such as income tax returns, are transferred to microfilm before being destroyed. But in many cases, once a written record is entered into a computer, no proof of the original is kept. If you discover that information has been entered inaccurately, it may be difficult for you to prove it. So, it is always smart to keep your own paper records, such as cancelled checks, as a backup.

In many instances, we may not even know that our records are being kept in a computer. Unfortunately, there is no law stating that you must be notified before some information about you is given or sold to someone else. In fact, some companies make a living by selling people's information to others. Publishers of magazines can sell your name and address to other publishers who will bury you in an avalanche of what they call "direct-mail marketing;" you know it as "junk mail." You can protect your privacy, however. Just send a letter to the publisher stating that you don't want your information included on any lists they sell or give to anyone else. It is their ethical responsibility to honor your request.

In 1989, Lotus Development Corporation announced plans to market a CD-ROM product called *Lotus Marketplace* that would have listed personal information—including name, address, sex, and race—for more than 120 million Americans. It would have put within reach of small businesses something that large corporations have had for years: targeted direct-mail marketing. Although *Marketplace* did not include individual incomes and buying habits by name in its data, it did match income levels with specific zip codes to help businesses plan mass mailings to target groups.

Instead of an overwhelming demand for the product, Lotus received 30,000 phone calls and hundreds of pieces of electronic mail opposing its release. In addition, the Computer Professionals for Social Responsibility objected to the fact that some of the information on the CD-ROM came from credit agencies. In other words, your private credit information could be read by anyone with a copy of the program.

Direct-mail marketing—an effective tool or an invasion of privacy

Focusing on Information, Accuracy, and Privacy

After sinking an estimated $10 million into the project, Lotus finally dropped *Marketplace* in February 1991. Consumers triumphed in protecting their fundamental right to privacy.

Besides the issue of privacy, many people are concerned about the accuracy of computerized personal records. With so much information being gathered in the 1990s, it is inevitable that some of it will contain errors. If a teller accidentally enters $1 instead of $1,000 when recording your latest bank deposit, you can be negatively affected. Likewise, if a store's computer breaks down and erases the record of payments you have made on a new CD player, you may be in for more negative effects. Whether they are due to human or computer error, inaccuracies such as these occur all the time.

But, who is responsible for catching these errors and seeing that they are corrected? Ultimately, the burden is on you to prove that computer records are wrong. You may have to fight through a bureaucracy to clear your name, but if you don't, bad information can haunt you forever. Inaccurate computer files can affect your ability to buy a home, get insurance, or even apply for a job. Therefore, you should keep track of any information that you know about that is kept in computer files. If you don't want certain information made public, don't be afraid to make that known to whomever owns the computer file.

At some point in your life, you may also handle other people's computer records, such as employment applications, mailing lists, and other personal data. Treat this information as if it were your own.

Maintaining the accuracy and privacy of a personnel file

As an employee or business owner, you have a responsibility to your company and to the people you deal with to maintain accurate records. If someone comes to you and tells you that there is an error, find out the right information and correct the computer file. Remember, the three most important points in dealing with computerized information are accuracy, accuracy, and accuracy.

You also have a responsibility to use information ethically. If friends call and want to find out how much someone in the word-processing department is being paid, tell them that the information is confidential and, if they really want to know, they will have to ask that person. Never, never give out information about someone without that person's permission.

Also, never use private information for a purpose that isn't part of your job. If you are an employee, the people you work for own anything you do on their time. Therefore, using company information for personal purposes is theft, which can lead to criminal or civil prosecution.

Whether you deal with an individual's computer file or a company's confidential information, you must always treat it with the special care it deserves. If you practice sound judgment in your own dealings and try to influence others to do the same, you will be a valuable resource to both your employer and the people whose files you control. In addition, your personal effort will help promote ethics and accuracy in the field of computerized information—and that's a worthwhile goal!

Help! My Computer Has Chicken Pox!

If you've been around computers for even a short amount of time, you've probably heard about viruses. Viruses are destructive codes that spread from computer to computer, capable of damaging software and "killing" computers.

Eighteen-year-old Brad Alexander had heard of viruses, but he thought he'd never see one first-hand. A recent trip to a computer fair changed his mind. To make others aware of these destructive codes, Brad wrote a report for his computer-programming class. You may want to read his report to learn how you can keep your computer healthy and virus-free.

Eliminating a virus before other computers are infected

Last weekend, I attended a local computer fair to get a look at some of the new products available for my Macintosh computer. While I was there, someone gave me a disk containing some freeware and shareware programs to try out. I took the disk home and copied it to my hard drive. After looking at the programs, I took them off my hard drive and promptly forgot about them.

I didn't forget about them for long, though. About a week later, my Macintosh suddenly started acting up. Every time I launched a program, a little picture of a bomb would appear on my screen and the computer would ask me if I wanted to restart. Frustrated, I started thinking that my hard drive might be in need of major repairs. Then, I remembered the public-domain software that I had gotten from the fair.

I immediately called a friend and got a copy of her old virus-detection program. Booting from a floppy disk, the program examined my hard drive looking for one of the handful of Mac viruses that it could recognize. Before long, my computer screen flashed a message: I had been infected by the *Scores* virus! Fortunately, it didn't destroy any of my data files; only my programs. After I ran a program called *KillScores,* it took me a full week to recover from the "infection." I also had to completely back up and reinitialize, or reset, my hard drive—at least a full day's work.

Needless to say, I learned a hard lesson about putting a free disk in my computer without checking it for viruses first. But the incident also made me want to find out more about computer viruses.

Probably the first virus was *Creeper,* written by Bob Thomas. It was first sighted in 1970 and was designed to move through a nationwide network of university, military, and corporate computers, showing up with the message, "I'm the Creeper, catch me if you can!" Unlike most modern viruses, we actually know the name of the author of *Creeper,* who wrote it as a demonstration program.

Over the years, viruses have appeared on nearly every type of computer. Some have had interesting names—such as *Rabbit, Pervading Animal,* and *Elk Cloner*—but all were created to cause trouble for you and your computer.

As I read more, I found out that computer viruses are usually designed to seek out bits of code in programs and attach themselves so that when a program or file is accessed, the virus does its work and spreads. However, computer vandals have had a lot of imagination over the years, so they have created a number of viruses that do damage in different ways.

For example, some viruses don't spread from file to file and disk to disk at all. These codes, called *Trojan horses,* are contained on a disk that looks just like a regular shareware or freeware program. When you remove the disk, the virus leaves without spreading. While it is in the computer, though, a Trojan horse can erase or scramble your files. It may even tell you that your hard disk is being erased! Once you see this message, there's nothing you can do but hope you have a backup.

Worms, on the other hand, are simple bits of code whose sole purpose is to stay alive by eating memory and traveling from computer to computer. A worm can travel around gathering information, such as passwords or private documents, and then cover its tracks so that you don't even know it's been there.

Some viruses are designed to be triggered by a specific event. Called *bombs,* these viruses can lie dormant for days or even months before they do their dirty work. *Software bombs* "explode" and scramble data when a program is launched. *Logic bombs* wait for you to do something—like delete a certain file—before they hit. A *Time bomb* simply waits for something to happen a certain number of times or for a specific date or time to roll around.

With so many viruses out there, you can almost count on coming into contact with one at some point. Believe me—I know! But don't panic. I found out that there are two things you can do to safeguard your computer against the work of a mischievous programmer.

First, avoid using any program whose origin is in doubt. Most electronic services, such as *CompuServe, Genie,* and others, check files for viruses before making them public. However, a new virus may escape detection. Don't be the first to download a file. Wait a few days and see if others experience problems.

Also, don't just accept a disk blindly—like I did at the computer fair—assuming that it is virus-free. Scan it with a virus-protection program before using it in your computer. I got *Disinfectant,* for my Macintosh. *Disinfectant* is a freeware program written by John Norstad that can scan disks and repair damaged files.

Besides these few precautions, you can also join a computer-users group or read computer magazines to find out about the latest viruses. Remember, the more you know what to look for, the better prepared you'll be to ward off viruses and keep your computer healthy!

MULTICULTURAL BYTE

In August 1991, more than 90 businesses in a province bordering Hong Kong were hit by 20 different computer viruses. This epidemic caused a major setback in the production of software in that particular area of China.

Analysts attributed the epidemic to the large amount of computer software that had been pirated from Hong Kong and other places. With everyone copying everyone else's programs, the viruses were able to spread freely, jeopardizing the productivity of an entire business community.

ETHICS AND PRIVACY

HOW TO BE A RESPONSIBLE COMPUTING CITIZEN

In the good old days, when you mainly used your computer to play games, you didn't have to worry much about other people or their computers.

However, your level of responsibility will likely change as you learn to interact with other computer users. Whether you come into contact with others over a local-area network (LAN) or an on-line bulletin-board system (BBS), you'll find that the rules will become a bit more complicated.

It's not unlike the days before you started school. Aside from following a few rules in your household, about the only person you really had to please was yourself. Then, when you started school, you came in contact with other children and learned that some things that were fine at home weren't acceptable in public.

Just as some things are unacceptable in society, the computer community has its own set of rules and regulations that you must adapt to. Fortunately, most of these rules are based on everyday common sense.

Common sense usually tells you that there's a right way of doing things and a wrong way. Unfortunately, some people insist on doing things the wrong way. The news is filled with hackers, virus programmers, computer vandals, and thieves who have been arrested and are facing fines and prison sentences.

Who are these people, you ask? Generally, they are people who act unethically, refusing to obey laws and general rules of computer courtesy. For instance, some hackers say their ethic is that it's OK to search, but not destroy. However, tampering with someone's system in any way might destroy months of work or cause a system crash—or total hard-drive failure. This is why the law defines unauthorized access as trespassing—even theft in some cases.

In May 1990, Secret Service agents served search warrants in several different cities in the US, confiscating 40 computers and over 23,000 illegal disks from hackers. This network of hackers

Showing courtesy and respect for other computer users

was suspected of trading stolen credit-card numbers and long-distance phone cards. The hackers also traded information on how to break into mainframe computers around the country. Though only a few arrests were made, the crackdown let hackers know that their crimes would not be tolerated.

Several publications have featured articles on Samurai hackers—computer wizards that are hired by companies to infiltrate competitors' and employees' files. Sometimes these actions are technically legal; sometimes they are illegal—but they are always most unethical. One of these cases involved a hacker who was hired by a Republican Party official in New Jersey to break into Democratic Party computers and steal their campaign strategies. *Rolling Stone* called this case, "Watergate on silicon," but in reality, it was just petty theft by computer.

Regardless of whether a person browses through other people's private files as a hobby or is hired by someone else to do the job, hacking is usually illegal and always wrong. No one should become an illegal hacker when there are better ways to make a living. In short, accessing, viewing, destroying, or stealing private computer information is wrong.

So, now that we've examined the wrong way to use a computer, let's take a look at the right way. One right way is to help others overcome the same hurdles you faced when learning to use the computer. Offer the benefit of your experience and remember that, at one time, you didn't know what a "monitor" or a "diskette" was, either.

Above all, don't be afraid to try. You may not realize it, but you probably already know enough about computers to help someone else learn. If a person has a computer question that you can't answer, don't worry about it. Just try to direct him or her to someone who might know the answer. By the same token, if you have a computer question, don't be afraid to ask for help. After all, that's the way friendships get started.

MODULE 11

MODULE SUMMARY QUESTIONS

In order to check your comprehension of computer ethics, you may wish to discuss the following ideas:

1. There is a mass of information stored in computers on different areas of peoples' lives. Where are some places that information about you and your family might be recorded in a computer? What are the responsibilities of those who keep this information? How can you ensure the accuracy of this information?

2. Who owns the software programs that you buy in the stores? Describe the four types of software.

3. What is a computer virus? How can your computer catch one? What can you do to prevent your computer from getting a virus?

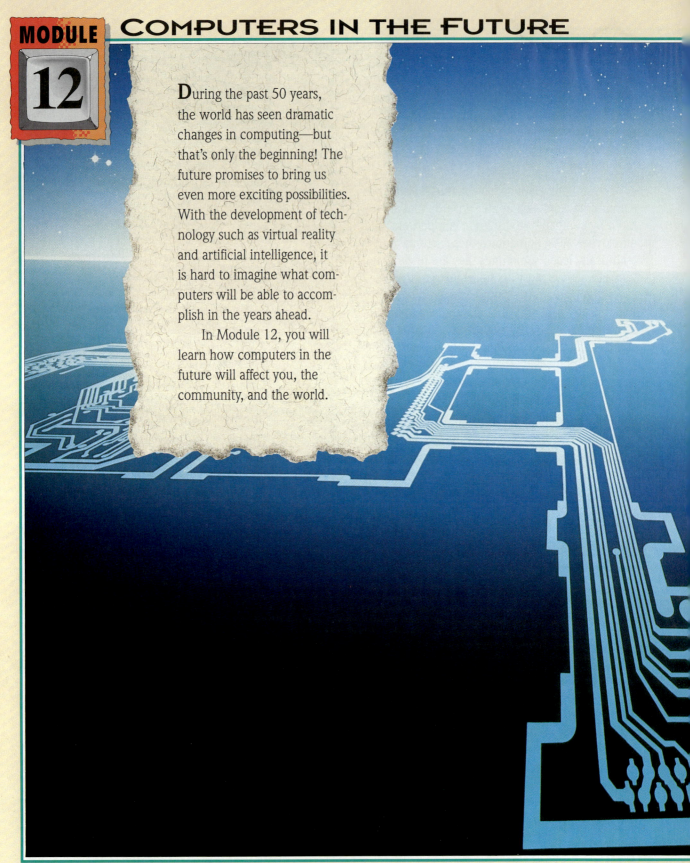

MODULE 12
Computers in the Future

During the past 50 years, the world has seen dramatic changes in computing—but that's only the beginning! The future promises to bring us even more exciting possibilities. With the development of technology such as virtual reality and artificial intelligence, it is hard to imagine what computers will be able to accomplish in the years ahead.

In Module 12, you will learn how computers in the future will affect you, the community, and the world.

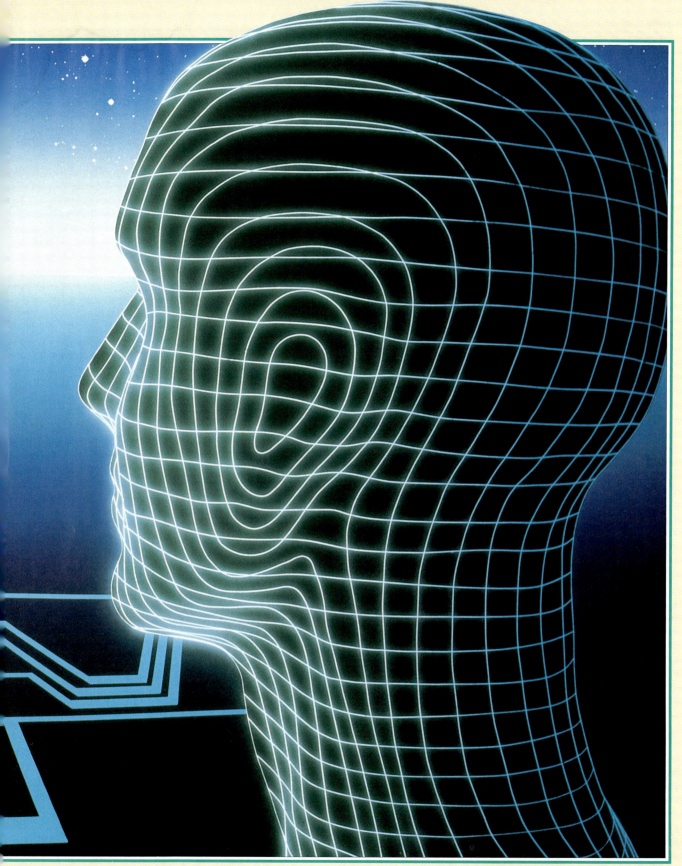

LOOKING INTO THE FUTURE

It was not until the mid- to late 1970s that people began using computer technology in their everyday lives. It was during that time that computers became small enough to fit onto an ordinary desk and more affordable to purchase. Today, over 50 million personal computers help people at home and at work. Every year, millions of computers are put into more of the items that we use most, such as cars, televisions, telephones, and microwave ovens.

You are living in a computer revolution. Computer use continues to grow rapidly and computer technology is changing daily. Some experts predict that, before the end of the 1990s, personal computers will become desktop *supercomputers*. Supercomputers are extremely powerful computers that can manipulate billions of commands per second. Tomorrow, desktop supercomputers may be as common as microwave ovens, resulting in changes in the way people learn, work, and entertain themselves.

Not only have there been significant advances in the technology of computers but also in the technology of networks. Networks are able to connect people in various buildings and communities, and millions of miles of fiber-optic glass fibers transmit most long-distance communications at a rate of up to a billion bits per second. The combination of improved computers and networks will increasingly affect how we interact with our co-workers, our neighbors, and people around the world.

Imagine the year 2020. How do you see computer technology affecting your life? How do you think computers will change people's jobs and lives in your community? What kinds of changes do you predict will happen in the world? In this module, you will explore how the continual growth of computer technology will impact individuals, their communities, and the world.

Using fiber-optic cables to transmit information with speed and clarity

COMPUTERS & YOU

The way we live in our homes, how we look, and how we perform tasks, such as paying bills, will be different in the future from what we know now. Read on to find out what the future may hold for you!

LIVING IN "SMART HOUSES"

Computers make it possible to program your house to complement your lifestyle. A *smart house* can be wired to automatically turn lights on and off, lock and unlock doors, control temperature, and so on. You can computerize a house to have the coffee pot turn on, lights go on, windows open up to let the fresh morning air in, and the television turn on the morning news—all before you even get out of bed! Appliances will also be computerized to become "smart machines." For example, vacuum cleaners will be programmed to vacuum on a regular basis.

One new technology being developed for smart houses—the coded house key—will benefit both working parents and their children. When a child comes home from school and unlocks the door with a specially coded key, a parent's work phone is triggered. A recorded message then notifies the parent that the child has arrived home.

Designing Houses Have you ever wondered what your house would look like if you changed the design? For example, what if you had a sliding glass door in your living room that led out to a deck that overlooked a pool in the backyard? The new age of computers will let home owners and prospective home buyers view a computer screen to see how a house's appearance can change.

COMPUTERS THEN & NOW

When computers were first being used in the 1940s and 1950s it was only people such as scientists and mathematicians who operated computers. Then, 30 years later, people regularly began to use computers at home and at work.

Now, computers are being developed that allow physically disabled people to take advantage of computer technology. For instance, there is a computer for the blind and visually impaired that has a braille keyboard and voice synthesizer that reads the text aloud.

Another kind of computer allows the physically disabled to control their environment through their personal computer. The screen is designed to look like the user's home or office. The user, for instance, clicks on the telephone icon to make a call and the telecommunications mode displays the user's personal phone list. The user clicks on the correct phone number and the computer dials the number. Computer companies are looking for future ways to develop systems to make everyday living easier for all of us.

COMPUTERS IN THE FUTURE

Computers can also help builders determine the most cost-efficient way to construct a house. A company in Atlanta already sells the hardware and software to design detailed drawings and to analyze materials to decrease costs and wasted materials.

SEEING IS BELIEVING

Have you ever wondered what you would look like with blue eyes, a smaller nose, freckles, or shorter hair? Thanks to computer imaging, you can experiment with your looks without making actual changes to yourself. Here's how it works. A video scanner *digitizes* the images, or converts the lines and shades into electronic digits (0s and 1s). The computer rearranges the digits by increasing or decreasing their values to alter the image. By touching an electronic slate with a high-tech pen, parts of the image can be erased, moved, changed, or added to as quickly as it took you

MULTI CULTURAL BYTE

In Japan, bar codes (labels with lines and numbers that are scanned by a computer for product identification) are being used to pay bills and to eliminate carrying cash. Customers of Tokyo Electric Power and Tokyo Gas can pay their bills at convenience stores. There, cashiers scan the bar codes that appear on the customer's bill. The scanner sends a message to the store's computer and then to the utility company's computer indicating that the customer has paid.

Bar codes also can eliminate the need to carry cash. For instance, many Japanese people find it inconvenient to carry cash with them when they go to health clubs. So, some clubs offer their members bar-coded identification wristbands to use for charging food and drinks. When leaving the club, the member returns the wristband and a computer calculates the bill.

Trying out a new look through computer imaging

Computers & You

Videophones—adding a personal touch to everyday communication

to read this sentence. Sections from other photos also can be placed on top of the original image. For example, if, while flipping through a magazine, you find a photograph of a haircut you admire, it is possible to use the computer to see exactly what that style would look like on you.

The computer also has a palette of millions of different colors and shades. The computer could even show you what your hair would look like if it were a different color. The beauty of this technology is that the altered images can be printed out and saved in the computer's memory.

SEEING TELEPHONES

Telephones that show you a still picture of the caller and show the caller a still picture of you are not new inventions. The picture telephone was first introduced at the 1964 New York World's Fair by American Telegraph & Telephone (AT&T). These telephones were sold for $8,000 at that time. About two decades later, Sony reintroduced its version of a videotelephone and, seven years later, Mitsubishi did the same. These videotelephones were not particularly popular. They were thought to be too costly for providing only a black-and-white still image.

In 1992, AT&T introduced a new and improved seeing telephone—the VideoPhone. The VideoPhone differed from the original picture telephone because it offered moving images in color. However, the image's movement was not continuous like the images seen on television. This videophone could transmit its signals over copper lines—and the rates to use it cost no more than the phone call itself. The cost of AT&T's VideoPhone was $1,500. But, as with all videophones, both the caller and the person being called must have the equipment to show and receive images. It is believed that, in 10 years, videophones will be as popular as cordless and cellular phones are today.

COMPUTERS IN THE FUTURE

Computers & the Community

Computers & the Community

The revolution of computers will bring many changes to the structure of communities. Computers will change the way people work and learn at school. The sections below and on the following pages tell you how computers may make a difference in your community in the future.

ACCESSING INFORMATION

It is predicted that, in the future, most people will have access to incredible amounts of information. Information networks will become a structured part of most communities. Just as community members now have access to network systems such as highways, telephone lines, and electric power lines, they will soon have access to information networks.

An essential part of setting up an information network is making the information available to everyone. Resources, such as phone directories, government tax codes, census data, and the millions of books in the Library of Congress, will easily be accessible to anyone.

Telephone companies and other network builders are now laying down fiber-optic lines that will allow users thousands of times more information than the copper wires that are being replaced. In the future, *gigabit* networks (networks capable of conveying a billion bits of information per second) will allow people to send and receive video images over these fiber-optic lines. The fiber optics will allow the images to be reproduced with amazing clarity.

★ READ ALL ABOUT IT ★

From *The Dallas Morning News*
August 25, 1991
By Tom Steinert-Threlkeld

Dressing for Tech-cess

Laptop and notebook computers are all the rage. Notepad computers that can be written on seem poised for takeoff. Yet pocket computers have never taken off. Users often are turned off by keys that are too small for the tips of their fingers.

Does that mean personal computers are approaching the lower limits of miniaturization and portability?

Hardly. Scientists from AT&T Bell Laboratories to NEC Corp.'s design studios in Tokyo envision a not-too-distant future where humans wear the computers they use.

"It's not that far off," said Arno Penzias, the Nobel Prize-winning vice president of research at Bell Labs. He sees the boundaries between communications and computing crumbling so fast in the next 10 to 15 years that it will be commonplace for people to be wearing microphones and videocameras that can connect them to almost anyone or any computer in the world.

"I suspect that a platinum microphone collar-bar will make a nice present for the 21st century yuppie who has everything," he said, in remarks prepared for a talk at the Infomart in Dallas. "Since we can build them into anything—broaches, tie pins, earrings—the trick will be to wear enough of these things in various locations on the body."

Part of the electronically steered array of microphones would stay trained on the wearer's lips, to record what is said.

Continued on next page

Computers & the Community

★ Read All About It ★

Wearable computers being developed by NEC Corp., including (from left) a wearable data terminal, waist-position terminal, video camera, PC, porta-office, PC, breathing information monitor, and TLC PC.

Others would aim at wherever the wearer's eyes are looking, in case a conversation is being carried on, adding a person to the "line" instantly, if wanted.

An unobtrusive earphone handles incoming sound. Tiny cameras are mounted on the frames of eyeglasses, for video.

All these wireless devices generate enough signals to reach a hip-pocket transceiver. The precursor of such transceivers is the cellular telephone, notes Mr. Penzias. Already Motorola Inc., Fujitsu Ltd. and other vendors provide half-pound phones of that size, purely for voices.

Across the Pacific, a team of engineers at NEC's Design Center in Tokyo have been working for four years on prototypes of wearable computers.

There are "no preconceptions" about how those computers should look or work, except that whatever is developed should be "what is comfortable for humans" to wear, designing supervisor Hideji Takemasa said.

As described by NEC and reported in *NeoJapan*, a journal that tracks emerging technologies, the prototypes include:

- A wearable data terminal. An optical sensor is located near the left hand. On the left forearm is a variety of touch sensors. A collar worn around the neck positions a screen on the chest. A compact disc reader stores data for reference. Clerks in factories, warehouses, retail shops and the like might use them to count inventory, as improvements upon current handheld terminals. "It will make it easy for walking in the storehouse," said Mr. Takemasa.
- A "tender loving care" computer. NEC's "TLC PC" is a response to Japan's critical shortage of doctors and information to help medics save patients en route to hospitals in its congested cities, said Mr. Takemasa.

Medics would wear a trackball in one hand that acts as a sensor to check vital signs of a patient at an accident scene. The ball includes a video sensor and spotlight to visually record injuries. Other sensors record the body's temperature, pressure, and heartbeat. The medic sees the video images and vital signs in the eyeglasses he or she wears.

Continued on next page

COMPUTERS IN THE FUTURE

Read All About It

The medic talks into a microphone describing the patient's condition, the injuries and vital signs are matched against information in a medical encyclopedia, stored on compact disc. The information also can be transmitted to a physician at a hospital, for further diagnosis and recommendations.

- The lapbody computer. This is "close to a real product," Mr Takemasa said. This is kind of a laptop computer with an outgrowth. The computer is worn like a purse. When needed, it swings around and folds out. The keyboard and screen stick out from the stomach. This presumably is ideal for sports writers, who want to prowl the sidelines and type at the same time.
- The porta-office. The distinctive feature in this design is the tube that goes down the user's spine. The tube contains the guts of the system, allowing users to attach a wide range of office equipment to its ends, including fax machines, still cameras, speaker phones, keyboards, or what have you.

Also in the works: hands-free phones for skiers; vest and belt computers; Compute-Man devices, like personal stereos; and computers that are actually embedded in surfaces—or the human body itself, a la heart pacers.

Such "humanware" shows that "instead of designing software around hardware platforms, advanced PC designers in Japan are beginning to design computers around human activities," said Sheridan M. Tatsuno, president of NeoConcepts, an Aptos, Calif., consultancy that tracks Japanese technological advances and publishes *NeoJapan*.

The wearable computers will be designed for specific uses, such as patient care, rather than general use. But their emergence nonetheless will mean "the notion of desktop, laptop, and notebook may be made irrelevant," said Mr. Tatsuno.

CHANGING THE WAY PEOPLE WORK

Personal computers in the 1990s and in the 21st century will reshape the business world. Employees in different offices will communicate more and more by using computers. Computers will become the main form of communication rather than the telephone and the fax machine.

DID YOU KNOW?

Did you know that, in the future, employees may be wearing clip-on computers that function as identification badges? The badge, only a little larger than the size of a credit card, will contain batteries, a microprocessor, and an infrared transmitter.

Receivers placed throughout a building will make it possible to keep track of people who wear a computerized badge. The badge transmits the wearer's identity and will open automatic doors and forward telephone calls. Rooms will also greet badge wearers by name.

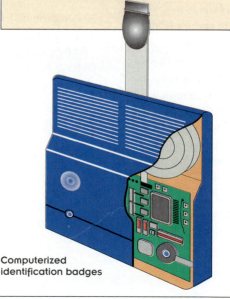

Computerized identification badges

As using the computer to interact with co-workers increases, the workplace for many employees will undergo changes. People who have careers such as computer programming, engineering, stock and bond trading, writing, artistry, composing, and accounting could live and work anywhere, provided that they could access information for their jobs. These workers will have the opportunity to telecommute—that is, work from home or other location and communicate with a main office by using a computer, modem, and special software.

If numerous workers telecommute, then there could be a positive impact on the community. If many people work from their homes, then commuting to work and taking most business trips will become unnecessary. This will benefit the environment by reducing pollution, congestion, and automobile accidents.

FILMMAKING

Developments in computerized filmmaking are having an increasing effect on the future of the movie industry. By using a new technology, a movie is fed into the computer and converted into a digital image. Each frame is coded into millions of digits that the computer "reads." The image can then be "massaged"—colors can be changed, parts of the image moved, copied, resized, or completely eliminated. After all the changes are made, the new movie can be printed to film and used like a motion picture. Digital film techniques such as this can help filmmakers accomplish some tasks more easily and safely. Directors can create special effects that would otherwise be impossible or just too dangerous to do with real actors. They can also create scenes with the computer that would be too costly or difficult to shoot on location.

Transferring digitized images to film, creating amazing special effects

Even more advanced technology will be used in creating movies in the future. Filmmakers will be able to call a stock house (a company that collects photographs and allows them to be used for a fee), order a photograph, have it downloaded, and then blend it into a movie scene. To do this, filmmakers will have to know how to utilize computers, networks, and databases. Since digital filmmaking seems to be the way of the future, most film schools are adding computer courses for students to take.

★ Read All About It ★

From *The Christian Science Monitor*
November 29, 1990
By Paul A. Eisenstein

'Smart Cars' Combat Gridlock

The sleek two-seater merges into the freeway traffic and nudges its way over to the express lane. Settling into the flow of Monday morning rush hour, the driver slips his hands off the steering wheel, reaches into his briefcase, and pulls out the morning paper. Opening to the sports section, he settles back to read as the car races along at a comfortable 100 miles an hour.

A scenario for disaster? Certainly, on today's highways. But sometime in the not-too-distant future, this may be a perfectly common sight.

Known as Intelligent Vehicle Highway Systems (IVHS) or "smart cars, smart highways," advanced electronics in tomorrow's automobiles could vastly improve the "productivity" of highways around the world, visionaries say. Such systems could pack more cars on densely crowded roadways, improve fuel economy, and reduce highway fatalities.

The largest-scale IVHS system now in use is Berlin's Ali-Scout—produced by Siemens AG as a navigation aid.

"Get in the right hand lane," the male, faintly metallic-sounding voice drones from a hidden speaker. "Make a left turn," it commands, an arrow echoing the order on a small video screen mounted on the dashboard. "You have reached your destination," the voice concludes, as the hotel comes into view.

Installed in a fleet of 700 Berlin vehicles, Ali-Scout uses a combination of visual cues

Computerized dashboards—traveling the fast lane of technology

and verbal warnings to warn motorists of traffic tie-ups, or guide them to unfamiliar destinations.

Ali-Scout's in-car hardware is linked by infrared signal to 2,000 "beacons" around the city. In turn, they are tied to a central traffic monitoring station where a mainframe computer digests information about city road conditions. Should a main artery be blocked by an accident, the system will automatically detour Ali-Scout cars onto alternate routes.

The first IVHS program in the United States is Project Pathfinder, which will soon go into use along a 10-mile stretch of California's

Continued on next page

Computers & the Community

★ READ ALL ABOUT IT ★

crowded Santa Monica Freeway. The cars used in the Pathfinder experiment will be equipped with a video map capable of displaying all local roads in precise detail. Should there be a tie-up, an alternate route will be highlighted on the dashboard-mounted video screen.

Although Ali-Scout and Pathfinder offer little more than route guidance, future IVHS systems will take on more responsibilities. Chrysler's Millenium concept vehicle uses TV cameras to eliminate blind spots, and its radar-controlled collision avoidance system can actually slam on the brakes before a driver would react.

Among other IVHS concepts under development:

- Infrared night vision sensors can cut through the darkness or even the worst pea-soup fog, projecting a computer-generated image on the windshield.

- On board camera systems, like the GM LaneLok, can help prevent a driver from inadvertently crossing lanes.

- Using microchip-controlled transmitters buried beneath the surface of the road, police and road crews could warn drivers of impending problems, such as accidents or lane closings.

This is more than a flight of fantasy; there is a growing need for IVHS.

Since 1970, the number of registered vehicles in this country has grown by 80 percent, to 181 million. Travel has increased by 70 percent. And by 2020, highway use is expected to double again.

"Highway congestion . . . and highway safety are national problems," Richard Morgan, executive director of the Federal Highway Administration noted at a recent automobile conference at the University of Michigan. "One solution is to build more highways, . . . but that will be extremely difficult to accomplish."

The alternative, Mr. Morgan and other experts say, is to find ways to improve roadway productivity.

Providing in-car navigation is only one of the ways in which technology may help smooth highway traffic. Along the New Jersey Turnpike, for example, motorists may wait five minutes or more in rush hour to pay their tolls.

A few hundred miles to the North, the Bay State is trying to speed up toll collection for 1,600 businesses regularly using the Massachusetts Turnpike. As the motorists enter a toll booth, they hand the collector a magnetically encoded card which is then run through a card reader. The businesses are billed monthly.

Motorists won't even have to stop if their cars are equipped to use an even faster system being tested at New York's Lincoln Tunnel, the Coronado Bridge in San Diego, and the Dallas North Tollway.

Developed by the Amtech Corporation of Dallas, the system aims a microwave burst at the windshield of cars passing through special "tollbooths." The beam bounces off an electronic tag about the size of a state inspection sticker and identifies the vehicle to a billing computer. The tolls can be billed to the motorist by mail, or deducted from his bank account or an account paid in advance. ■

COMPUTERS IN THE FUTURE

LEARNING AT SCHOOL

It's the year 2020. As you're sitting on the bus on the way to school, you decide to review for the social studies test that you have second period.

You press one of the icons on your palm-sized PC that "opens" your "textbook." (The icon instructed the computer to access your social studies lesson that is stored on a small compact disc in your PC.)

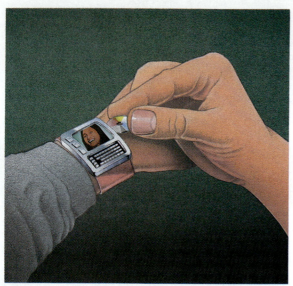

Armed with a state-of-the-art wristband computer

You decide to study with a friend. "Call Debbie," you instruct your wristband computer. Your friend's image is projected along with your lesson. "Want to study for the social studies test?" you ask.

"Well, I have to finish a science report first," Debbie replies, "but I'm almost through dictating it now."

Your friend goes back to work, using a cordless microphone to speak into her computer. When Debbie finishes the report, she'll send it to her teacher using electronic mail—no wires, no printer. Using a PC, the teacher can read the report, grade it, and send back comments.

C·A·R·E·E·R·S

SALESPERSON · ELECTRICIAN · ARTIST · SECRETARY · PROFESSOR · PILOT · OPTOMETRIST · SURGEON · TEACHER · DOCTOR · NURSE · FARMER · DENTIST · PHYSICIST · ENGINEER · MECHANIC · ASTRONAUT

In the future, more and more police officers and dispatchers may have computers in their cars and at headquarters.

The Colorado State Patrol has experimented with a system that bounces signals off satellites to locate patrol cars. When a call comes in to headquarters, a television screen displays a map of the area where the call originated and then shows the location of any patrol cars in that area.

Eventually, the system will also send messages to computers in patrol cars. The messages and assignments would be stored in the memory of the patrol car's computer and would appear on the screen when the officer wanted to check them.

Do-it-yourself Textbooks The situation just described may seem in the distant future, but there are changes in education that may come about much sooner. Some textbook companies are putting their educational materials on computer disks, allowing teachers to choose lessons that they want to teach. In effect, teachers are creating personalized textbooks. Soon, bringing your notebook-sized computer to school will be like carrying your pens, pencils, and paper today.

COMPUTERS & THE GLOBAL VILLAGE

As national information networks are built, countries will be able to link them together to create a "global village." This will allow people of the world to share valuable knowledge and services. New technology such as virtual reality and artificial intelligence may also have a global impact.

Spreading computer networks to every nation in the future

ACCESSING INFORMATION FROM AROUND THE WORLD

In the future, computer networks will continue to increase communication around the world. In a world that has hundreds of millions of computers, it will be easy to access information through a *global network*. Global networks allow ongoing communication and cooperation among people located in different parts of the world. Messages can be sent around the world in just minutes. Advanced electronic mail (E-mail) will also be available in the future. With advanced E-mail, it will be possible to transmit not only text through a network, but also graphics, animation, sound, and video.

Being able to access information is important not only to the leading nations of the world but also to poorer countries. With direct access to others' knowledge and experience, people in underdeveloped areas will be able to learn about health care, how to fix machinery, how to improve distribution of food and medicine, and so on.

MULTI CULTURAL BYTE

The East-West Education Development Foundation, a non-profit organization located in Boston, collects computers that aren't being used to send to Eastern Europe. "What's happened is that the computer revolution has progressed at a different pace in Eastern Europe," explained Alex Randall, East-West's executive director. The equipment that the Americans have outgrown can help Eastern Europeans catch up in the computer revolution. The recipients of the computers use them to learn English, write their own software, and to provide communications within organizations, and so on. The organization provides Eastern Europe with the technology to become an important participant in the global village.

VIRTUAL REALITY

Can a computer be used to create a real world? We may not know the answer to that question yet, but we do know that computers are already being used to create worlds that look real. We call this technology "virtual reality." Virtual reality is a lifelike world created with computers. What is amazing about a virtual world is that it lets people explore the world as they move through it.

Virtual reality systems are currently in the beginning stages of development. Once they are fully developed, they will make excellent tools for many professionals such as doctors, scientists, and designers. NASA (National Aeronautics and Space Administration) researchers have developed a virtual-reality system that allows them to "stand" on the surface of Mars or Venus and learn about these planets without actually going to them. Some architectural designers also use virtual reality today to test models of their designs. Virtual reality allows them to see how a design will work in a "real-life" situation without having to go to the expense of building an actual building.

If doctors were to explore a virtual world of a body, here's what might happen. The sensors on the doctors' hands would tell the computer what part of the body they were working in. Let's say they begin to explore a vein. As they explore the walls of the vein, the computer tracks their movements and projects a 3-D image of the vein wall on a monitor. The wall of the vein isn't really there on the computer screen, but the image is actually larger and easier for the doctors to see than the real vein would have been.

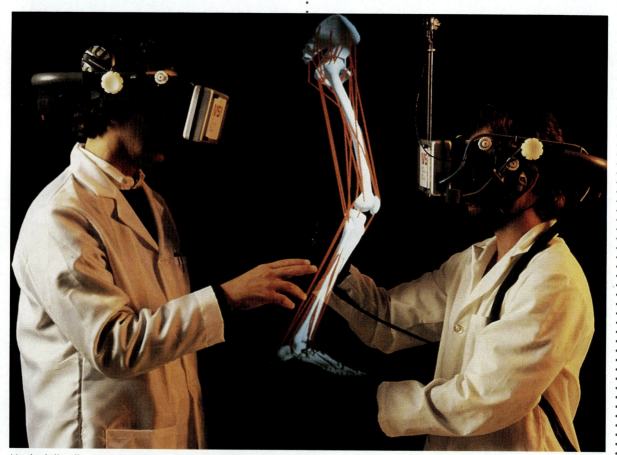

Manipulating the anatomy of a human leg through virtual reality

Creating a virtual-reality system requires several components. First, the user needs to be equipped with special sensors. These devices help the computer keep track of the user's movements as he or she explores the virtual world. Standard gear to wear when experiencing virtual reality is a helmet with a built-in computer screen and gloves that are wired to track hand movements.

In the future, virtual reality systems may be as common as the PC is today. Instead of reading a book or watching a video about the ocean, you could explore it as a virtual world. Virtual worlds offer many possibilities for exploration.

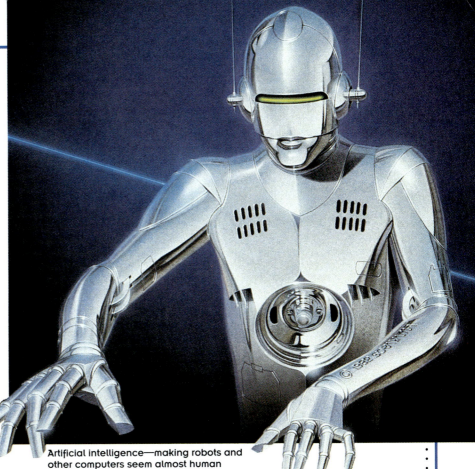

Artificial intelligence—making robots and other computers seem almost human

ARTIFICIAL INTELLIGENCE

Artificial intelligence is the field of computer science concerned with developing computers that have the ability to infer, reason, solve problems, and understand language. The University of Colorado's Institute of Cognitive Science is one of the top artificial-intelligence centers in the nation. Scientists there have been working on a computer program that will analyze speech fragments, reduce them to electronic signals, and store them in a computer's memory. The next step is for the computer to combine the signals and produce printed materials.

"Max, throw some popcorn in the microwave, put *2001: A Space Odyssey* in the VCR, and take out the trash," you say. "And, listen, I've got this letter I need to write. . . ."

"Yes, master," replies the robot.

Someday, in the 21st century, artificial intelligence, like Max, may surround us in our daily lives.

EXPERT SYSTEMS

An *expert system* is a computer system that has a very large database and the ability to ask questions. It also contains a set of rules that allows the system to use this data to arrive at conclusions. For example, hospitals around this country and in other parts of the world currently have expert systems that help doctors diagnose and treat illnesses.

A typical system is fed a large amount of data on certain kinds of illnesses. It is then programmed with the rules that doctors follow when observing a patient's symptoms to determine what illness that patient has. The system also has the ability to question either the doctor or the patient about the illness. "Has the patient had a sore throat lately? Has the patient had a persistent fever?" Depending on the answers it gets, the computer either asks further questions or offers a diagnosis. Using an expert system can be like having a medical team of expert doctors at your fingertips!

A LETTER TO MY FUTURE SON OR DAUGHTER

The following is a first-prize-winning essay written by Breezy Carter from Aberdeen, WA. Her letter was printed in a book called The Best of the Time Capsule Contest, *published by the National Foundation for the Improvement of Education and Prodigy Services Company.*

Dear my-yet-to-be-born child,

As I sit here writing to you, I think about the future and what it will be like in twenty years. I am Breezy Carter and I am writing this letter to you in the year 1990. I expect that you are reading this letter from me, your mother, in the year 2010.

Your computers will be really different from the ones we enjoy today. In your day, all people will probably have computers in their homes as well as a computer for each student in every classroom; however, your computers will probably have a six-by-six foot screen built into the wall of the living room. All computers will have modems and will replace telephones. On the computer screen you will be able to see the person you are talking to. You will no longer type into your computers; you will probably speak into them and they will do the typing for you. Also, your computer screens can be used for video games that can be played in three dimensions with you choosing to be a character in the game. You will be able to play with people in other countries.

In your year, television sets will come with built-in videocassette recorders so that people do not need to buy separate machines. Also, the television sets will be in 3-D.

I think everyone will have more education beyond high school so they will be smart enough to control the telecommunications devices.

I do not believe you will need to wash and dry clothes in your day. You will probably have a little ray gun that you will point at the clothes, and when you pull the trigger, all the dirt will be made to jump right out of the clothes.

I think you will be a caring person, someone like a doctor who helps others. You will not have to work as much as we do. You will not even have to go to the hospital to do your work. As a doctor, you will sit in front of a screen and talk to other doctors, nurses, and patients. There will be a huge screen that will show a doctor how a cell is working inside a patient's body.

Won't it be interesting to see how close my predictions are for the year 2010?

Your loving mother-to-be,
Breezy Carter

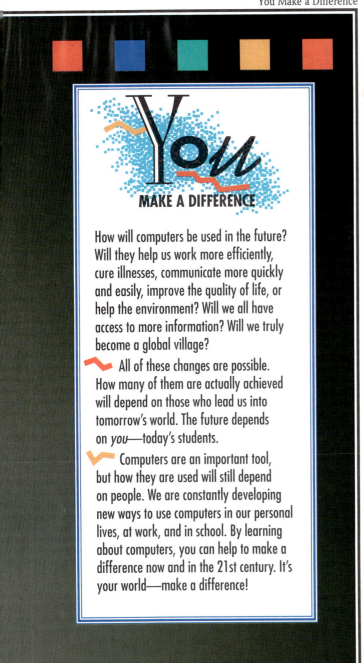

YOU MAKE A DIFFERENCE

How will computers be used in the future? Will they help us work more efficiently, cure illnesses, communicate more quickly and easily, improve the quality of life, or help the environment? Will we all have access to more information? Will we truly become a global village?

All of these changes are possible. How many of them are actually achieved will depend on those who lead us into tomorrow's world. The future depends on *you*—today's students.

Computers are an important tool, but how they are used will still depend on people. We are constantly developing new ways to use computers in our personal lives, at work, and in school. By learning about computers, you can help to make a difference now and in the 21st century. It's your world—make a difference!

MODULE 12

MODULE SUMMARY QUESTIONS

In order to check your comprehension of computers in the future, you may wish to discuss the following ideas.

1. How do you think *you* will be using computers in the future?
2. How do you think computers will affect your community?
3. What global changes do you predict will occur in the future because of computers?

COMPUTERS IN THE FUTURE

STUDENT GLOSSARY

Terms in **boldface** are vocabulary words that students are responsible for in this program, and on which they will be tested.

A

abacus The oldest known mechanical aid for calculating, consisting of beads strung on wires or wooden rods. (M1)

active cell The cell that is highlighted and currently designated by the software to receive data or be edited. (**M8**)

address The location of a cell on a grid or matrix (such as on a memory matrix or an electronic spreadsheet) as identified by its coordinates. See also: coordinate. (M2, **M8**)

algorithm A step-by-step set of instructions for solving a specific problem. (M9, **M9**)

ALU See: Arithmetic Logic Unit. (M2, **M2**)

American Standard Code for Information Interchange (ASCII) See: ASCII. (M2, **M2**)

animation The making or designing of an object in such a way as to make it appear to be alive or have movement. (M3, **M3**)

antivirus program A program that automatically checks each floppy disk as it is inserted into the disk drive and scans all data from telecommunications devices to locate and give warning of any virus that may be likely to enter a computer. (**M11**)

applications software Programs that enable a computer to do specific jobs, such as word processing. (M2, **M2**)

Arithmetic Logic Unit (ALU) The place in the computer (within the CPU) where all arithmetic and logic functions are performed. (M2, **M2**)

arrange See: sort. (**M6**)

arrow key A key on a keyboard, labeled with a left, right, up, or down arrow that causes a corresponding movement of the cursor on the computer screen when it is pressed. (**M2**)

artificial intelligence (AI) The field of computer science concerned with developing computers that have the ability to mimic human intelligence by learning, reasoning, solving problems, and understanding language. (M12, **M12**)

ASCII Stands for American Standard Code for Information Interchange—a code used to exchange information from one type of computer to another. (M2, **M2**)

authoring system A system that ties together hardware and software to make the tasks involved in producing interactive programs easier. (M4)

automatic teller machine A machine located at a bank or other convenient location that allows people to make cash withdrawals or deposits and do their banking business electronically and, usually, at any time, day or night. (M7)

B

background The layer on the screen which seems "farther" from the viewer in a *HyperCard* program. (M9)

backup copy A duplicate of original files or data, made to guard against loss and usually stored on a disk or magnetic tape. (M2)

BASIC Most widely used computer programming language; stands for Beginner's All-purpose Symbolic Instruction Code. (M4)

baud rate The speed at which signals are sent and received by a modem. (**M7**)

binary system A numbering system based on two numbers: 0 and 1. (M2, **M2**)

bit Short for binary digit. Either of the two digits in the binary number system (1 or 0). (M2, **M2**)

bit-mapped (or raster) graphics Graphics consisting of patterns of dots. (M4)

boldface Refers to type that is darker and heavier than other text. (**M5**)

bomb Destructive code that is set to activate at a certain time or when a specific action is taken. (M11, **M11**)

Boolean logic A logic system based on the idea that propositions are either true or false. It uses the number 1 to represent true and 0 to represent false. (**M9**)

booting The process of loading the operating system software into memory to start up a computer. (M2, **M2**)

bug A mechanical or electrical flaw in a computer system or an error in a program. (M10, **M9**)

bulletin board A place on the network where public messages can be left and one message can reach all users. (M7, **M7**)

button In *Tutor-Tech, LinkWay, HyperCard,* and other hypermedia programs, a feature (object) used to create links between cards and to initiate other actions, such as running a video segment, playing an animation, or reproducing a sound. (M4, **M9**)

byte A unit of measurement for the memory and/or storage capacity of a computer; equals one character, or eight bits of data. See also: bit. (M2, **M2**)

C

calculator A small electronic machine, usually hand-held, used for doing arithmetic/mathematic calculations. (M1)

capacity The maximum amount of storage space available in memory. (**M2**)

card In hypermedia, an electronic "card" on which data is entered. A card is made up of several "fields," "buttons," and "graphics." Multiple cards form a "stack." A *HyperCard* "card" is generally equivalent to a "page" in *Tutor-Tech* or *LinkWay.* (M9, **M9**)

CAT scan A medical test that uses a computer-aided machine to take close-up pictures of body organs through an X-ray process; CAT stands for computerized axial tomography. (M1)

Cathode Ray Tube (CRT) A type of large vacuum tube, such as a computer monitor screen or TV picture tube, in which a stream of electrons can be focused on a screen (on the inside of the tube) to produce images. (M2)

CD-ROM Stands for Compact Disc Read-Only Memory—an optical disc that can only be read from and not written to. (M2, **M2**)

STUDENT GLOSSARY

cell The intersection of a row and a column on a grid or matrix such as an electronic spreadsheet or a chart of a memory matrix. (M8, **M8**)

Central Processing Unit (CPU) The main component, or "brain," of a computer. It is the chip that performs all of the information processing. (M2, **M2**)

character A letter, number, symbol, or space that is recognized as one byte of information by a computer. (M2)

chip A very small silicon wafer containing an integrated circuit. (M2, **M2**)

clicking Refers to placing the cursor on an item and then pressing and releasing the mouse button one time. (**M2**)

clip art A series of picture files that are stored on disks and can be "clipped," or cut and pasted into other documents. (**M4**)

coding Writing directions, in a language the computer understands, for each step in an algorithm. (**M9**)

column The vertical divisions of a grid or matrix that intersect the horizontal divisions (rows) to form cells in which data can be entered. (M8, **M8**)

command (prompt) Displayed text indicating that a computer program is waiting for input from the user. For instance, a line in the status area of an electronic spreadsheet that shows which command is being performed. (M2)

command key See: control key or function key. (M2, **M2**)

commercial software Copyrighted software available for purchase. (M11, **M11**)

communications software Software that enables computers, modems, and telephone lines to work together; sometimes stores information, automatically dials telephone numbers, or transmits incoming information to a printer. (M7, **M7**)

compiler A compiler reads a source program, translates all of the source statements to machine language, and produces the final output in one step. (M10)

computer An electronic machine that can perform calculations and can process a large amount of information accurately and much more rapidly than the human brain. (M1, **M1**)

computer-aided design (CAD) Software that allows a user to create designs using a computer. Designs of products made with CAD programs can often be viewed three-dimensionally and cross-sectionally, and can be rotated, enlarged, or reduced. (M1, **M4**)

computer-aided manufacturing (CAM) A program that allows a computer to translate a finished CAD design into a set of instructions that can direct machines that will produce the products. See also: computer-aided design. (M1, **M4**)

computer graphics The creation, display, and storage of pictures, with a computer. Primary applications are entertainment, charts and graphs, and design and manufacturing. (M1, **M4**)

computer program See: program. (**M9**)

consumer-services network A network that connects computers to banks, stores, government offices, and other such locations. See also: network. (M7)

control key Special purpose key on a keyboard labeled *control* or having a symbol, such as an apple; also called a command key or function key. (**M2**)

control unit The part of the computer (within the CPU) that makes sure the program's instructions are followed correctly and at the right time. It also controls the movement of data from input to the computer's memory, and from memory to output. (M2, **M2**)

coordinate The row and column designations that define a cell location in a grid or matrix, such as "A2," to indicate the cell where column A crosses row 2. (**M8**)

copy and paste 1. (word processing) To highlight one section of text and leave it unaffected where it is, but also put a copy of it in another place. In some programs, this feature is called copy and move. 2. (database) To duplicate a data entry and place it in a different location while leaving the original in place. (**M5, M6**)

copy protect To protect software against unwanted or illegal duplication by writing computer code within the programs that prevents simple copying. (**M11**)

copy protection A coding scheme that requires the user to have the original disk handy to run a program. (**M11**)

copyright The exclusive right to the reproduction, publication, and sale of an intellectual work. (M11, **M11**)

CPU See: Central Processing Unit. (M2, **M2**)

CRT See: Cathode Ray Tube. (M2)

cursor A highlighted or bright (sometimes blinking) square or other mark on the CRT that indicates where information is being input. In some programs, the cursor may be a special shape or be represented as a certain icon that is related to the activity in which it is being used. (M2, **M2**)

cut and move See: cut and paste. (**M5, M6**)

cut and paste 1. (word processing) To highlight one section of text and move it to a different location. In some programs, this feature is called cut and move. 2. (database) To move a data entry from one location to a different location. (**M5, M6**)

data A general term for pieces of information that a computer processes. (M1, **M2**)

databank Electronic storehouse of information, usually accessed by using a computer network. (M7)

database An organized collection of related data entries, such as a list of names and addresses. (M1, **M6**)

database management system A type of software that provides a fast and efficient means of organizing, retrieving, and printing large amounts of information. (M6, **M6**)

data file See: file. (**M6**)

debug 1. Locate and correct errors in program code. 2. Locate and correct defects in hardware. (**M9**)

delete 1. (word processing) To remove text from a document or file. 2. (database) To remove an entry from a field or to remove a record from a file. (M4, **M5, M6**)

desktop publishing (DTP) A computerized layout program that allows the user to integrate text and graphics, make editorial changes right on the screen, and produce camera-ready copy. (M5, **M5**)

219

UNDERSTANDING COMPUTERS THROUGH APPLICATIONS

Student Glossary

digital Referring to the representation of data as discrete signals such as on or off. (**M4**)

digital compositioning One process used to create exciting visual effects in movies. Scanned images from a film are manipulated by artists, then reintegrated in the film. (**M3**)

digitize To change analog information into digital information that the computer can use. (M12, **M3**)

digitizing tablet See: graphics tablet. (**M4**)

disk drive The device that reads from and writes to a floppy disk or hard disk. (**M2**)

document (file) Anything that is produced using a word-processing program. (**M5**)

dot-matrix printer A printer that uses a moving bundle of small wires or pins to form characters by making patterns of small dots in the shape of each letter or number. Dot-matrix printers can also produce graphic designs in the same way—by making patterns of dots in desired shapes. (**M5**)

downloading Transferring information electronically from a databank, or another computer, to your computer. (M7, **M7**)

drag Refers to placing the cursor on an item, then pressing and holding the mouse button while moving the mouse, to cause a corresponding movement of the item on the screen. (**M2**)

draw program A program that creates graphics by using sets of lines, called vectors. The program uses mathematical equations to draw objects. See also: vector. (M4, **M4**)

edit To make any change to the contents of a document, database, or spreadsheet. (M5, **M6**)

electrical impulse A momentary surge (sometimes very small) of electrical current. A series of such impulses may be used to create signals that can be converted into sound or other output. (**M1**)

electronic messaging Sending and receiving information, or messages, over a computer network. (**M7**)

E-mail Private messages, called electronic mail, that are sent and received over a computer network. (M1, **M7**)

entry A piece of information, or data, typed into a field in a database. (**M6**)

ethics Moral principles and values. (M11, **M11**)

expert system A computer system that contains very large databases, the ability to ask questions, and sets of rules to follow when using data to arrive at conclusions. (M12, **M12**)

field 1. A single category of information in a record. 2. In *HyperCard* and *LinkWay,* an area (object) on a card or page where text is entered. (M6, **M6**, **M9**)

file A collection of related records in a database. (M1, **M6**)

file transfer Copying or moving documents, through telecommunications, from one computer to another, such as exchanging files on a network. (**M7**)

find See: search. (**M6**)

find and replace See: search and replace. (**M5, M6**)

floppy disk (diskette) The most common storage device used with microcomputers. A flexible disk, made of thin plastic and magnetically coated. It is protected by a jacket that has openings to allow the disk drive to read or write information. (M2, **M2**)

flowchart A diagram showing the relationships between different parts of a problem, or a program. It is used by programmers to break the problem down into small steps. (M9, **M9**)

flush left Refers to text that aligns with the left margin of the page. (**M5**)

flush right Refers to text that aligns with the right margin of the page. (**M5**)

folder See: stack. (**M2**)

font A specific design for a whole set of text characters, including letters, numbers, and punctuation marks. (M5)

forecast 1. To calculate the effect of a change before the change takes place. 2. To make financial predictions based on "what-if" questions, often with the aid of an electronic spreadsheet. (**M8**)

foreground The top layer through which you can see the background in a *HyperCard* program. (M9)

formatting 1. To prepare a blank diskette for use. 2. To set up the elements of style that are added to a document's layout and typeface to make it more appealing and easier to read. (M2, **M5**)

formula A mathematical equation based on numbers and/or symbols. (**M8**)

formula line See: status line. (M8, **M8**)

freeware Copyrighted software that is given away free of charge but is still the property of the owner. (M11, **M11**)

function An operational instruction for programming a computer, or an operation performed by a computer as a result of such an instruction. (M2)

function key Generally, any key on the keyboard that does not produce a letter, number, or special symbol. Often refers to keys labeled F1, F2, F3, and so on. (M2)

futurist A person whose job it is to plan for future developments. (**M12**)

generation Within the overall continuing development and improvement of computer products, a generation is a group of computers that are able to perform certain closely related functions. (M10, **M10**)

gigabit A unit of measurement equal to one billion bits. (M12)

gigabyte (GB) A unit of measurement for the memory and/or storage capacity of a computer; equals about one billion bytes. (**M2**)

global network Online computers, set up around the world, allowing ongoing communication and access to information. (M2)

STUDENT GLOSSARY

global village Implies that people around the world are joined together, through electronic communications, into a great community. (M1, **M1**)

grammar checker A software program that checks for correct grammar and punctuation within a document created with a word-processing program. Mistakes are highlighted and, in some cases, suggestions are made for ways to correct the errors. (M5)

graphical user interface (GUI) A type of display that uses pictures, called icons, that the user can employ to activate programs, view file listings, delete files, and initiate various other computer activities. (M8, **M4**)

graphics See: computer graphics. (M1)

graphics tablet A flat input device that allows the user to draw a picture or design with a finger or special pen, called a stylus. The drawing appears immediately on the computer screen and is converted to a digital format that the computer can understand. Also called a "digitizing tablet." (M4, **M4**)

graphing A feature in a software program that allows the program to produce graphs. (M8)

grid A series of evenly spaced horizontal and vertical lines that intersect each other. (**M8**)

hacker Originally, an amateur computer user who was very talented and knowledgeable. More recently, one who uses a computer to gain illegal access to other computer systems and files, usually through the use of telecommunications. (M11, **M11**)

hard copy (printout) Text or graphics printed on paper. (M2, **M2**)

hard disk A round, platter-shaped, magnetic storage device that is permanently sealed in a case and can store much more data than a floppy disk. (M2, **M2**)

hardware The physical equipment of a computer, such as the screen, the keyboard, and the storage devices. (M2, **M2**)

hidden field A field whose contents are normally not visible but can be called up by some particular action, such as by clicking on a certain button. (**M2**)

highlight To select text for change by marking its beginning and end. (M5)

high resolution Refers to images or data that appear sharp and detailed because they are made up of a large number of dots per inch. See also: resolution. (M4)

host computer The main computer to which all the computers or terminals of a network are connected. (M7, **M7**)

hypermedia Encompasses the same concept as hypertext but is expanded to include cross-linking of graphics and other media as well as text. (M9, **M9**)

hypertext An indexing system that cross-links one word to another within a computer program. (M9, **M9**)

IC See: integrated circuit. (M2, **M2**)

icon A stylized figure or image used on a computer screen to represent available functions or activities. An icon can be selected in some manner, such as by clicking with a mouse, to cause a particular result, such as opening a certain file. (**M4**)

impact printer A printer that works by having a print head impact, or strike, a ribbon to make an impression on the paper. (**M5**)

ink-jet printer A nonimpact printer that can form characters by shooting out tiny droplets of ink at the paper. (M2)

input The information entered or put into a computer for processing. (M2, **M2**)

insert 1. (word processing) To add new text into the middle of existing text. 2. (database) To add information to a field or to add a new record into the middle of a file. (M5, **M5, M6**)

integrated circuit (IC) A complete electronic circuit contained on a minute chip of silicon. (M2, **M2**)

integrated software A software package that combines several different computer programs, such as a word processor, a graphics application, a database, and a spreadsheet. The individual programs within the package use similar sets of commands and interact easily with each other. (**M5**)

intellectual property Ideas put into action, such as writing, music, art, computer code, and inventions, that can be protected under copyright or patent laws. (**M11**)

interactive Capable of two-way communications such as between the computer and the user or between system components. (**M1**)

interactive animation A combination of live action and animation, or cartoons, such as in a film in which both humans and cartoons appear together and interact through movement and speech, as if both have life. (M3, **M3**)

interactive fiction A combination of literature and software in which the person reading can manipulate the story or is a character in the story. (**M3**)

interactive videodisc A technology that combines data from a computer and laserdiscs, making a great deal of information available in the form of images, sounds, and text. The laserdisc is normally accessed and controlled by the computer, using special software. (M7)

italic Refers to a typestyle in which the characters are evenly slanted toward the right. (**M5**)

justified Relating to text in which one or both margins are aligned vertically. (**M5**)

keyboard An input device resembling a typewriter and consisting of a standardized layout of buttons or keys with symbols, such as letters or numbers, that can be entered into a computer by pressing on the keys. (M2, **M2**)

kilobyte (K) A unit of measurement for the storage or memory capacity of a computer; equals 1,024 bytes (or about 1,000 bytes); usually referred to as "K," such as in "64K memory." (M2, **M2**)

STUDENT GLOSSARY

LAN See: local-area network. (M7, **M7**)

laptop A computer that can run on batteries and usually weighs less than 20 pounds (9 kg). (M1)

laserdisc A disc with recorded pictures and sound that is read by a laser beam. (M3)

laser printer A nonimpact printer that produces a high-quality image, using a method similar to that of a photocopy machine. Laser printers are widely used in business. (M2, **M5**)

local-area network (LAN) A number of terminals or microcomputers, usually located in the same building or room, connected by cables or wires. See also: network. (M7, **M7**)

logic bomb A virus that is designed to be triggered by a specific event. It can lie dormant for days, or even months, waiting for a user to perform a certain function—such as delete a certain file—before it does its dirty work. (M11)

logic function A function in which the computer compares data using conditions such as numbers, equations, or words. The computer tests the relationship between items of data to determine whether they are equal to each other or not equal, or whether they relate in any of the other logical ways in which data can be compared. (M2)

Logo A structured computer language that usually uses a turtle as the cursor; used to create graphic designs. (M4)

loop In a program, a series of steps, or statements, that is executed repeatedly, either for a certain number of times or until a certain condition becomes true or false. (**M9**)

low resolution Images or data that do not appear sharp and detailed because they are made up of a small number of dots per inch. See also: resolution. (M4)

macro A software feature that allows a series of keystrokes to be recorded then "played back" by pressing a key, or a combination of keys, assigned to the macro. This allows repetitive commands to be executed, or repetitive text entries to be typed, with just a few simple keystrokes. (M8)

mainframe A large, powerful, and expensive type of computer that can support many users at one time, can store vast amounts of data, and can perform many tasks at the same time. (M1, **M1**)

media The means by which information is presented. (**M9**)

megabyte (M or meg) A unit of measurement for the memory and/or storage capacity of a computer; equals about one million bytes. (M2, **M2**)

menu A list of options from which a program user can choose in order to give a command to the computer. Selecting a menu item gives the computer a specific command. (M5, **M5**)

microcomputer A small computer with enough power and storage capacity to meet the personal needs of many different kinds of users; also called personal computer, home computer, or desktop computer. (M1, **M1**)

micromachine A tiny machine—smaller than the width of a human hair—that can be used as a sensor. Micromachines perform a variety of tasks, including collecting information, triggering air bags in cars, and directing robots. (M10)

microprocessor A Central Processing Unit that is comprised of one chip. It carries out the four functions of a computer: input, processing, storage, and output. (M2, **M2**)

MIDI Musical Instrument Digital Interface—a standard computer language that is used in connecting sequencers, synthesizers, and samplers, allowing them to communicate with one another. (M3)

minicomputer A computer that is generally smaller than a mainframe computer and larger than a microcomputer, can store large amounts of information, and supports multiple users. (M1, **M1**)

mobile data terminal A mobile computer terminal, usually mounted in a vehicle, that is linked to a central computer by radio. (M1)

mode The type of information (such as text, graphics, or video) sent over a network. (**M7**)

modem Stands for MOdulator-DEModulator. A device that permits a computer to transmit and receive data over a telephone line. (M2, **M7**)

monitor A display screen (Cathode Ray Tube) designed specifically as an output device for a computer. See also: Cathode Ray Tube. (M1, **M2**)

mouse A small, hand-held input device moved around on a surface to cause the cursor to move correspondingly on the screen. (M2, **M2**)

multimedia The merging of traditional computer creations, such as word processing and graphics, with TV, sound, and video. (M4)

multitasking A feature that allows several programs to be opened and worked with at the same time. (**M5**)

network A number of computer users linked together, usually, by a powerful central computer and many microcomputers or terminals. A set-up for either local or long-distance communications. Also called "information network." See also: consumer-services network; local-area network; and wide-area network. (M1, **M7**)

nonimpact printer A printer that has no mechanism that physically strikes a ribbon and then the paper, such as an ink-jet printer or laser printer. (**M5**)

numeric keypad A group of keys, resembling the keys of a calculator, that are used to input numbers. (**M2**)

object A small amount of code that performs a particular function. (M9)

Student Glossary

object-oriented program   A graphics program that manipulates graphics/objects as a whole, instead of as dots. (M4)

Object-Oriented Programming (OOP)   A method of programming that uses a library of pre-programmed objects (small amounts of code that perform particular functions) to construct an application. Each object can run independently and is designed to perform a specific function and also interface with the rest of the objects. Programmers construct programs by selecting objects that provide the features needed to accomplish an application program's tasks. (M9)

online   Electronically connected, as with a mainframe and another computer, through the use of a modem and telephone lines. (M6, **M7**)

operating system   A program that provides the instructions that enable the computer to handle tasks necessary for it to work. (M2)

optical disc   A disc that provides random access to information and is read by a laser. (**M2**)

optics   The science of controlling light to produce images. (M3)

output   Information produced by the computer, as a result of processing, that is sent to devices that display, print, or store it. (M2, **M2**)

page   In *Tutor-Tech* and *LinkWay,* an electronic "page" on which data is entered. A *Tutor-Tech* or *LinkWay* page is generally equivalent to a card in *HyperCard*. (**M9**)

paint program   A program for creating graphic images on the computer. Paint programs manipulate pixels to create graphics. See also: pixel. (M4, **M4**)

PC   See: personal computer. (M1)

peripheral   Any hardware device that is connected to a computer in order to make the computer easier to use or to expand the computer's capabilities. (M2)

personal computer (PC)   Usually, a microcomputer consisting of a keyboard, a CRT, and a unit containing a microprocessor. (M1)

photo imaging   The process of scanning and digitizing photographs into a computer. See also: scanner. (**M4**)

piracy   Unauthorized and illegal copying and use of software. (**M11**)

pixel   One of the tiny points or boxes of light that make up a computer screen; stands for picture element. Pixels are the smallest elements that can be displayed and manipulated in creating letters, numbers, or graphics. (M4, **M4**)

plotter   An output device that controls the movements of one or more pens over a piece of paper and can produce intricate hard-copy drawings. They are used to create certain kinds of graphics that are most often used by engineers, architects, and physicians. (M4)

point   Referring to type size, a point is a unit of measure, equal to 1/72 of an inch, that is used to indicate character height and the amount of space between lines of text. (**M5**)

port   The place on a computer or peripheral where connecting cables or wires can be attached. (M7)

portable computer   A computer that is small enough to be carried. Some examples are palmtops, laptops, and notebook computers. (**M1**)

primary storage   Refers to the Random Access Memory, or RAM, of a computer. (M2, **M2**)

printer   A mechanical output device that can print text, and sometimes graphics, on paper. (M2, **M2**)

printout   See: hard copy. (M2, **M2**)

procedure   A sequence of steps to be followed, such as a series of keystrokes necessary to execute a particular command. (M9)

processing   The manipulation of data by a computer in accordance with its instructions, or programming. (**M2**)

program   A set of instructions that a computer follows to solve a problem or perform a number of functions. (M1, **M9**)

programmer   A person who designs and develops computer programs. (**M9**)

programming   The writing of instructions (a program) for the computer. (M9, **M9**)

programming language   The set of words, objects or other code elements, and the rules governing their application that are used in constructing a computer program. (M4)

programming language software   Programs that allow the user to write applications software. (**M2**)

prompt   See: command. (M2)

public-domain software   Software, donated for public use, that can be freely copied and distributed. (M11, **M11**)

RAM   See: Random Access Memory.

Random Access Memory (RAM)   The temporary memory of a computer that holds software programs and other input data while in use. Data in RAM can be accessed randomly, or directly, by location, rather than sequentially. When the computer is turned off, all data in RAM is lost. (M2, **M2**)

Read-Only Memory (ROM)   "Read-only" means that the computer can only *read* what is contained in this memory and cannot change what is there. ROM is also permanent memory; it does not erase when the computer is turned off. Computers usually contain ROM chips with permanent instructions on how to load the systems software. (M2, **M2**)

record   A collection of related fields in a database. All the information and entries that pertain to one subject or concept, such as the name, address, and phone number for one particular person in a database of many people. (M6, **M6**)

resolution   The quality of the image on a display screen. An image with higher resolution has more dots or pixels per inch and finer detail can be seen. Lower-resolution images appear coarser and sometimes have jagged edges. (**M4**)

robotics   The field of computer science concerned with the construction, maintenance, and behavior of robots. (**M12**)

ROM   See: Read-Only Memory.

STUDENT GLOSSARY

row The horizontal divisions of a grid or matrix that intersect the vertical divisions (columns) to form cells in which data can be entered. (M8, **M8**)

sampler A device that uses compact-disc technology to digitally record, or sample, a sound. It allows a musician to play back reproductions of stored sounds, in a full range of pitches, using the sampler's keyboard. (**M3**)

scanner A device that converts art, photography, or other graphic material into bit-mapped data that is input into the computer. The digitized images can be edited by a computer graphics artist. See: photo imaging. (M2, **M4**)

script In *HyperCard,* the programming for various objects, such as fields and buttons. (M9, **M9**)

scroll To move the text on the screen up or down, or left or right to show more characters or lines than can be seen. (**M5**)

search A software feature that allows the user to locate a particular string of characters or set of data in a file, sometimes also called "find." (**M6**)

search and replace 1. (word processing) A feature that allows a certain string of characters (letters, numbers, or words) to be found quickly in a document and replaced with a different string of characters. 2. (database) A feature that allows a certain data entry or set of data to be found quickly in a database and replaced with a different entry or set of data. (M5, **M6**)

secondary storage Permanent storage on disks or tapes. (M2, **M2**)

sector A division of a track on a computer storage disk. (**M2**)

selected cell See: active cell. (**M8**)

sequencer A device that can record and store individual musical parts on separate tracks. Musicians can later decide which versions to keep, or can combine pieces of different versions. (**M3**)

shareware Copyrighted software that is distributed free of charge on a trial basis. A nominal fee is charged if the user decides to keep it. (M11, **M11**)

silicon The second most common element (after oxygen) from which resistors, capacitors, and transistors are made. (**M2**)

site license Grants the user the right to make a specified number of copies of a software program for use on multiple computers. (**M11**)

smart home office A home office that is self sufficient and not connected to a central office. In addition to its own computerized sources of information, it can receive any necessary additional information through telecommunications.

smart house A house with a computer, or computers, that can be programmed to handle many domestic tasks. (M12, **M12**)

soft copy Refers to output from a computer's monitor and speakers. (**M2**)

software Program material for computers; instructions to the CPU to tell it what to do with the data it receives. Software programs are usually stored on disks until needed. Sometimes a disk, with its program, is called "software." (M1, **M2**)

software bomb A virus that is designed to be triggered by the startup of a program. (M11)

sort To organize a set of data in a database in a certain order, such as a list of names alphabetically by the surname. (**M6**)

spelling checker Part of a word-processing program that uses a disk-based dictionary to check for and correct misspellings in documents. (M5, **M5**)

spreadsheet An applications program that can quickly handle calculations and perform evaluations. (M1, **M8**)

stack In *HyperCard* and *Tutor-Tech,* a collection of "cards" or "pages" on related concepts or subjects. In function, a "stack" is similar to a stack of index cards. Individual cards can contain text and/or graphics. A stack in *HyperCard* or *Tutor-Tech* is generally equivalent to a folder in IBM *LinkWay.* (M4, **M2**)

standard formula (function) A formula used by a spreadsheet that allows the user to enter a simple mathematical equation to execute a complex calculation. An equation tells the program to use a particular formula to perform a calculation on the contents of certain cells. The formula may also contain special spreadsheet functions. (M8)

status line Located in the upper left-hand corner of most electronic spreadsheets, a line that gives the user information about data being entered. (M8, **M8**)

storage Any physical device in which or on which data is kept, such as a disk, or the placing of information in or on such a device. (M2, **M2**)

stylus A special pen used with a graphics tablet to create computer graphics. See also: graphics tablet. (**M4**)

subscript Text that is printed slightly lower on the line than surrounding text. (**M5**)

supercomputer The most powerful type of computer in existence at any given time. (M12, **M1**)

superscript Text that is printed slightly higher on the line than surrounding text. (**M5**)

synthesizer A device that can generate original sounds that are new and different or that imitate existing sounds, allowing musicians to produce customized tones, pitches, and timbres to suit their preferences. (**M3**)

systems software Programs used to organize and run the internal workings of the computer or to manage systems-related tasks such as formatting or initializing disks. (M2, **M2**)

telecommunications Sending information electronically across distances using any form of communication, such as video and telephone. (M7, **M7**)

telecommunications software See: communications software. (M5)

telecommuting Working at home by being connected to a computer at a place of business through modems and phone lines. (M7, **M7**)

Student Glossary

teleconferencing Having a discussion, electronically, with a group of network users. (M7, **M7**)

template A pattern, or outline, of the fields in a database record. It is used as a guide when designing the database. (**M6**)

terabyte A unit of measurement for the memory and/or storage capacity of a computer; equals about one trillion bytes. (**M2**)

time bomb A virus that is designed to be triggered at a particular time or by a specific event. A time bomb can lie dormant for days, or even months, waiting for something to happen a certain number of times or for a specific date or time to come. (M11)

timesharing Sharing the power of a central computer among the users of an electronically linked network. (M7)

toolbox A collection of drawing and painting tools included in a graphics software package. (**M4**)

top-down design A method used by programmers in which the program is planned "from the top" starting with the most general problem. The general problem is then broken down into sub-problems. Then steps are listed for solving each subproblem. (M9, **M9**)

touch pad An input device used in graphic design. A user draws a picture with a finger or stylus on this device in order to input the image into the computer (M4, **M4**)

track An individual ring on a computer storage disk. (**M2**)

trackball Basically, a mouse turned on its "back" with a ball on its "stomach." The ball is rolled around by the user to move and guide the cursor. (M4)

transistor A compact electronic device that controls the flow of current without the use of a vacuum. (M2)

traversing In *HyperCard*, to move from one card to another, or from one stack to another by activating a button. (M9)

Trojan horse Destructive code that gains access to a computer disguised as something such as a desirable software program. Once inside the computer, the Trojan horse can do its damage but it cannot spread from disk to disk or computer to computer. (M11, **M11**)

tween Process by which frames between the beginning and end points are animated using the computer. (M4)

typeface A specific, named design for a whole set of text characters, including letters, numbers, and punctuation marks, that have a certain shape, thickness, slant, and other attributes. (M5, **M5**)

typesize The largeness or smallness of a character. (M5)

typestyle A special look given to a set of characters. (M5)

uploading Sending a file from your computer to another computer. (**M7**)

vacuum tube A glass tube, containing metal electrodes and grids in a vacuum, that is designed to control the flow of electrons. Used by the first-generation computers. (M10)

variable A location in the computer's memory where information that can vary is stored. (M8)

vector Line connecting specific points on the screen. Points for drawing a vector are identified by coordinates or numbers. (**M4**)

vector graphic An object that is created as a collection of lines, rather than as patterns of individual dots. (M4)

video game A form of interactive entertainment that uses a monitor (either a computer screen or a TV screen) to display the action of the game, and some kind of input device (a keyboard, mouse, joystick, button, touchpad, or "glove") to manipulate the game shown on the monitor. (**M3**)

video teleconferencing A conference over phone lines wherein the participants, through the use of special computer and video equipment, are able to hear and see other members of the conference who are at other locations. (M7)

virtual reality Refers to a lifelike world, created by computers, in which the participant can become part of the action. (M3, **M3**)

virus A program that contains destructive code which copies itself onto other computer files. (M11, **M11**)

virus disinfectant program A program used to search for viruses that may be established on a hard drive. (**M11**)

voice recognition The technology that allows some computers to understand human speech. (**M12**)

voice synthesis The technology that allows some computers to mimic the sound of the human voice. (**M12**)

volatile Refers to temporary memory (RAM). When you turn on the computer, RAM is empty. Because RAM is volatile, or temporary, anything that is put into RAM while the computer is on will be erased and lost whenever the computer is turned off again. (M2)

wide-area network (WAN) A number of terminals or microcomputers, usually widely separated, that are connected through modems and telephone lines. See also: network. (M7)

window A portion of the computer screen that can contain its own document. (M8, **M5**)

word processing A computer application that resembles typewriting but allows instant correction of errors, moving text to different locations, and other editing functions. (M5)

word processor 1. A computer that is set up to be used only for word processing (also called a "dedicated word processor"). 2. Software that allows a computer to function as a word processor, or tool for inputting and editing text. (**M5**)

word wrap In word processing, the automatic movement of a word to the next line when it is begun near the end of a line of text on which it is too long to fit; it eliminates the need for typing a carriage return. (**M5**)

worm Destructive code that bores its way through a computer's files. It can move from computer to computer, dropping off segments of itself as it goes. (M11, **M11**)

WORM (Write Once, Read Many) An optical disc/drive that allows data to be written to the disk only once. However, data can be read afterward many times. (**M2**)

INDEX

A

abacus, 5
accuracy of information, 192–195
address, 24
AI, See: artificial intelligence
Aiken, Howard, 171
algorithm, 150
Altair kit, 175–176
ALU, See: Arithmetic Logic Unit
American Standard Code for Information Interchange (ASCII), 31
analog, 113
Analytical Engine, 168–170
animation, 44–45, 47, 52–53, 67, 71
   interactive, 52
Apple Computer, 176–179
applications software, 32
Arithmetic Logic Unit (ALU), 24
artificial intelligence (AI), 215
ASCII, See: American Standard Code for Information Interchange
authoring system, 71–73, 157–158
automatic teller machine (ATM), 118

B

Babbage, Charles, 168–170
background, 158–160
backup copy, 26, 185–186
BASIC, 64, 152, 158
binary system, 31
bit, 31
bit-mapped (or raster) graphics, 60–61
bomb, 197
Boole, George, 31
booting, 32
Bricklin, Dan, 135
bug, 173
bulletin board, 117, 198; See also: electronic mail
button, 71–72, 156–157, 159–163
byte, 24, 31

C

CAD, See: computer-aided design
calculator, 4, 145, 157, 166
CAM, See: computer-aided manufacturing

card, 156, 158–163
cards, punched, 168–169
careers, 6–14, 30, 47, 61, 62, 86, 106, 120, 139, 150, 181, 193, 212
Careers features (in order of appearance),
   occupational therapist, 8
   computer professional, 30
   computer game designer, 47
   cartographer, 62
   writer, 86
   database administrator, 106
   weather forecaster, 120
   business analyst, 139
   computer consultant, 150
   inventor, 181
   computer scientist, 181
   computer security professional, 193
   dispatcher, 212
   police officer, 212
Cathode Ray Tube (CRT), 28
CAT scan, See: computerized axial tomography scan
CD-ROM, See: Compact Disc Read-Only Memory
cell, 132–133
Central Processing Unit (CPU), 22–24, 26, 172
character, 24
chip, 23, 29, 180
choose your own adventure, 161
COBOL, See: COmmon Business Oriented Language
column, 130–132, 144
command, 32, 160; See also: prompt
command key, 27
commercial software, 186
COmmon Business Oriented Language (COBOL), 152, 173
communications software, 113
Compact Disc-Read-Only Memory (CD-ROM), 26–27, 42, 46, 71, 105
compiler, 173
CompuServe, 34, 118
computer, 4
   buying, 35–36
   future, 179, 200–217
   history, 164–181
      first generation, 171–173, 180
      second generation, 174, 180
      third generation, 175, 180
      fourth generation, 175–179, 180–181
   languages, 64, 150, 152, 154, 158, 173
      BASIC, 64, 152, 158
      COBOL, 152, 173

226

INDEX

high-level, 152
Logo, 64, 154
Pascal, 150, 152, 158
protection, 196–197
types, 5–6, 36, 41, 51, 114–117, 174–179, 180, 202
general purpose, 175
mainframe, 5, 114, 117, 174, 180
microcomputer, 5, 116, 180
minicomputer, 5, 180
personal (PC), 6, 36, 41, 51, 175–179, 180, 202
computer-aided design (CAD), 9, 66–67
computer-aided manufacturing (CAM), 9, 66–67
computerized axial tomography (CAT) scan, 7
computer games, 40–47
creating, 44–45
history, 40–42
computer-generated music, 48–51
computer graphics, 14, 56–73
computer imaging, 204
computers in protective services, 12, 103–104
consumer-services networks, 118
control unit, 23
copy protection, 187
copyright, 185–188
CPU, See: Central Processing Unit
CRT, See: Cathode Ray Tube
cursor, 22
cut and paste, 77
AppleWorks (Apple II), 79
DeskMate (IBM), 80, 99
ClarisWorks (Macintosh), 81, 100

data, 4
databank (information service), 117, 119
database, 4, 92–109, 127, 192–193
quick-reference charts, 98–100
AppleWorks (Apple II), 98
DeskMate (IBM), 99
ClarisWorks (Macintosh), 100
database management system (DBMS), 95–96, 106, 150
data file, 95
DBMS, See: database management system
delete, 59, 78
AppleWorks (Apple II), 79, 98
DeskMate (IBM), 80, 99
ClarisWorks (Macintosh), 81, 100
desktop publishing (DTP), 86–91
dictionary, See: spelling checker

digital, 63, 113
digitize, 204
disk, 26–27, 33
care, 33
floppy (diskette), 26
hard, 26
disk operating system (DOS), 32, 135
display screen, See: monitor
document, 77
creating, 77
DOS See: disk operating system
dot-matrix printer, 28
downloading, 127
draw program, 65–69

Eckert, J. Presper, 171–172
education and computers, 14–16, 116, 121–123, 212
electrical impulses, 7
electronic mail (E-mail), 11, 13, 117, 125, 213
bulletin board, 117, 198
Electronic Numerical Integrator And Calculator (ENIAC), 5, 171–172
E-mail, See: electronic mail
ENIAC, See: Electronic Numerical Integrator And Calculator
entertainment, 38–55
ethics, 182–199
Excel, 135
expert system, 215

farming and ranching with computers, 10, 107–109
fiber optics, 112, 202, 206
field, 95–96, 159
file, 12, 77, 192, 194–195
first-generation computers, 171–173, 180
floppy disk (diskette), 26
flowchart, 150
font, 87
foreground, 158–160
formatting, 32, 78
formula line, 132
fourth-generation computers, 175–179, 180–181
Frankston, Bob, 135
freeware, 186
function, 32
function key, 27

Index

future access to information, 206
future computing, 55, 179, 200–217

games, 40–47
generation, 171–180; See also: computer, history
gigabit, 206
global network, 213
global village, 18, 115, 213
grammar checker, 83
graphical user interface (GUI), 135, 178
graphics, 14, 56–73, 87
graphics tablet, 61
graphing, 135
graphs, 58–59, 64, 134, 144
GUI, See: graphical user interface

hacker, 184, 198–199
hard copy (printout), 28
hard disk, 26
hardware, 32
highlight, 77
high resolution, 60
history of computers, 5–6, 36, 40, 63, 83, 96, 113, 135, 157, 164–181, 188, 203
Hollerith, Herman, 170
Hopper, Grace Murray, 173
host computer, 114, 121, 125
HyperCard, 72–73, 156–160
hypermedia, 155–163
HyperTalk, 160
hypertext, 155–163

IBM, See: International Business Machines Corporation
IC, See: integrated circuit
icon, 71, 160
information network, 10, 34, 119, 126–127, 206
initialize, See: formatting
ink-jet printer, 28
input, 22, 27, 61–63
   devices, 22, 27
insert, 78
   AppleWorks (Apple II), 79, 98
   DeskMate (IBM), 80

ClarisWorks (Macintosh), 81
integrated circuit (IC), 23, 29, 174–175, 180
interactive animation, 52
interactive videodisc, 71, 121
International Business Machines Corporation (IBM), 30, 36, 170, 177
   founder, 170

Jacquard, Joseph, 168
Jobs, Steve, 176, 178–179
joystick, 61–62
justified text, 90

keyboard, 22, 27
kilobyte (K), 24

LAN, See: local-area network
laptop, 6
laserdisc, 46
laser printer, 28
Leibniz, Gottfried, 31
light pen, 61–62
linking, 156–157
local-area network (LAN), 116, 198, 202
logic bomb, 197
logic function, 24
Logo, 64, 154
loom, punched-card, 168
Lotus, 135, 137, 194
Lovelace, Lady Ada, 168–169
low resolution, 60

Macintosh, 178–179
macro, 135–136
mainframe, 5, 114, 117, 174
map making, 62
Mark I, 5, 171–172
Mauchly, John, 171–172
medical use of computers, 7–8
megabyte (M or meg), 24

INDEX

memory, 24–26
menu, 77
microcomputer, 5, 116, 180
micromachine, 181
microprocessor, 23, 175, 180–181
minicomputer, 5, 180
mobile data terminal, 12
modem, 34, 113–114
monitor (display screen), 7, 28
mouse, 22, 27, 61
movies, 52–53, 59, 67, 70, 161, 209
multicultural, 72–73
Multicultural features, 12, 24, 30, 42, 61, 87, 104, 112, 137, 154, 167, 197, 204, 213
multimedia, 70–73
music, See: computer-generated music

network, 10, 116–120, 121
NeXT, 137, 179
Nintendo Entertainment Systems (NES), 42

object, 150, 156–157
object-oriented program, 65
Object-Oriented Programming (OOP), 150
online, 106
operating system, 32
optical disc, 26
optics, 46
output, 22, 28, 63
 devices, 22, 28

PC, See: personal computer
paint program, 65–66, 68–69
Papert, Seymour, 154
Pascal (language), 150, 152, 158
Pascal, Blaise, 135, 152, 166–167
Pascaline, 166–167
password protection, 187
peripheral, 26–28
personal computer (PC), 6, 36, 41, 51, 175–178, 180, 202
pixel, 60

plotter, 62
police, (military and computers), 5, 12, 103–104, 189–191, 193, 198–199
port, 113
primary storage, 24
printer, 22, 28
printout, 32
privacy rights, 192–195
procedure, 149
Prodigy, 34, 126
program, 4
programming, 146–163
programming language, 64, 71, 160, 173
public-domain software, 186

quick-reference charts, 79–81, 98–100
 word processing, 79–81
  AppleWorks (Apple II), 79
  DeskMate (IBM), 80
  ClarisWorks (Macintosh), 81
 databases, 98–100
  AppleWorks (Apple II), 98
  DeskMate (IBM), 99
  ClarisWorks (Macintosh), 100

RAM, See: Random Access Memory
ranching and farming with computers, 10, 107–109
Random Access Memory (RAM), 24–26
Read-Only Memory (ROM), 24–26
record, 95
ROM, See: Read-Only Memory
row, 130, 132, 144

save, 78
 AppleWorks (Apple II), 79, 98
 DeskMate (IBM), 80
 ClarisWorks (Macintosh), 81, 100
scanner, 27, 61–62, 63, 87
screen, 87
script, 160
scripting, 136
search and replace, 78
 AppleWorks (Apple II), 79

INDEX

DeskMate (IBM), 80
ClarisWorks (Macintosh), 81
secondary storage, 26
second-generation computers, 174, 180
shareware, 186
silicon, 29
smart cars, 210–211
smart house, 203
software, 9, 32–36, 151–154, 185–188
software bomb, 197
Software Publishers Association (SPA), 189–191
spelling checker, 82
spreadsheet, 4, 128–145
stack, 72, 156–159
standard formula (function), 132
status line, 132
storage, 24–27, 61
supercomputer, 202
systems software, 32

Tabulator, 170
telecommunications, 34, 110–127
    business uses, 125
    school uses, 116, 121–123, 212
telecommuting, 124, 209
teleconferencing, 119–120
thesaurus, 83
third-generation computers, 175, 180
time bomb, 197
timesharing, 117
top-down design, 150
touch pad, 61
trackball, 62
transistor, 174–175, 180
transportation and computers, 9, 11
traversing, 157
Trojan horse, 197
tween, 71
typeface, 87–89
typesize, 87–89
typestyle, 87–89

UNIVAC (UNIVersal Automatic Computer), 171–172

vacuum tube, 172, 174, 180
variable, 133
vector graphics, 60–61
videodisc, 71, 105
video teleconferencing, 112
videotelephones, 205
virtual reality, 46–47, 214–215
virus, 184, 196–197
VisiCalc, 135
voice-recognition device, 28, 78, 203
volatile, 26
Von Neumann, John, 172

WAN, See: wide-area network
Wang, An, 24
wide-area network (WAN), 116
window, 135
word processing, 4, 74–91, 97
    functions, 77–81
    quick-reference charts, 79–81
        AppleWorks (Apple II), 79
        DeskMate (IBM), 80
        ClarisWorks (Macintosh), 81
    special features, 82–83
        grammar checker, 83
        spelling checker, 82
        thesaurus, 83
worm, 197
WORM (Write Once, Read Many) drive, 26–27
Wozniak, Steve, 176, 178

Acknowledgments

Module 1

Page 13: Reuters America, Inc. "Astronauts Test Mail by Computer." *The Boston Globe,* Aug. 6, 1991. Reprinted with permission.

Pages 14–16: Chiu, Tony and Gail Cameron Wescott. "Students Don't Fear Her Byte." *People Weekly Extra,* Fall 1991. © 1991 The Time Inc. Magazine Co. Reprinted with permission.

Module 2

Page 30: Peterson, Robert W. "My Work as a Computer Technician." *BOY'S LIFE,* Aug. 1991. Reprinted with permission.

Module 3

Pages 44–45: "*Spaceship Warlock:* Exploring Space and Technology." (Michael Saenz, telephone interview, Sept. 1991.) Used with permission.

Pages 48–51: Tully, Tim. "Good Vibrations: The PC Joins the Band." *PC Computing,* Feb. 1989. Reprinted with permission.

Module 4

Pages 68–69: Curry, Gloria M. "Computer Graphics Field Keeps Growing." *The Office,* March 1990. Reprinted with permission.

Module 5

Pages 88–91: Morgenstern, Steve. "Rules of Thumb for Making Readable, Attractive Pages." *Home-Office Computing,* Feb. 1991 Reprinted with permission.

Module 6

Pages 103–104: Betts, Mitch. "Justice Aims Database at Gun Sales." *Computerworld,* Dec. 4, 1989. Copyright 1989 by CW Publishing, Inc.: Framingham, MA. Reprinted with permission.

Pages 107–109: Burgess, John. "High Tech on the Range." *The Washington Post,* Oct. 22, 1989. © 1989 *The Washington Post.* Reprinted with permission.

Module 7

Page 122: Tischler, Linda Hayes. "Classroom TV Brings in World." *The Boston Herald,* Sept. 12, 1990. Reprinted with permission.

Page 123: Kurshan, Dr. Barbara, Beverly Hunter and Suzanne Bazak. "Today's Software, Tomorrow's Children's Workstation." *Teaching and Computers,* Oct. 1989. Reprinted with permission.

Module 8

Pages 140–143: Burgess, John. "High Tech on the Range." *The Washington Post,* Oct. 22, 1989. © 1989 *The Washington Post.* Reprinted with permission.

Module 9

Page 148: Joy, Bill. "On the Next (Human) Generation." *BYTE* Magazine, Sept. 1990. New York: McGraw-Hill, Inc. All rights reserved. Reprinted with permission.

Pages 151–154: Boehr, Gretchen. "How Do You Create Software?" *PC Novice,* Oct. 1991. Reprinted with permission.

Module 10

Page 170: Condon, Ron. "Babbage's Difference Engine Launched—142 Years Later." *Computerworld,* July 8, 1991. Copyright 1991 by CW Publishing, Inc.: Framingham, MA. Reprinted with permission.

Module 11

Pages 189–191: Fitzgerald, Michael. "Open Up—This Is the Software Police!" *Computerworld,* June 17, 1991. Copyright 1991 by CW Publishing, Inc.: Framingham, MA. Reprinted with permission.

Module 12

Pages 206–208: Steinert-Threlkeld, Tom. "Dressing for Tech-cess." *The Dallas Morning News,* Aug. 25, 1991. Reprinted with permission.

Pages 210–211: Eisenstein, Paul A. "'Smart Cars' Combat Gridlock." *The Christian Science Monitor,* Nov. 29, 1990. Reprinted with permission.

Page 216: "A Letter to My Future Son or Daughter." *The Best of the Time Capsule Contest.* © 1990 Prodigy Services Co. Reprinted with permission.

Credits

Cover Photo: ©K.S. Studio; Inset courtesy of Autodesk, Inc.; Inset generated in *Mathematica* by Stewart Dickson

Module 1

Pages 2/3: Jim Karageorge/Courtesy of Seagate Technology; Page 2: Photo Researchers/©D.O.E. Science Source; Page 3: Top: NASA/Johnson Space Center; Right: Howard Sochurek/The Stock Market; Bottom: NASA/Johnson Space Center; Page 4: Jim Whitmer; Page 6: Courtesy of Apple Computer, Inc.; Page 7: Leonard Todd; Page 8: Steve Frazier Photography; Page 9: Andrew Sachs/Tony Stone Worldwide; Page 10: Colin Raw/Tony Stone Worldwide; Page 11: Courtesy of Southwest Airlines; Page 12: Jack Holtel; Page 13: Louis Eisele; Page 14: Steve Guarniccia/The Image Bank; Page 15: Tony Chiu, Gail Cameron Wescott/People Weekly ©1991 The Time Inc. Magazine Co.; Page 17: Comstock; Page 18: Jim Whitmer

Module 2

Pages 20/21: Jim Karageorge/Courtesy of Seagate Technology; Page 22: Jack Holtel; Page 23: Brian Sauriol; Page 25: Leonard Todd; Pages 26/27: Zebra Design; Page 28: Rick Becker; Page 29: T. Tracy/FPG; Page 30: Tom Sobolik/Black Star; Page 31: Zebra Design; Page 33: Zebra Design; Page 34: Art Direction; Page 36: Top left: Courtesy of Apple Computer, Inc.; Top right: Courtesy of International Business Machines Corporation; Bottom right: Courtesy of Apple Computer, Inc.; Page 37: Jack Holtel

Module 3

Pages 38/39: Mitch Kezar/Black Star; Page 40: Courtesy of Atari Games, Inc.; Page 41: Zebra Design; Page 42: Jack Holtel; Page 43: Jim Higgins; Page 44: Chris O'Leary; Page 46: Margaret Benyon/Ron Erickson; Page 47: Courtesy of NASA/Ames Research Center; Page 48: Jim Higgins; Page 49: Zebra Design; Page 51: Paul Swan; Page 53: COURTESY OF LUCASFILM LTD.; ™ & ©Lucasfilm Ltd. (LFL) 1983. All Rights Reserved; Page 54: Robin Smith/Tony Stone Worldwide; Page 55: Jim Higgins

Module 4

Pages 56/57: Jook Leung/FPG; Page 60: Faith Echtermeyer; Page 62: Top left: Jack Holtel; Middle bottom: Courtesy of International Business Machines Corporation; Page 63: Top right: R. McClain/The Stock Solution; Bottom: Courtesy of Apple Computer, Inc.; Page 65: Jack Holtel; Page 67: Gregory Macnicol; Page 69: Art Direction; Page 70: FPG; Page 71: Courtesy of Macromind/Paracomp; Page 72: Courtesy of Capital Cities/ABC News Interactive

Module 5

Pages 74/75: Pentagram Design, Inc.; Page 75: Jack Holtel; Page 84: Jim Whitmer; Page 85: Jim Whitmer; Pages 86/87: Jack Holtel; Page 88: Jim Higgins; Page 90: Jack Holtel

Module 6

Pages 92/93: Jack Holtel; Page 94: Jack Holtel; Page 95: Jack Holtel; Page 101: Jack Holtel; Page 102: Chris O'Leary; Page 103: S. Linthicum; Page 105: Courtesy of The Voyager Company; Page 106: Jack Holtel; Page 107: Courtesy of Billy Perrin; Page 108: Jim Higgins

Module 7

Pages 110/111: Art Direction; Page 113: Jim Higgins; Page 114: Wally Nelson; Page 118: Courtesy of CompuServe/Jack Holtel; Page 119: Hyper Graphics; Page 121: Gabe Palmer/The Stock Market; Page 122: Chuck Keeler/Tony Stone Worldwide; Page 124: Mark Romine/Superstock; Page 125: Jim Higgins; Page 126: Jack Holtel

Module 8

Pages 128/129: Matt London; Page 131: Jim Higgins; Page 133: Jack Holtel; Page 134: Jim Higgins; Page 136: Hyper Graphics; Page 137: Courtesy of Lotus Development Corporation; Page 139: The Stock Broker; Page 140: Top right: Courtesy of International Business Machines Corporation; Middle: D. Frazier/The Stock Solution; Page 141: Jack Holtel; Page 142: Daniel Kirk/The Image Bank; Page 143: Peter Beck/The Stock Market; Pages 144/145: Jack Holtel

Module 9

Pages 146/147: Randy Palmer; Middle: ©Berenholtz/The Stock Market; Page 146: Top: Focus on Sports; Middle: New York Convention & Visitors Bureau; Bottom: Jack Holtel; Page 147: Top right: Frank Lloyd Wright Archives; Top middle: Frank Lloyd Wright Archives; Top left: New York Convention & Visitors Bureau; Bottom right: Bettman Archives; Bottom middle: New York Visitors & Convention Bureau; Bottom left: Barbara Martin; Page 148: Jean-Francois Podevin/The Image Bank; Page 149: Jack Holtel; Page 151: Jack Holtel; Page 153: Jack Holtel; Page 156: Charlotte Langen; Page 161: Hyper Graphics; Page 163: Bob Daemmrich

Module 10

Pages 164/165: Robin Brun; Pages 164/165: Jack Holtel; Page 167: Courtesy of International Business Machines Archives; Page 169: Courtesy of International Business Machines Corporation; Page 171: Courtesy of UNISYS; Page 173: Paul Swan; Page 174: AT&T Archives; Page 176: Courtesy of Apple Computer, Inc.; Page 177: Courtesy of International Business Machines Corporation; Page 179: Courtesy of NeXT Computer

Module 11

Pages 182/183: Randy Palmer; Page 184: John Mattos; Page 185: Jack Holtel; Page 187: Top: Peter Tenzer/International Stock; Middle left: Superstock; Page 189: Tim Grajek/Stockworks; Page 190: Jack Holtel; Page 191: Jim Higgins; Page 192: Jack Holtel; Page 193: Kenneth Garrett/FPG; Page 194: Jack Holtel; Page 195: T. Tracy/FPG; Page 196: Jim Higgins; Page 198: Courtesy of International Business Machines Corporation

Module 12

Pages 200/201: Uniphoto; Page 202: Christopher Herrfurth; Page 204: Courtesy of United Digital Systems; Page 205: Courtesy of AT&T; Page 207: Courtesy of NEC/Tokyo; Page 208: Charlotte Langen; Page 209: Jim Higgins; Page 210: Christopher Herrfurth; Page 212: Christopher Herrfurth; Page 213: John Dykes; Page 214: Peter Menzel; Page 215: Hajime Sorayama/The Image Bank; Page 216: Jack Holtel